16.93
24.95

W9-ANE-014
3 1230 000

MODERN NOVELISTS

General Editor: Norman Page

MODERN NOVELISTS

Published titles

SAUL BELLOW   Peter Hyland
ALBERT CAMUS   Philip Thody
FYODOR DOSTOEVSKY   Peter Conradi
GEORGE ELIOT   Alan W. Bellringer
WILLIAM FAULKNER   David Dowling
F. SCOTT FITZGERALD   John Whitley
GUSTAVE FLAUBERT   David Roe
E. M. FORSTER   Norman Page
ANDRÉ GIDE   David Walker
WILLIAM GOLDING   James Gindin
GRAHAM GREENE   Neil McEwan
ERNEST HEMINGWAY   Peter Messent
CHRISTOPHER ISHERWOOD   Stephen Wade
HENRY JAMES   Alan W. Bellringer
JAMES JOYCE   Richard Brown
D. H. LAWRENCE   G. M. Hyde
ROSAMOND LEHMANN   Judy Simons
DORIS LESSING   Ruth Whittaker
MALCOLM LOWRY   Tony Bareham
THOMAS MANN   Martin Travers
V. S. NAIPAUL   Bruce King
GEORGE ORWELL   Valerie Meyers
ANTHONY POWELL   Neil McEwan
MARCEL PROUST   Philip Thody
BARBARA PYM   Michael Cotsell
JEAN-PAUL SARTRE   Philip Thody
SIX WOMEN NOVELISTS   Merryn Williams
MURIEL SPARK   Norman Page
JOHN UPDIKE   Judie Newman
EVELYN WAUGH   Jacqueline McDonnell
H. G. WELLS   Michael Draper
PATRICK WHITE   Mark Williams
VIRGINIA WOOLF   Edward Bishop

Forthcoming titles

MARGARET ATWOOD   Coral Ann Howells
IVY COMPTON-BURNETT   Janet Godden
JOSEPH CONRAD   Owen Knowles
JOHN FOWLES   James Acheson
FRANZ KAFKA   Ronald Speirs and Beatrice Sandberg
NORMAN MAILER   Michael Glenday
GABRIEL GARCIA MARQUEZ   Michael Bell
IRIS MURDOCH   Hilda Spear
VLADIMIR NABOKOV   David Rampton
PAUL SCOTT   G. K. Das
MARK TWAIN   Peter Messent

MODERN NOVELISTS

GEORGE ELIOT

Alan W. Bellringer

St. Martin's Press   New York

First published in the United States of America in 1993

Printed in Hong Kong

ISBN 0–312–09474–4

Library of Congress Cataloging-in-Publication Data
Bellringer, Alan W.
George Eliot / Alan W. Bellringer.
p.   cm. —(Modern novelists)
Includes bibliographical references and index.
ISBN 0–312–09474–4
1. Eliot, George, 1819–1880—Criticism and interpretation.
I. Title.   II. Series.
PR4688.B37   1993
823'.8—dc20   92–40375
                                                          CIP

For Keith

Contents

Acknowledgements

I would like to acknowledge support from colleagues and friends in the composition of this book, especially from Bill Tydeman and Tom Corns. I am indebted to Gail Kincaid and Michelle Harrison for secretarial assistance. My wife's help and understanding have been invaluable. I am grateful to the University of Wales, Bangor, for contributions to research costs.

General Editor's Preface

The death of the novel has often been announced, and part of the secret of its obstinate vitality must be its capacity for growth, adaptation, self-renewal and self-transformation: like some vigorous organism in a speeded-up Darwinian ecosystem, it adapts itself quickly to a changing world. War and revolution, economic crisis and social change, radically new ideologies such as Marxism and Freudianism, have made this century unprecedented in human history in the speed and extent of change, but the novel has shown an extraordinary capacity to find new forms and techniques and to accommodate new ideas and conceptions of human nature and human experience, and even to take up new positions on the nature of fiction itself.

In the generations immediately preceding and following 1914, the novel underwent a radical redefinition of its nature and possibilities. The present series of monographs is devoted to the novelists who created the modern novel and to those who, in their turn, either continued and extended, or reacted against and rejected, the traditions established during that period of intense exploration and experiment. It includes a number of those who lived and wrote in the nineteenth century but whose innovative contribution to the art of fiction makes it impossible to ignore them in any account of the origins of the modern novel; it also includes the so-called 'modernists' and those who in the mid- and late twentieth century have emerged as outstanding practitioners of this genre. The scope is, inevitably, international; not only, in the migratory and exile-haunted world of our century, do writers refuse to heed national frontiers – 'English' literature lays claim to Conrad the Pole, Henry James the American, and Joyce the Irishman – but geniuses such as Flaubert, Dostoevsky and Kafka have had an influence on the fiction of many nations.

Each volume in the series is intended to provide an introduction

to the fiction of the writer concerned, both for those approaching
him or her for the first time and for those who are already familiar
with some parts of the achievement in question and now wish
to place it in the context of the total *oeuvre*. Although essential
information relating to the writer's life and times is given, usually
in an opening chapter, the approach is primarily critical and
the emphasis is not upon 'background' or generalisations but
upon close examination of important texts. Where an author is
notably prolific, major texts have been made to convey, more
summarily, a sense of the nature and quality of the author's work as
a whole. Those who want to read further will find suggestions in the
select bibliography included in each volume. Many novelists are,
of course, not only novelists but also poets, essayists, biographers,
dramatists, travel writers and so forth; many have practised shorter
forms of fiction; and many have written letters or kept diaries that
constitute a significant part of their literary output. A brief study
cannot hope to deal with all these in detail, but where the shorter
fiction and the non-fictional writings, public and private, have an
important relationship to the novels, some space has been devoted
to them.

NORMAN PAGE

1
George Eliot's Life

Mary Anne Evans (the novelist George Eliot) was born on 22
November 1819 at South Farm, Arbury Hall, the estate of the
Newdigate family near Nuneaton, North Warwickshire. Her father,
Robert Evans, was Francis Newdigate's agent. Apart from oversee-
ing the estate, Evans had many business interests; he was widely
respected as a skilled carpenter, surveyor, mining manager and
farmer. He was on terms of friendship with his employer, often
bringing his daughter Mary Anne with him to the great house or
on his other varied errands in the vicinity. Robert Evans had two
elder children from a previous marriage, and two more, Chrissey
and Isaac, from his marriage with Christina Pearson; Mary Anne
was their youngest surviving child. In 1820 the Evans family moved
to Griff House, Chilvers Coton, on the edge of the estate. It was here
that Mary Anne Evans grew up, enjoying especially the companionship of her brother Isaac on the farm and surrounding land.

In 1824 she was sent to join her sister Chrissey at Miss Lathom's
boarding school, Attleborough, not far from Griff. Her youthful
reading included Bunyan, Defoe, Goldsmith and Scott. At the age
of seven, having read part of Scott's *Waverley* (1814), she wrote a
completion of the story for herself.[1] In 1828 she was transferred
to Mrs Wallington's boarding school, Nuneaton, where she became
the pupil of Maria Lewis, a devoutly evangelical Anglican. At thir-
teen she moved to the Miss Franklins' school, Coventry, continuing
her contact with Maria Lewis as a friend and correspondent. She
now made rapid progress in French, music and English composition. Privately she wrote a few pages of a historical romance, set
in mid-seventeenth-century Chepstow.[2] She had the opportunity
of a good educational grounding, especially in literature and the
Christian religion, and took full advantage of it.

Her mother, Mrs Christina Evans, died a painful death in

February 1836. During the period preceding and following this harrowing event Mary Anne Evans returned to Griff to look after her father. Her religious views now grew increasingly puritanical. For example, she gave up attending performances of oratorios; their style she regarded as too virtuosic for the solemnity due to Holy Scripture. For novels, both of the religious and of the worldly variety, she was ready to express hatred; 'The weapons of Christian warfare were never sharpened at the forge of romance',[3] she wrote. It can be assumed that her own interest in writing romance had been renounced. In 1837 she began writing her name as Mary Ann Evans, possibly because Anne was the French (and Catholic) form. Her reading deepened, taking in church history, of which she made a chart, and works in Italian and German, in which she received private tuition. Latin she was teaching herself. In January 1840 she had a poem of hers (it praises the Bible) published in the *Christian Observer*. In the following year Robert Evans retired from serving the Newdigate family, whose Conservative political principles he pronouncedly approved. He moved with his youngest daughter to a house at Foleshill, Coventry. Isaac Evans, now about to be married, was left at Griff.

In Coventry Mary Ann Evans, much to her father's uneasiness, was introduced by neighbours to a group of freethinkers and political radicals who were making a stir in the town. Her faith in Christianity, which had already begun to be modified by new reading in science and poetry at Griff, was soon lost entirely. A new and personally engaging friend, Charles Bray, the author of an eclectic work, *The Philosophy of Necessity* (1841), influenced by utilitarian and socialist writers, discussed his various pet topics with Mary Ann Evans. They were excited in particular by his brother-in-law Charles C. Hennell's *Inquiry into the Origins of Christianity* (1838). She had probably already acquired a copy of this publication, which is an early Victorian exercise in demythologising, before it came up in conversation. Bray's wife Cara, an accomplished pianist and artist, and her sister Sara Hennell, a more scholarly type, though no match for Mary Ann Evans in intelligence, provided constant and enjoyable company. Advanced views were not only aired but taken to heart. Mary Ann Evans felt she must act to preserve her integrity. On Sunday 2 January 1842 at Foleshill she shocked her father by declining on principle to accompany him to church. A period of severe strain with her relatives ensued. For over a month she stayed with her brother at Griff. Pressure was applied, and by

May 1842 a reconciliation between Mary Ann Evans and her father had been effected at Foleshill. In order to keep up appearances she agreed to take up attending church with him again. Her inner alienation from religious worship remained, however. She needed to get away, certainly. One excursion led to complications. On Charles Hennell's marriage to Rufa Brabant in November 1843, Mary Ann Evans went to stay with the bride's parents in Wiltshire. Dr Robert Brabant, aged sixty-three, needed assistance in reading works in foreign languages. He was very distinguished in appearance whereas his visitor was rather on the plain side, though with an appealing expression. Surprisingly, Mary Ann Evans, forty years his junior, formed a sudden emotional attachment to Dr Brabant, aroused the jealously of his wife, and within a month had to leave abruptly for Coventry. It was shortly after this episode that Brabant's daughter Rufa Hennell agreed to the helpful suggestion of her new sister-in-law Sara Hennell that Mary Ann Evans should take over the task of translating into English D. F. Strauss's *Das Leben Jesu* (1835), one of the seminal texts of nineteenth-century agnosticism. Rufa Hennell had been using the fourth edition of 1840, but had not got very far. Mary Ann Evans set to work early in 1844, progressing at a rate of at least six pages a day, until she finished the huge translation in the summer of the following year. It was not till after nine more months of checking and proof-reading, with Sara Hennell as editorial helper, that Mary Ann Evans could say that she was free at last of feeling 'Strauss-sick'.[4] The three volumes were published by Chapman Bros in London on 15 June 1846, as *The Life of Jesus, Critically Examined*, Strauss himself having contributed the preface (in Latin). Twenty pounds was the fee paid to the anonymous translator.

During this time there were visits with Charles and Cara Bray to the Lake District, London and (especially exciting because of the Scott associations) Scotland. Since October 1844 Mary Ann Evans had been giving German lessons to Mary Sibree, daughter of an Independent minister who was a friend of Rebecca Franklin, Mary Ann Evans's old Baptist teacher. Mary Sibree reported that *her* new teacher never pressed her godless views on others, but could be vividly frank on matters like navvies' actual speech and English people's arranged marriages.[5] At this period she especially admired the passionate style of Rousseau and George Sand. Such opinions may also have come up at meetings at the Brays' Coventry home, Rosehill, with visiting celebrities like Cobden and Bright, Emerson and Robert Owen. The last named's socialism she regarded with coolness; she had engaged in a good deal of private social work among the poor, and questioned imposed theory. Another new acquaintance was the novelist and journalist Harriet Martineau, whom the Brays took her to meet at Atherstone. A valuable intimation that Mary Ann Evans picked up on this occasion was that the move from the provinces to London had been crucial for the literary lady's career.[6] Meanwhile Mary Ann Evans had to be content with making contributions to the *Coventry Herald*; namely five essays 'From the Notebook of an Eccentric' (1846–7)and some reviews. By 1847 her father's health had deteriorated, owing to a weakening of the heart. There were a few excursions with him, then without him. She had to nurse him at home, reading Scott aloud to him. She also read and admired Currer Bell's *Jane Eyre* (1847)though no doubt she kept from her father her disapproval of Charlotte Brontë's heroine's absolute respect for the marriage vow. Eighteen forty-eight was the year of Revolutions in Europe, which she welcomed as part of a movement towards social reforms, but which he distrusted. As he neared his end, her father's moral pull began to reassert itself upon her. 'The one deep love I have ever known has now its highest exercise', she wrote. On the night of Robert Evans's death, 30–31 May 1849, Mary Ann asked, 'What shall I be without my Father? It will seem as if a part of my moral nature were gone.'[7] Alongside her emancipated views on religion, divorce and welfare, the distrust of progressive politics learned from her father remained a significant factor in George Eliot's work.

A short time spent translating Spinoza at Rosehill followed her bereavement. Then the Brays took her on her first trip abroad. They accompanied Mary Ann Evans to France, Italy and Switzerland, but on the way back she decided to remain behind at a *pension* in Geneva in order to improve her French. The Geneva stay lasted from July 1849 till March 1850. From the October she lodged with an artist, F. D'Albert Durade and his wife; they were an evangelical and conservative couple of wide tastes. In Geneva she attended lectures on experimental physics, studied mathematics and read Voltaire. D'Albert sketched a portrait of her and painted a copy for her to take home. He escorted her the whole way to London as a mark of his esteem.

Back in Coventry Mary Ann Evans found it hard to settle. D'Albert stayed with her at Rosehill for three days in May. John Chapman the publisher was a visitor in October, along with R. W.

Mackay, whose *Progress of the Intellect* (1850) he had just published. Mackay's belief in the cultic origin of religious myths showed the influence of D. F. Strauss. When Chapman asked Strauss's translator to write a review of Mackay's work, she not only accepted but took it in person the next month to the Chapmans' boarding house in the Strand and stayed a fortnight. She began to see herself more as an author than a teacher. Though accepting Polly and Pollian as variants of her first names from her friends, she now increasingly preferred to refer to herself as Marian Evans, two names presumably being enough for a writer.

She returned to the Chapmans' at 142 Strand from Warwickshire on 8 January 1851, accepting the publisher's offer of help in the search for work. The quest turned to cooperation, and she found herself reading manuscripts for him and teaching him German. Strikingly handsome and gallant, he reciprocated by accompanying her to the theatre as well as to lectures on science and geometry. Inevitably Marian Evans became entangled in Chapman's already complex emotional life and decided to go back to Coventry on 24 March 1851. The relationship continued, however, in a lower key. In May 1851 Chapman purchased the radical *Westminster Review*, in which he had placed Marian Evans's unsigned review of Mackay. He travelled to Coventry to put up at the Brays' and suggested to Marian Evans that she should assist him in editing the *Review*. There were several more meetings to discuss the wording of the prospectus for the new series of the quarterly. She returned to 142 Strand on 29 September 1851 as Chapman's assistant editor. In practice it was Marian Evans who ran the periodical anonymously for ten numbers.

The first issue which she edited appeared in January 1852, with articles by J. A. Froude, F. W. Newman and G. H. Lewes. Subsequent contributors included John Stuart Mill, John Oxenford and Herbert Spencer. She herself wrote reviews of Carlyle and Margaret Fuller. Editorial contacts were wide; she became known personally to Louis Blanc, Mazzini, Henry Crabb Robinson, T. H. Huxley and W. C. Bryant, and developed friendships with feminists like Bessie Parkes and Barbara Leigh Smith. G. H. Lewes's polymath versatility was frequently in her mind; she wrote about him in a letter to John Chapman of 24–25 July 1852, 'Defective as his articles are, they are the best we can get *of the kind*.'[8] In retrospect that might seem very uncomplimentary, but Marian Evans's affections at this time were centred on the editor of *The Economist*, Herbert Spencer, advocate of scientific education and author of *Social Statics* (1850). It was Spencer who was with her now at concerts and operas or on visits to Kew Gardens. A crisis arose during a trip of his to Broadstairs, where she was on holiday. She wrote to Spencer that her feeling of thorough love had concentrated itself on him: 'I suppose no woman ever before wrote such a letter as this.'[9] But her emotion was unreciprocated; she had to be content with Spencer's intellectual friendship. A month divided between Edinburgh, Ambleside (at Harriet Martineau's) and Coventry (at the Brays') gave relief from headaches. But the year 1852 ended darkly with the death of her brother-in-law Dr Edward Clarke. She spent Christmas at Meriden in Warwickshire with the widowed Chrissey and her six children, very conscious of the need to support them.

She had first met G. H. Lewes on 6 October 1851. He was not only a novelist, drama critic, reviewer of foreign books and scientist, but also the author of a *Biographical History of Philosophy* (1845–6) and the editor of a radical weekly, *The Leader*, which he had founded with Thornton Hunt in 1850. When he met Marian Evans, Lewes had three sons living by his wife Agnes, whom, however, he no longer recognised as such because of her adultery with Hunt, with whom by 1857 she had four other children. During 1852 Lewes was a frequent visitor at the Chapmans'. In 1853 it was he who was escorting Marian Evans to the theatre and meeting her to discuss literary work. In October she moved from the Strand to the more discreet 21 Cambridge Street, Hyde Park Gate. By this time the new relationship was deepening into mutual love. She was working on a translation for Chapman of the second edition (1843) of Ludwig Feuerbach's *Das Wesen des Christentums* (1841), which was to appear in July 1854 as *The Essence of Christianity*, bearing for the first and only time the name of Marian Evans (as translator) on the title page. She was also reading the proofs of Lewes's new book on *Comte's Philosophy of the Sciences* (1853). These two European thinkers, the one, Feuerbach, the hostile critic of religion which he viewed as the fantastic projection of alienated humanity, the other, Comte, the founder of the positivist science of society which he believed would free humanity from its historical thralldom to the supernatural and metaphysical, were to remain *the major* influences on her subsequent writing. Lewes was very close to her in his beliefs (he had a healthy suspicion of the phrenology which was one of Charles Bray's enthusiasms). Though not, like Bray, personally prepossessing, Lewes fascinated Marian

Evans by his lively disposition, skill in making literary contacts and open-mindedness on radical politics. Her desire was to live with him in a partnership or union that was a marriage in all but name. A legal divorce was virtually impossible for Lewes to obtain as he had condoned his wife's adultery. Options for Marian Evans and Lewes included alternating between separate establishments and having spells together abroad. They decided to live together abroad first. She resigned her post with the *Westminster Review*, while continuing to work for it independently and for the *Leader*. She and Lewes left for Weimar together on 20 July 1854, having given the minimum necessary information to relatives and friends. It is not certain that Lewes at first intended to continue the experiment after their return.[10]

Living openly as partners for the first time, Marian Evans and G. H. Lewes found life in Germany extremely enjoyable. They shared their current interests in writing and reading, saw plenty of art, architecture and natural scenery together and met people of the highest distinction, such as Clara Schumann and Liszt. It was a pattern they were to repeat in their many future continental travels. He interviewed people who had known Goethe and his circle; she kept a descriptive journal for turning into articles. He was bringing to its last stages his long-prepared *Life of Goethe* (1855), for which she did the translating of the prose. Goethe's ideas had always impressed her with their tolerance and patience. Now in Lewes's summing up of the Goethean doctrine of renunciation at the end of his chapter on *Faust* she could find a morality which she could wholly approve. Lewes stresses Goethe's belief that the quest for absolute happiness and for absolute knowledge must be given up in favour of a course of active duty; 'a consciousness that our labour tends in some way to the lasting benefit of others makes the rolling years endurable'.[11] In the cultural atmosphere of Weimar the ground was laid for ways of coping in the future.

In October 1854 the couple moved to Berlin; here they were in the company of scholars, scientists and actors. He took her to the theatre and museums; now aged thirty-five, she read intensively in German and English literature, wrote a few articles and worked on a translation of Spinoza's *Ethics* (1677). Spinoza's doctrine that God and nature were one may have seemed rather remote when news started to reach them from England that there was a disapproval of their *liaison* even among their liberal-minded friends. Carlyle wrote sympathetically, but referred to her as a strong-minded woman.[12]

On their return to England on 12 March 1855 she at first stayed
at Dover, naturally worrying while Lewes sorted out his financial
affairs in London. Not till Lewes's wife declared her intention never
to reunite with him and intimated that 'she would be very glad if
he could marry Miss Evans'[13] did the latter come up to London
to take lodgings with him and insist on being called 'Mrs Lewes'.
Contemporary outrage was explicit. The first woman to brave it
by visiting her in her unconventional state was Rufa Hennell. The
couple found obscure lodgings in East Sheen in May and later in
October moved further out to 8 Park Shot in Richmond, Surrey.
Fortunately Marion Evans had plenty of literary work to occupy her,
since Chapman had invited her to review contemporary literature
in the 'Belles Lettrers' section of the *Westminster Review*, which
she did from July 1855 till January 1857, covering new volumes
by, among others, Arnold, Tennyson, Browning, Thoreau, Ruskin
and Whitman. She also reviewed for other journals and wrote
four sharply worded essays, notably 'Evangelical Teaching: Dr.
Cumming', where she argues that certain clergymen preach so
fallaciously and uncharitably as to be intellectually disreputable
(*Westminster Review*, October 1855). Virtually isolated now, she
must have felt she had little to lose by such attacks. Few women
friends sought her society; invitations were lacking. She bore it with
character, reading widely in Latin and Greek literature, especially
Sophocles, and completing her translation of Spinoza, for which,
however, Lewes found no publisher. On a holiday in Ilfracombe,
where Lewes was collecting natural specimens for biological studies, she finished her article for Chapman on Riehl's account of
German provincial life, in which she criticised (though not by
name) Dickens for encouraging in his novels the 'fallacy that
high morality and refined sentiment can grow out of harsh social
relations'.[14] The charge was a little reckless, for Dickens was no
simple determinist, but faced with so much personal prejudice
she had become impatient of hopeful idealism. Riehl's realistic
sociology was conservative in its political implications. She recognised in it another check to radical optimism. She argued the
need for an English writer who would study the English social
classes realistically and reveal the pressures which accelerate and
impede social progress. Fiction which presented the complexity of
life undogmatically in this way would itself, she believed, have a
social function. Lewes was aware what she was thinking and what
was in the air. During July 1856 at Tenby, where he continued

to gather zoological data, he one day urged her, 'You must try and write a story',[15] and the idea came to her for the first of the *Scenes of Clerical Life*. She began the writing back in Richmond on 23 September 1856.

On 6 November 1856 Lewes submitted 'Amos Barton' to John Blackwood, editor of the Edinburgh monthly, *Blackwood's Magazine*, where he had previously had fiction of his own accepted as well as his 'Sea-side Studies'. In commending the new story Lewes mentioned Goldsmith's and Jane Austen's works as precedents. It was accepted and was to be serialised anonymously. Lewes soon had to explain to the publisher that the 'clerical friend' of his to whom he had attributed the tale was not actually a 'clericus'.[16] John Blackwood addressed the new and very retiring author in a letter as 'Amos Barton', but his brother William Blackwood received a reply from 'George Eliot';[17] it was dated 4 February 1857, which is worth considering her second birthday. The *nom de plume* which she adopted is explained variously; its very ordinariness is half its strength. To a Victorian aware of George Eliot's sex, it would imply a compliment to George Sand. An echo of the heroine of *Jane Eyre* would also be discernible; she called herself Jane Elliot at the Rivers' when she wished to conceal her identity. A nod in the direction of George Henry Lewes is more obvious. She may have unearthed a buried memory of a 'George Eliot's close' shown on an old map of Chilvers Coton probably used by Robert Evans.[18]

Echoes of Warwickshire places and people were certainly discernible as the three 'Clerical Scenes' unfolded during 1857, increasing speculation on the identity of the author. She and Lewes spent the spring and summer months out of the way that year on the Scilly Isles and Jersey. They read aloud Mrs Gaskell, Charlotte Brontë, Hawthorne, but especially Jane Austen repeatedly, and corresponded with Blackwood over the harsher details in the new stories, as a result of which George Eliot agreed to some omissions concerning spitting and drunkenness. Her confidence was boosted by Lewes's judicious comments; she defended her stories as being real and concrete, not ideal and eclectic; their moral effect depended on her 'power of seeing truly and feeling justly', she argued, not on any cynicism or irreverence.[19] She could not have wished for more favourable notice than the unsigned review of the book version of *Scenes of Clerical Life* (1858) which appeared in *The Times* on 2 January 1858, linking her work to

Goldsmith, Crabbe, Galt, Lockhart and, by association, Sir Walter Scott. The reviewer was Samuel Lucas.

George Eliot's reputation as a major novelist was already prospectively well on its way by November 1858 when she had composed *Adam Bede* (1859), which was to be her astonishing contemporary success. Much of it was written during a long tour which took in Munich, Vienna, Prague and Dresden, while Lewes was also preparing a book, his *Physiology of Common Life* (1859–60). *Adam Bede* attracted enthusiastic and serious reviews and much private praise among the literati and members of the general public. It was soon translated into several languages, including Russian. Tolstoy himself read it in October 1859 and was deeply impressed.[20]

Meanwhile in Warwickshire there were confused claims by a local clergyman Joseph Liggins that he was George Eliot, as well as a report that Isaac Evans, unreconciled to his sister since May 1857 when she informed him of her 'marriage' to Lewes, recognised her in the pseudonymous novelist;[21] these developments persuaded her to drop the incognito. She admitted to friends like the Brays who George Eliot was. When the news was out in London there was unpleasant gossip. The weekly *Athenaeum* carried an unjustifiable report that the Liggins business had been a mystification deliberately got up as a publicity stunt by 'a clever woman with an observant eye and unschooled moral nature' (2 July 1859). George Eliot, subject now to unwelcome, unfair and insensitive personal comments, still made a point of being called 'Mrs Lewes'. It was the period when the satirical passages in *The Mill on the Floss* were being penned. She was also shocked and depressed by news of her sister Chrissey's death in Attleborough that year, to be followed by that of Chrissey's daughter Kate Clarke in the next. Her surviving Clarke niece Emily she supported at school. She and Lewes had taken a house of their own called Holly Lodge in Wandsworth in February 1859. Here she enjoyed exercising their puppy Pug, one of the many animals for which concern was continually reflected in George Eliot's fiction. There were visits from Dickens and Herbert Spencer. They had as neighbours a Warwickshire couple, the Congreves, who became valued new friends, Dr Richard Congreve being a leading activist among the English followers of Comte. Lewes's eldest son Charles, a clerk in the Post Office in London, was living with them by then, and in order to be nearer his place of work they moved on 24 September 1860 to lodgings in Marylebone and then in December to 16 Blandford Square nearby. Guests there included Browning, Trollope and Wilkie Collins. *The Mill on the Floss* (1860) had been published and *Romola* conceived while they were on a visit to Italy, financed out of the considerable earnings from Blackwood. On their way back they had called on the D'Albert Durades at Geneva, D'Albert gaining George Eliot's permission to be her French translator.

Silas Marner, published on 2 April 1861, brought further prestige and affluence to George Eliot. In February 1862 she received an offer of ten thousand pounds for her next novel from Smith and Elder, who had published some of Lewes's scientific essays in the *Cornhill Magazine*. She agreed to accept seven thousand pounds and the reversion of the copyright in six years. John Blackwood, who had been kept informed on the progress of her Italian story, had to be told. He predicted that the decision would turn out to be a mistake, and so it proved, for Smith and Elder made a loss on *Romola* (1863). Blackwood preserved courteous relations, and George Eliot returned to his firm for *Felix Holt* (1866) and her subsequent works.

In August 1863 she and Lewes bought The Priory, 21 North Bank, which was to be her London home for nearly seventeen years, right up to the last year of her life. It had many advantages, being near Regent's Park, yet secluded, with large rooms. They had the drawing room specially reconstructed and professionally decorated, to be used for receptions. The men guests were at first very much in the majority on these occasions, since the unofficial nature of the host and hostess's union continued to draw widespread social disapproval. George Eliot abstained from public actions because she feared that her associating herself with good causes would do them some harm. An exception was Emily Davies's plan to found a women's college at Cambridge, to which she subscribed fifty pounds from 'the author of *Romola*'.[22] At this period, with Lewes's help, she was sketching a drama, but nothing came of it. She began work on the poetic *Spanish Gypsy*, but broke off to return to English themes with *Felix Holt*. She needed advice on the legal entanglements in the plot of this novel and turned to Frederic Harrison, a barrister closely involved with the Positivist movement. He expressed particular appreciation of the quality of her writing when *Felix Holt* was published and suggested she should dedicate her talent to the cause by composing next a Comtist novel; 'the grand features of Comte's world,' urged Harrison, 'might be

sketched in fiction in their normal relations though under the
forms of our familiar life.'[23] George Eliot replied coolly; 'I think
aesthetic teaching is the highest of all teaching because it deals
with life in its highest complexity. But if it ceases to be purely
aesthetic – if it lapses anywhere from the picture to the diagram
– it becomes the most offensive of all teaching.'[24] The point has
not always been taken by those writing literature of ideas; to their
disadvantage, it should be said. It is not certain that George Eliot
herself totally endorsed it, since she added that her whole soul went
with Harrison's idea that the Comtist work should be written. She
bore it in mind when, after an arduous tour with Lewes in Spain
early in 1867, she resumed her draft of *The Spanish Gypsy*, which
Richard Congreve was to call 'a mass of Positivism'.[25] There were
further visits to Germany before it was published in 1868. It had
a mixed critical reception, but good sales, especially in the United
States.[26] American visitors to The Priory were now more common,
including C. E. Norton and his sister Grace Norton, the friends of
Henry James. When James himself first met George Eliot on 9 May
1869, she and Lewes were just back from the Continent (at Rome
they had met her future husband, John Walter Cross, then aged
twenty-nine, a stockbroker moving job from New York to London
– he was the son of a friend of Herbert Spencer). James's visit
to the Priory was marred by the suffering of Lewes's second son
Thornton, who had moved there after having contracted incurable
spinal tuberculosis in Natal (Charles Lewes had left to be married
in 1865). Nevertheless James gave his father immediately in a letter
the best physical description that we have of George Eliot:

I called on her yesterday (Sunday) afternoon, with Grace Norton
and Sara Sedgwick – the only way in which it seemed possible
to do it as she is much hedged about with sanctity and a
stranger can go only [under] cover of a received friend. I was
immensely impressed, interested and pleased. To begin with
she is magnificently ugly – deliciously hideous. She has a low
forehead, a dull grey eye, a vast pendulous nose, a huge mouth,
full of uneven teeth and a chin and jaw-bone *qui n'en finessent
pas* .... Now in this vast ugliness resides a most powerful beauty
which, in a very few minutes steals forth and charms the mind,
so that you end as I ended, falling in love with her. Yes behold
me literally in love with this great horse-faced blue-stocking. I
don't know in what the charm lies, but it is thoroughly potent.

An admirable physiognomy – a delightful expression, a voice soft
and rich as that of a counselling angel – a mingled sagacity and
sweetness – a broad hint of a great underlying world of reserve,
knowledge, pride and power – a feminine dignity and character
in those massively plain features – a hundred conflicting shades
of consciousness and simpleness – shyness and frankness – gra-
ciousness and remote indifference – these are some of the more
definite elements of her personality. Her manner is extremely
good tho' rather too intense and her speech, in the way of accent
and syntax peculiarly agreeable.[27]

Thus wrote the 26-year-old James, already the author of a dozen
short stories; Sir Frederic Burton's well-known chalk portrait of
George Eliot, for which she had given sittings for over more
than a year's duration (1864–65) before she was satisfied with it
sufficiently to let Lewes hang it in his study, scarcely told so much.
By the time she met Henry James, George Eliot had already
made a start on a plan for the Lydgate part of *Middlemarch*, which,
however, ground to a halt in the agonising last stages of Thornton
Hunt's illness. She was with him till he died, aged only twenty-five,
on 19 October 1869. She had resumed preparations for the new
novel before March 1870 when she and Lewes left for yet another
central European journey, the last for over two years as it turned
out. The Franco-Prussian War caused her much anguish since
she had sympathies with both sides, but it may indirectly have
helped *Middlemarch* along, for it curtailed foreign travel. She and
Lewes stayed at Shottermill in Surrey during the summer months
of 1870; she was adding the Dorothea Brooke material to the
Middlemarch chapters. As a novelist she was at the very height
of her powers, challenging comparison with any other. In rest
periods Lewes read her Victor Hugo aloud and began arranging
publication of *Middlemarch* with Blackwood on lines similar to those
adopted by Hugo, mostly in two-monthly parts, but for its American
publication he arranged weekly parts. George Eliot had largely
lived down the objections to her partnership with Lewes; visitors
now included Tennyson and Arnold and their wives, but no longer
the ever-respectful Dickens, who dined with her and Lewes for the
last time on 6 March 1870. Blackwood bought out the first (large)
instalment of *Middlemarch* on 1 December 1871. In the same month
appeared *Wise, Witty, and Tender Sayings in Prose and Verse selected from
the Works of George Eliot*, edited by Alexander Main, an enthusiast

who had elicited her approval for this project; she had been pleased to intimate to him her 'worship for' Sir Walter Scott.[28] Worshipful discipleship regarding herself was, by inference, not ruled out, though Lewes had reservations. *Middlemarch* was still being written in September 1872, the last parts at a house at Redhill, 'shut out from the world amid fields'.[29] The 'Finale', which has a jarring note or two, was added at a place very much *in* the world, the German spa and gambling resort of Homburg.

The warm reception accorded to *Middlemarch* during the whole of its unfolding and after its final appearance in four volumes in 1872 was the highlight of George Eliot's career. It brought her deep personal satisfaction and yet further financial success. She now received men and women of high rank at The Priory. It was also in 1872 that two younger women, Elma Stuart and Edith Simcox, were introduced to her; they both formed emotional attachments to her which she reciprocated only in part. Another close friend now was J. W. Cross, whom both she and Lewes knew as 'nephew Johnnie'.[30] He took charge of their financial affairs, investing their literary earnings very profitably, so that they were well able to purchase a new piano and set up their own carriage.

The framework of *Daniel Deronda*, first conceived when George Eliot watched Byron's grand-niece at a Homburg gambling table in September 1872, gradually built itself up. Since 1866 George Eliot had been friendly with Emanuel Deutsch, a Jewish scholar who visited Jerusalem and cherished the idea of a national home for Jews: he gave her Hebrew lessons, before falling victim to cancer. She visited him several times in Marylebone, during his terminal decline late in 1872, and in the following summer while in France and Germany began developing and discussing the Jewish part of the new novel, inspecting synagogues and bookshops. In June 1874 the search was on in the west of England for settings for the scenes concerning Gwendolen Harleth. By the end of that year she was well into the actual composition; progress was steady, in spite of interruptions owing to headaches, toothache and kidney stone pain. On 29 June 1875 there occurred another grievous event, the death of Lewes's second son Bertie in Natal, the repercussions of which inevitably set back her writing schedule. *Daniel Deronda* came out in eight monthly parts from February to September 1876, the actual writing being finished on 8 June 1876, after which she and Lewes took a long holiday in Switzerland. *Daniel Deronda* was less liked than *Middlemarch*, though its overall purport of discrediting anti-Semitism was respected, and in Jewish circles in Britain and abroad gratefully appreciated; it was acknowledged as a stimulus to Jewish nationalism. In London George Eliot was now an international figure; at Oxford and Cambridge she was privately treated with honour. Her presence was sought overseas. Her only regular public appearances were at the concerts at St James's Hall, where her arrival was the occasion of excited murmurs and rapidly executed pen or pencil sketches. At a dinner held on 15 May 1877 the Princess Louise asked to be presented to *her*, and during Wagner's series of London concerts in that month George Eliot met the composer twelve times, once with William Morris and Edward Burne-Jones also present;[31] music, literature, design and art, as it were, all supremely represented. Higher things were to follow; a year later at a dinner she and Lewes met the Princess Royal and the German Crown Prince. But an exception was being made, and they got no higher.

They had bought, on Cross's advice, The Heights, Witley, late in 1877. They settled into this secluded and spacious country home, near the Tennysons at Blackdown, in June 1878. Here George Eliot wrote her rather uneven collection of late essays, *Impressions of Theophrastus Such* (1879), while Lewes fought bravely against encroaching cancer. There was an excursion to meet Turgenev and another, not entirely propitious, visit from Henry James (they apparently did not like *The Europeans*). In November they moved back to London, where Lewes's grim symptoms worsened. His last letter was a commendation of *Theophrastus Such* to Blackwood. He died on 30 November 1878, aged sixty-one, the same age at which George Eliot herself was to die.

She did not attend the funeral at Highgate Cemetery. Deeply stricken, she stayed in her room in The Priory for a week and then devoted her time to preparing Lewes's *Problems of Life and Mind* for the press. On 8 February 1879 she ventured out of her house for the first time since her bereavement. On the 23rd of that month she renewed her highly valued acquaintance with Cross, who helped her with the financial and legal arrangements consequent upon Lewes's demise. They included the establishment of the George Henry Lewes studentship in Physiology at Cambridge.

George Eliot's friendship with Cross was being strengthened by serious literary study. They began to read Dante in Italian, a task which continued when she moved down to Witley in May 1879 and he came over regularly from his home at Weybridge. Cross may have proposed marriage to her in August, though the Cross family was to consider it more likely that it was she who proposed it to him.[32] At any rate a letter of George Eliot's dated 16 October 1879, written to Cross from Witley, and signed 'Beatrice' certainly expresses her intimate love for him, her 'dear tender one'.[33] Her spirits had revived, but then were dashed again temporarily by the news of John Blackwood's death in Edinburgh on 29 October 1879. She returned to The Priory on 1 November, being willing now to receive calls, and many there were, including ones from Herbert Spencer, Charles Darwin and Leslie Stephen. Cross came frequently also; she played the piano for him. He escorted her to art galleries. He celebrated his fortieth birthday on 12 November 1880. Within a month their marriage was decided. It took place in St George's, Hanover Square, on 6 May 1880. She was given away by Charles Lewes. Though one or two friends felt doubts, most wrote in tactful support. Particularly piquant was a letter of reconciliation from her brother Isaac at Griff.

The marriage journey took the Crosses through northern Italy to the Hotel d'Europe in Venice. But here a psychological catastrophe ensued. Cross evidently grew mentally deranged (it may not have been for the first time) and jumped from his balcony into the canal at the very moment when George Eliot was consulting an Italian doctor about his condition.[34] He was rescued by gondoliers. Moving slowly across Europe George Eliot resolutely maintained an atmosphere of normality. He began properly to recover in Witley in late July 1880. Tension was relieved with tennis. He strengthened his muscles with tree-felling, using a special axe. George Eliot, however, was growing thin, beset by painful renal disorders and, no doubt, worry. In due course they returned to London and on 3 December 1880 moved into a new home at 4 Cheyne Walk, Chelsea, where George Eliot had, quite unknown to herself, less than three weeks to live and very little work left.[35] There was letter-writing to do, piano-playing, concert-going to resume; on 17 December she and Cross attended at St George's Hall a performance of Aeschylus's *Agamemnon* in Greek. She thought she must have caught a cold there, when a sore throat developed two days later. In two more days she felt better, but then, rapidly and steeply, declined. Her heart malfunctioned, and her last words were, 'Tell them that I have great pain in the left side'. She died, painlessly, according to Cross,[36] at ten in the evening on Wednesday 22 December 1880. She was buried a week later in a plot near Lewes's in Highgate

Cemetery. There were numerous mourners, many of them very distinguished people. Also, up from Warwickshire had come Isaac Evans, effectively to bring half-true the Biblical epitaph which his sister had afforded to her Maggie and Tom Tulliver at the end of *The Mill on the Floss.* In their death they were not divided.

George Eliot's unlooked-for death distressed everyone. She left a truly great gap, it can be said. So powerful was her moral influence and so extensive her intellectual reach that had she lived another twenty years she conceivably might have stiffened resistance to the decadence, jingoism and socialist uplift which swept British culture in the *fin de siècle.* Without her, the atmosphere definitely changed for the worse.

2

Country Life: *Adam Bede*

George Eliot's first novel, *Adam Bede* (1859), has a special appeal. The predominantly rural scenes have the quality of picturesque charm, yet the manipulation of incidents, characters and points of view is so highly intelligent that the reader of the novel finds his or her normal mental life not only extended but surpassed, being prompted all the time to compare, reconsider, question, in an exciting way. *Adam Bede* is still probably George Eliot's most popular work, and that is certainly no reason for underestimating it. Various categories such as Pastoral, Romance and Myth have been applied to it to suggest a limitation of its method. But it seems to resist them. There is too much complexity, irony, width of reference and challenging implication for any reductionist interpretation to carry conviction. It keeps curiosity alive, from the opening promise to reveal 'far reaching visions of the past' to the last reference to yet another 'hard day' for Adam Bede.

Despite the title, the hero's effort to secure his independence and a partner for life is not central to the novel, but is balanced by the story of Hetty Sorrel's seduction by the squire's twenty-year-old grandson and her subsequent transportation for infanticide. George Eliot's aunt, then Elizabeth Tomlinson, a Methodist preacher, had actually heard the confession of one Mary Voce, 'a common coarse girl, convicted of child-murder',[1] in a Nottingham gaol in 1802, before accompanying her to the gallows, where she was hanged. The aunt impressed on George Eliot the 'great respect'[2] with which the people about the gaol had regarded her ministry on this occasion. The novelist, thinking of the beneficial effects of moral sincerity among those whose beliefs were quaint or narrow, accepted G. H. Lewes's advice that the scene in the prison would make 'a fine element' in a piece of fiction and determined to blend it with some points in her father's 'early

life and character'. The problem was to make the unhappy girl
a chief character and 'connect her with the hero'. The two-fold
solution, to make the upright Adam Bede deludedly in love with
Hetty Sorrel (her character is constructed as that of a socially
ambitious, sexually vain, hard-hearted orphan), and to make the
woman-preacher in love with Adam Bede, came slowly, but proved
very neat. It illuminated the curious connection there often is
between mistaken judgment and moral integrity, and allowed for
a softening of the appalling details of the aunt's story. By placing
Hetty as a dairy-maid in the country south of Ashbourne, where
George Eliot's father and uncle had been in business as joiners early
in the nineteenth century, the author was able to explore economic
and environmental interests which were, she knew, closely related
to the main question of human motivation. She wrote to her
publisher that the new novel would be 'a country story, full of
the breath of cows and the scent of hay'.[3] The combination of the
sour with the sweet in these olfactory images is typical of the rich
ambiguity of *Adam Bede*. George Eliot had herself been brought
up on tenant-farms like the Poysers'; her father had befriended
his squire, as Adam does Arthur Donnithorne, who in the novel
secretly fathers a child on the attractive Hetty against his own
better judgment. From her writing-desks in London and Germany,
the forty-year-old novelist looked back on the man-made Midland
landscapes and the social history of the period at the turn of the
century with unsentimental affection. Her memories of the land
were the foundation of what her husband, J. W. Cross, called her
'latent Conservative bias', which, however, always amused her.[4]
The country community of Hayslope in 1798 imagined in *Adam
Bede* seems very suitable for interconnecting her themes of work,
property, conscience, sexuality, religion and power, and for developing the personality of the narrator, whose relation to the setting
is varied with much subtlety.

The confessor-figure, Dinah Morris, the earnest comforter of
the poor and listener for the inner 'call', was not the easiest
part of the project to bring off. But because of the closeness
of George Eliot's conception of Dinah to her old Evangelical
self, when she too had tried self-denial, good works and faith
in the living Jesus, she was able to preserve a certain tension
in the episodes where the preacher appears. Though lacking the
humour carefully applied elsewhere, the presentation of Dinah
is full of indications of the character's unawareness amid her

concern, as in the reference to 'that sincere, articulate, thrilling treble, by which she always mastered her audience', which reminds us that she is both ahead of her time as a woman in a man's role and behind it in her antique piety, 'joined to the Lord' (Ch. 8). There is more to Dinah than a charismatic personality, whose exceptional disinterestedness impresses everyone strongly, even, in the end, Hetty. As we extend to her archaic phraseology[5] that 'impatient patience' which Arthur later applies to his mournful Aunt Lydia (Ch. 44) and perhaps see her in modern terms as too submissive a social worker, offering palliatives instead of radical challenges,[6] we realise we are underestimating her influence. Dinah's power is the power of tact, which, proceeding from 'acute and ready sympathy', is 'careful not to oppose any feeling' (Ch. 10), but it is also the power of touch, which provides physical reassurance. In Dinah's errands of mercy there is a drive to physicality. She grows out of the habit of vision, of envisaging the presence of the stigmatised Christ, to real motherhood, from preaching to teaching, from inspirational talk to silent feeling. At Dinah's supreme exaltation in the scene of expected execution it is the embrace which counts for the trembling Hetty, who 'clung to her and clutched her as the only visible sign of love and pity' (Ch. 47). If Hetty has her eyes closed as commanded, Dinah is a *tangible* sign to her, a visible sign to the crowd. She embodies comfort, in the way she had imagined Christ to do, successfully effacing the other sign, 'the hideous symbol of a deliberately-inflicted sudden death', the gallows. She does so, not by evoking 'a bleeding Face, crowned with thorns' (Ch. 2), but by being touched. Indications of Dinah's firming human substance as the novel proceeds force us to revise our stock-reaction to her religious quaintness. In a scene of mockery worthy of Shakespeare, when Hetty disguises herself provocatively in Dinah's net-cap to tease Adam with 'coquettish dark eyes', Mrs Poyser ominously breaks a jug, thinking she has seen Dinah's ghost. But her recovery is significant; though she feels that Dinah on the whole needs more self-love, yet she insists here that her niece is 'one o' them things as looks the brightest on a rainy day' (Ch. 20). Dinah's spirituality has an expanding material core.

Dinah bases her ministry on the example of Wesley, whom in her girlhood she had heard preach. He went among the poor, speaking tenderly to them the good news about a loving God. Her message is in itself other-worldly, in that it venerates a putative love of God for His creation above shared material prosperity humanly achieved.

Of the former (to Dinah) credible, but (to George Eliot) unknow-able benefit, Dinah proclaims there is 'Enough for all, enough for each'; the latter comes, in her view, a poor second. 'It is not like the riches of this world, so that the more one gets the less the rest can have' (Ch. 2). Dinah's public persuasiveness depends on a denial of economic truth and a pessimistic view of poverty:

> We have been brought up in poor cottages, and have been reared on oat-cake, and lived coarse; and we haven't been to school much, nor read books, and we don't know much about anything but what happens just round us. We are just the sort of people that want to hear good news. (Ch. 2)

But in a poor cottage nearby, Lisbeth Bede's, Dinah is made to learn that coarseness is not inevitable; there are refinements to be passed on even in cooking oats 'by putting a sprig o' mint in' (Ch. 11), as well as progress in reading. Dinah's frankness about the appeal of religion to the uncultured[7] (she admits there is less 'deadness to the Word' in lead-mining villages like Hetton-Deeps and industrial towns like Leeds, where 'life is so dark and weary', than in quiet villages (Ch. 8)) includes the idea (unrecognised by her) that an improvement in social conditions might lead to a decline in Christian belief.

The novel also distances itself from Dinah's puritanism. On Hayslope green, she deplores in an anecdote the act of a vain 'serv-ant of God' in saving all her money to buy lace caps: she had been a girl who only wanted 'to have better lace than other girls', until she saw the face of the suffering Christ in her mirror. Dinah uses this example to urge Chad's Bess, a girl in her audience, to throw off her ear-rings, 'as if they were stinging adders'. This self-denying emotionalism has no permanent effect on Bess, however, who is later disappointed to discover that her prize for the 'sack-race' is a grim 'grogram gown' instead of something finer. On this occasion, Arthur Donnithorne discreetly resolves to compensate Bess with money, 'that she might buy something more to her mind', but, unaware of this just piece of generosity, she in any case lets a cousin have the material to make clothes for her son (Ch. 25). Arthur is seen to be dealing with Bess's psychological needs (and Bess with her cousin's) much more constructively than Dinah was. At the end Dinah in turn learns to accept and value Arthur's very appropriate remembrance-token of a watch, though he knows 'she doesn't care about such things' (Ch. 48), and to reassure him that she always uses it. So Dinah's original unpremeditated doctrinal enthusiasm, which the observing elderly gentleman notes as opening 'the inward drama of the speaker's emotions' (Ch. 2), is tempered by experience.

Dinah's handling of Hetty is also shown as a process of trial and error. Hetty, admiring her reflection in the mirror with 'great glass ear-rings in her ears', is literally a vainer servant than any Dinah has envisaged. Dinah's mistake, when, having deliberately opened the Bible anywhere and landed on a passage referring to the disciples' kissing Paul, she goes in and kisses Hetty, is to confuse chance with choice, imagination with fact, probability with conviction. Her effort to get Hetty to anticipate trouble, to visualise, as *she* does, the 'thorny thicket of sin and sorrow' and to forearm herself with trust in God's support, is naturally repulsed by the self-conscious seventeen-year-old as an interfering attempt to frighten her. It is just before this rebuff that Dinah's 'pale face full of subdued emotion' is compared with 'a lovely corpse into which the soul has returned charged with sublimer secrets and sublimer love'. The idea that Dinah's genuine desire to help others itself tends towards unreality and exaltation is finely caught in this paradoxically chill and warm simile.[8] The narrator comments pointedly that the higher nature has to learn to understand the lower as we learn the art of seeing itself, 'by a good deal of hard experience . . . fancying our space wider than it is' (Ch. 15). This process is underway at Snowfield when Dinah, dreaming of the Poysers and Hetty as if they were 'in trouble', waits, this time, to be taught 'some leading', seeing 'with new clearness' that the true Cross is 'the sin and sorrow of this world' (Ch. 30). She is ready for the ordeal with Hetty when it comes. Even so she may hold back too cautiously while there is a possibility of preventing the worst, still waiting for a supernatural sign. She never pushes her increasing common sense into a radical questioning of her faith. The main cause of her more realistic awareness of the moral space within which she can exercise her benevolent nature is her relationship with Adam, the only person before whom she blushes. With Dinah's inner changes George Eliot makes do with intimation rather than analysis. Dinah's body repeatedly gives signs of need which she herself eventually comes to respect.

Adam Bede too is not without superstitious intuitions. The unexplained raps upon the door, heard while he is working on the coffin, suggest omens of impending death to him. But he checks his curiosity in favour of training his eye for measuring: 'I think it's better to see when your perpendicular's true, than to see a ghost' (Ch. 4.). Adam's uprightness, his interest in figuring and admiration of inventive labour in both the industrial and domestic spheres disincline him to 'doctrinal religion' or over-spirituality. He realises the need of secular thought, of 'something beside Gospel', to produce the new engines, aqueducts and mills in places like Cromford, and locates God's 'sperrit' in the expert worker (Ch. 1). Dinah, hardly going beyond Mrs Poyser's point that people 'should rejoice in their families and provide for them', believes it her vocation to work for other' souls (Ch. 6.). But evidently her dedication to charitable service needs to be supplemented by Adam's commitment to enterprise and education. Both Dinah and Adam have large horizons, but with a difference. When Dinah looks out of her window on the moonlit Hayslope fields she *closes* her eyes to feel 'the presence of a Love and Sympathy deeper and more tender than was breathed from the earth and sky' (Ch. 15). Despite the echoes of 'Tintern Abbey', such a presence has an un-Wordsworthian quality, different from the influence of natural objects; it is entirely *assumed.* Adam, on the other hand, less impressed by improbability, likes rolling country, where hill-top views show him a bridge, town or steeple: 'It makes you feel the world's a big place, and there's other men working in it with their heads and hands besides yourself' (Ch. 11). He can imagine the future; indeed he loves the Anglican service for its reminder of that as well as of 'our entire past' (Ch. 18). Though a certain rigidity in his work-ethic and a hardness to those who fall short of his own standards limit his sensibility, Adam characteristically works on the problem. He sticks by his mother, despite her irritating querulousness, rejecting the purely utilitarian motive of 'making things easy and pleasant to yourself' (Ch. 4). With Hetty, however, Adam is deceived. Her beauty affects him impersonally, so that he cannot conceive of her inner life. He is certainly fortunate not to be trapped into marriage with Hetty. When his bitter disillusionment comes, Adam manages to overcome his feelings of jealousy and anger by leaning on a sense that his life has 'visible and invisible relations beyond any of which either our present or prospective self is the centre' (Ch. 50). This wider and more tentative outwardness brings Adam into closer alignment with Dinah, who in turn has to temper her renunciatory zeal to meet him.

The idea that Dinah is attracted to him is a difficult one for
Adam to take in, though the narrator keeps before us the fact
that his mother spots the truth. Having given no real thought
to Hetty's sexuality, but regarding it possessively as passive, 'just
what one wants to make one's hearth a paradise' (Ch. 15), he is in
turn inevitably slow to understand Dinah's maturing feelings. Yet,
regarding his brother Seth's affection for Dinah, Adam had not
doubted that her 'finer grain' (Ch. 11) would stretch to sexual love
as well as to neighbourly goodness: 'the best fire doesna flare up the
soonest' (Ch. 30). He regards sexual attraction humorously as an
unaccountable mystery like 'the sprouting o' the seed' (Ch. 11): he
is too sensitive to Seth's feelings to calculate the effect of his own
masculinity upon Dinah. The narrator makes Adam's attractiveness
a salient feature, of course; there are many descriptive strokes to
this end, 'his thick black hair all glistening with fresh moisture', 'the
dark penetrating glance of this strong man' (Ch. 11), his 'shaggy
air, and dark vigorous colour' and his 'deep strong voice', the
'intense thrill' of which seems one of the 'manifold temptations'
(Ch. 55) which might enslave Dinah 'to an earthly affection'
(Ch. 52). It is hardly enslavement that is involved, however, but
adaptation. To build a relationship on physical contact and care
means to be laboured for as well as to labour, to be ministered to
as well as to minister – 'What greater thing is there for two human
souls?' asks the narrator, implying that salvation is not (Ch. 54).

The coming together of Adam and Dinah, both exemplary figures, yet restrained by difficulties in their attitudes, is handled
with considerable delicacy. Their unclaiming mutual regard is
compared with 'little quivering rain-streams', 'the first detected
signs of coming spring', 'the tiniest perceptible budding' (Ch. 50).
The passionate partnership which these two can form is, I think,
well suggested.[9] It is essential for its success that Adam offer Dinah
freedom of religious conscience. She will continue teaching as a
Methodist, only with more means now to make the sick comfortable. Adam argues that 'feeling's a sort of knowledge', so that
her married life would equip her with experience which would
help her in counselling others. With this viable arrangement in
prospect, Dinah's vision of Jesus 'pointing to the sinful' (Ch. 52)
begins to appear less imperious and frightening. It is, in effect,
replaced in her consciousness by the sight of Adam as he appears
behind her near Sloman's End. 'She was so accustomed to think of
impressions as purely spiritual monitions, that she looked for no

visible accompaniment of the voice' (Ch. 54). But there *is* one, and she moves towards him for his embrace, admitting that without him she had lost 'fullness of strength' for her ministry. With Adam, Dinah is able to combine practical religion with family life, and it is clear that, despite the later Methodist Conference's ban on women-preachers, she is 'not held' from other kinds of teaching (Epilogue, set in 1807).[10] The whole treatment of religion in *Adam Bede* is scrupulously inoffensive, but implicitly radical. The historical setting is exploited to encourage the reader's detached judgment. One early Methodist reviewer, however, noticed unorthodoxy in the underplaying of guilt in sinning and argued that George Eliot's stress on the disastrous consequences of sin was unrealistic.[11] But consideration of that point brings us to Hetty.

The inescapable crime in *Adam Bede* is Hetty Sorrel's negligent abandonment of her nameless, sexless child to its death in circumstances which emerge so cruelly in the testimony of the witnesses at the trial and in the confession of the girl herself. George Eliot's characterisation of a seventeen-year-old who could do such a thing has been universally admired for its analytic and experiential detail. The compliment of Dickens, 'I know of nothing so skillful, determined, and uncompromising',[12] may be left to speak for all the rest. Infanticide arouses condemnatory emotions stronger than those evoked by any other kind of murder. It negates nursing motherhood, on which human beings in their most helpless stage are dependent. But George Eliot is concerned not with attributing monstrosity but with understanding influence and deficiency. Hetty, below-average in intelligence, though literate, has her sights on the easy life. Hard-worked by her aunt at butter-making[13] and other chores and indulged by her uncle because she is so extremely pretty, Hetty knows that she cannot rise far in the limited female labour market, but can exploit sex. She seizes her opportunity with the heir to the Donnithorne estate, who is on leave from his regiment recovering from an injury to his arm. He has already been attracted to her. There is little doubt that in a more sexually sophisticated age,[14] Arthur would have got away with the affair, had Hetty let him. 'Who seduces whom?' we may ask: neither really seduces the other; spontaneous nature and sexual enjoyment take over for both, but, unlike Arthur, Hetty has no scruples. To all intents and purposes an atheist, she is convinced the attachment is to her advantage.

Hetty's lack of moral feeling is indicated by many details. She

has no tender memories of childhood, pets or flowers, since they
hold no pleasures for her; she is the sort who would blossom if lain
rootless, on an 'ornamental flower-pot' (Ch. 15). She thinks of her
young cousins as worse than 'the nasty little lambs' brought in by the
shepherd. Indifferent to suffering, 'pleasure-craving . . . luxurious
and vain', she is unwilling to 'face difficulties' (Ch. 31). 'She's no
better than a peacock,' says Mrs Poyser. 'It's my belief her heart's
as hard as a pebble' (Ch. 15). She is unmoved by Adam Bede's
affection, beyond the 'cold triumph of knowing' that he would not
care to look at other girls, since she disbelieves in his ability to afford
her 'even such luxuries as she shared in her uncle's house' (Ch. 9).
Later, determined to conceal her pregnancy, she duplicitously
accepts Adam's proposal with no thought for the anguish in
store for him. Mistakes increase her confusion. Her 'little silly
imagination' had fixed on Arthur as an impressive provider. Life
at Donnithorne Chase, where she was learning lace-mending from
the lady's maid, furnishes her with previsions of idleness and rank;
her thought is recorded as indirect speech:

> it was impossible to think how it would be! But Captain
> Donnithorne would know; he was a great gentleman, and
> could have his way in everything, and could buy everything
> he liked. And nothing could be as it had been again: perhaps
> some day she should be a grand lady, and ride in her coach,
> and dress for dinner in a brocaded silk. (Ch. 15)

Beneath her 'false air of innocence', her kitten-like surface, Hetty's
hope for acquired privilege is clear. Her sly consciousness that 'no
turn of her head was lost' gives her a distracting beauty 'which
you feel ready to crush for inability to comprehend the state of
mind into which it throws you' (Ch. 7). The narrator's severity is
justified by the gravity of the tragedy to which Hetty's beauty contributes, guaranteeing her an immunity from criticism by the men
closely involved. The flexible indirect free style, as the narrator's
comments and images alternate with thoughts couched in Hetty's
language, catches subtly the combination of daring, inconsistency,
susceptibility and calculation in Hetty's attitude:

> she thought of nothing that was present. She only saw something
> that was possible: Mr. Arthur Donnithorne coming to meet her
> again along the Fir-tree Grove. That was the foreground of

Hetty's picture; behind it lay a bright hazy something – days that were not to be as the other days of her life had been. It was as if she had been wooed by a river-god, who might any time take her to his wondrous halls below a watery heaven. There was no knowing what would come, since this strange entrancing delight had come. (Ch. 13)

Hetty's lack of interest in reading (she 'knew no romances', Ch. 34) makes the romantic evocation of 'wondrous halls' and the like an authorial suggestion of the value of natural feeling even amidst so much knowingness and thoughtlessness. Hetty's poverty of culture (novels were too hard for her and the pictures in *The Pilgrim's Progress* too riddling, Ch. 14) render her expectations of Arthur's protection vulnerably unrealistic, but it is not an excuse. Dominated by an egotism that takes no account of others' interests and feelings, she can be budged only by fear of pain and of scorn. Hers alone is an unquiet mind at Thias Bede's funeral service, experiencing a 'selfish tumult', because Arthur does not turn up. When on this occasion Molly the housemaid sympathetically applies smelling-salts to Hetty's nostrils, her reaction is peevish; 'she would have pressed her own nails into her tender flesh rather than people should know a secret she did not want them to know' (Ch. 18). It is this fear of public criticism which impels Hetty to deceive everyone over her misfortunes and to remain silent even when they are discovered. It is fear that her baby's presence and cries will expose her that causes her first to mean to kill it and then to cause its death. Finally, only fear of everlasting punishment (unpardoned perishing 'for ever') induces Hetty to speak the truth about what she has done, apologise to Adam and forgive Arthur (Ch. 46). Apart from this influence of extreme terror, Hetty never softens.

Unsympathetic as she is, Hetty Sorrel does, however, have one feature on which sympathy may be built, the basic human desire to live. The difficulties of her journey to Windsor in search of Arthur incline her half-consciously to the waggoner's trembling spaniel, in contrast with her previous indifference to animals: 'she felt as if the helpless timid creature had some fellowship with her' (Ch. 36). During her subsequent 'objectless wandering, apart from all love, caring for human beings only through her pride, clinging to life only as the hunted brute clings to it', she lacks the will or courage to commit suicide, but awakens beside a pool, discerning

'the rapid motion of some living creature – perhaps a field-mouse'.
The 'pricking of the gorsy wall' of a hovel is then a delicious
sensation to her, and, inside it, she experiences 'hysterical joy that
she still had hold of life, that she was still on the familiar earth,
with the sheep near her. The very consciousness of her own limbs
was a delight to her: she turned up her sleeves and kissed her arms
with the passionate love of life' (Ch. 37). The power of George
Eliot's narrative technique moving from momentary vividness to
psychological generalisation, with the occasional phrase ('this *was*
the field where she had seen the hovel') recording Hetty's own
verbalised consciousness, produces one of the triumphs of English
fiction. Strong empathy is achieved with a figure whose every act is
self-centred, who curses her love, who seems to hate her baby 'like
a heavy weight' (Ch. 45), who is unpitying and strong-hearted, from
whose face 'a hard unloving despairing soul' looks out (Ch. 37).
Hetty's compulsive auto-erotic kiss becomes a sign of humanity. The
very unimaginativeness so convincingly inhabited by the narration
is inverted in the process of reading. Critical detachment has to be
reconsidered.

Hetty has no conscience except fear of shame, but as with Dinah,
though in the opposite direction, feeling does become a sort of
knowledge to her. The implication is that morality is bound up
with the broadening of knowledge, both of others and of the
self. Is there, then, something too narrow, too comfortable, too
complacent, too static about the ethic of Hayslope and the way
of life of its people, which explains Hetty's bid for excitement?[15]
In fact Hetty shows some of the characteristics of the Hayslope
outlook, its acceptance of inequality of inheritance (she simply
wants to become superior by marriage), its hardness on poverty
as bringing 'burthens on the parish' (Ch. 37), its high estimate
of the appearance of respectability. Readers are made so familiar
with Hayslope as they proceed through *Adam Bede* that they may
be inclined to idealise it.[16] Its name, however, suggests a certain
obliqueness as well as fertility. It is possible to exaggerate both
the charm and the tranquillity of the village. The mention of 'idle
tramps' (Ch. 1) against whose 'burglarious attempt' Martin Poyser
keeps a gun in the bedroom (Ch. 22) indicates a world that is not
entirely secure, but one where it is better to see a female preacher
'safe home' (Ch. 1) than not. But it is not only vagrants who can
cause trouble in Hayslope. The squire's servants like Bethell are
feared for 'making love to both the gells at once' and turning

the farm-kitchen into a public house (Ch. 32). Hetty's fall is not unprecedented, it seems. Hayslope is hardly paradisal. There are poachers about and the odd 'mutinous pauper' in the workhouse (Ch. 16). Violence, though contained, can be threatened nastily. In the opening scene in the carpenters' workshop, which one might be tempted to regard as picturesquely idyllic, the sarcastic Wiry Ben, menacing Seth Bede with disgrace in the form of a specimen of his defective workmanship hung up with 'Seth Bede, the Methody, his work' painted on it in red, is pinned roughly against the wall by the impetuous Adam until cringingly giving way. Soon afterwards the Rector has to resist a proposal that another Methodist, Maskery the wheelwright, who had called him an 'idle shepherd', should be turned out of his home for it, lose business orders and even be hunted out of Hayslope 'with rope-ends and pitch-forks' (Ch. 5), a measure which would certainly have occasioned a damaging scandal for the Anglican Church in the religious press. Potential unrest in the form of persecution of strangers or abuse of aristocratic privilege is checked in Hayslope by the existence of the right of free speech, but the hints should not be ignored.

Nevertheless threats to good order are in general defused by the magisterial tolerance practised by Mr Irwine, who is scrupulous in avoiding sectarian bitterness and muting disruptive protest. The Rector is a key-figure in the pleasant impression made by Hayslope; he harmonises well with 'that peaceful landscape', acting as 'everybody's friend' (Ch. 40) by being 'tender to other men's failings and unwilling to impute evil' (Ch. 5). It is true he may be a bit too relaxed. The narrator seems to have him partly in mind in her personification of 'Fine old Leisure', on whose easy conscience we are asked not to be 'too severe' (Ch. 53). With his classical taste and fine features (he 'had the mysterious secret of never wearing a new-looking coat', Ch. 24), Mr Irwine blames his own delicacy for not stopping Arthur in his tracks before the damage with Hetty was done. He is presented in a very balanced way as an individual making choices all the time, usually justifiable; as such he comes across more favourably than he would as 'an embodied system or opinion', as viewed by a critical historian, yet 'generic classification' does not entirely belie Mr Irwine since he shares experiences with other Anglican pluralists at that time who thought religious custom more beneficial to their congregations than doctrine (Ch. 5). He represents a conservative influence. The community over which he presides is inevitably very slow to change.

Much of the description of the landscape, buildings and rural manners of Hayslope is done in a picturesque way to reinforce the value of stability and quiet.[17] Correspondingly, the inhabitants are seen and see one another familiarly as typified by occupation, physique or mental trait. So the 'typical features of this pleasant land', in which the level sunlight lies 'like transparent gold', seem appropriate to 'the living groups' of villagers, in which every generation and trade is represented, including the 'slouching labourer' (Ch. 2), the brawny blacksmith and 'the stalwart work- man in paper cap' (Ch. 1), Adam Bede himself. Locations in the novel, emphasising regularity of life, the workshop, the dairy, the church, the night-school, the cottage, even the prison, acquire a prominence from their use in chapter-titles. Permanence is suggested again by the importance accorded to family and home, irrespective of status. Experience and traits of one generation are said to reappear in the next. People are not expected to thrive away from their roots. The constant notice taken of animals, wild, domesticated and productional, reinforces the impression of an apparently cyclic, unintellectualised life. The humorous closeness of human and animal life issues in numerous comparisons between them in both directions in dialogue and commentary. Totty's childish fat, 'which made her look like a metamorphosis of a white sucking-pig' (Ch. 6), is matched by the largest actual piglet's 'excellent spring-bed' discovered in its 'mother's fat ribs' (Ch. 18). Country lore assumes a world where breed and species can be known and assessed like the recurrent seasons and weather. The repetitive domestic round of washing, cleaning, cooking and sleeping, adds to the pattern, as when the members of the Poyser household are 'all going to bed by twilight, like the birds' (Ch. 14). Mrs Poyser, with her many memorable sayings, caustically phrased, depends on such a view of known types for her originality. She relies on analogy to 'stock' the country with new proverbs (Ch. 33), as the Rector puts it. She in turn associates the reassuring fertility of the farm with the superiority of the Rector:

and him a gentleman born, and's got a mother like a picter. You may go the country round, and not find such another woman turned sixty-six. It's summat like to see such a man as that i' the desk of a Sunday! As I say to Poyser, it's like looking at a full crop o' wheat, or a pasture with a fine dairy o' cows in it; it makes you think the world's comfortable-like. (Ch. 8)

Yet references to ageing and extraordinariness remind us that this grip on comfort and security derives from a pressing psychological need, not complacency. Mrs Poyser here is about to hear of Thias Bede's drowning in the Willow Brook, to which she can respond in 'the frank and genial' key of C. She is stiffened by her belief in fixity of character (the troublesome Thias is 'better out o' the way nor in'). Her sister Judith's charitable disposition, for example, was 'just the same from the first o' my remembering her; it made no difference in her, as I could see, when she took to the Methodists'. Dinah too, she is convinced, in unchanging; 'it 'ud be just the same if I was to talk to you for hours' (Ch. 6). Mrs Poyser's habit of stereotyping lets her down, of course, with Arthur, whom she trusts as being so open-looking that he could do them nothing but good, and with Hetty, whose pregnancy 'the familiar unsuspecting eye' leaves unnoticed (Ch. 36). Mr Craig the gardener is even more limited in his point of view. He exhibits an absurd Francophobia, which Adam refutes (Ch. 53), and gets his weather-forecast wrong ('a ticklish thing', Ch. 19). Mr Craig's prejudices prevent us from indulging too ready a partiality for Hayslope as a model village. He 'has the name and nater o' plants in's head' in a self-satisfied way (Ch. 23) and prefers repetitive Scottish tunes to English ones. On this point, Bartle Massey the schoolmaster disagrees, significantly alluding to scolding women (like Mrs Poyser); the Scottish tunes 'go on with the same thing over and over again, and never come to a reasonable end' (Ch. 23). Massey's own misogyny and contempt for Hayslope backwardness ('this stupid country', Ch. 40) are themselves stock-responses, which function to counter the loyalties of the Poysers, though none of these characters is just simple. Massey's humorous quarrel with Mrs Poyser on the respective demerits of men and women, a match which is interrupted as a draw (Ch. 53), proceeds so merrily simply because of its classifying facility. But Massey is more sensitive than he seems, recognising Dinah's effectiveness as a comforter to other women (Ch. 46) and admitting that Mrs Poyser is 'sound at the core' (Ch. 53). Massey's role as a typical local schoolmaster, typifying others, contains contradictions.

Bartle Massey's notable harshness over Hetty's punishment is due mainly to the harm she has caused his favourite pupil, Adam, which the schoolmaster sees as repeating the injury he had himself suffered from an unnamed woman earlier. But the most telling comparison in this novel of comparisons is the one that is always being implied between Hetty and Vixen, Bartle Massey's bitch of the turn-spit breed.[18] There is much more to this comparison than comical observation of animals, for whom George Eliot always shows a genuine respect. Vixen, who, Massey knows, would fret if he left her behind him, has adapted to the mixed domestic and wild state of the pet. She is to be found by turns pattering beside him for sustenance and protection, and putting her nose 'in every hole and corner' and 'running into bad company' (Ch. 40). The schoolmaster complains that her 'conscience has all run to milk'; having produced an unplanned litter of 'two extremely blind puppies', she divides her affections between the hamper and her master, accompanying him to the gate, but twice running 'back to the house to bestow a parenthetic lick on her puppies' (Ch. 21). Hetty's attachment to *her* protector and offspring is far less intelligent and effective, not to say amiable, than Vixen's to hers. It is especially significant that Bartle Massey forgets he is using a figure of speech when he keeps referring to Vixen as a woman, since it implies an equation between the domestic animal and the dependent woman, both creatures of mixed states. But this perception is not carried through in Massey's conventional doctrine of the Fall; he argues that it is 'an impious unscriptural opinion to say a woman's a blessing to a man now; you might as well say adders and wasps, and foxes and wild beasts, are a blessing, when they're only the evil which belongs to this state o' probation' (Ch. 21). Surely, in Massey's terms, women are more truly compared with pets than wild beasts. The human use of dogs has altered their status as hunters in packs and given them new patterns of behaviour, as Massey recognises in his companionship with Vixen. Equality for women would also, it would be reasonable to assume, change *their* behaviour. In fact, Bartle Massey proves a feminist in spite of himself in his insistence that men can do all women's work more carefully than they; the opposite would be equally true in different circumstances. That circumstances can change in Hayslope is shown by the fact that Dinah can go there and preach.

Adam Bede rejects Bartle Massey's dislike of women as too inflexible to be serious. Adam believes, while he is in love with Hetty, that the 'working man 'ud be badly off without a wife to see to th' house and the victual, and make things clean and comfortable' (Ch. 21). That Hetty would not fit this stereotype is less ironic in the long run than that Dinah does not entirely either. Adam is, however, though stubborn, capable both of change and of recognising change. He heeds his mother's warning that he can't go on thinking of nothing but figuring and work 'as if thee was a man cut out o' timber' (Ch. 51). His reliance on mathematics and mechanics to give him 'a grip hold' of things does not mean that he regards his own life and fortune as unchanging or unchangeable.[19] Though he believes 'the natur' o things doesn't change', he is referring here to squares and levers; his own life seems to him 'nothing but change' (Ch. 11). For Adam, abstract systems are for use and development as well as contemplation.

It is Arthur Donnithorne, so uneasily vacillating in his one tender, sexual relationship and yet so sturdily embodying the hopes of the whole neighbourhood for a more prosperous and amenable future, who falls most foul of the most rigid feature of Hayslope life, class-division. He is shattered by what should have been the foreseen consequences of his letting sexual desire 'like an ill-stemmed current' (Ch. 12) overcome his scruples with regard to Hetty, a woman he felt he could not marry. Overcoming too the opposite impulse to 'undo everything' by some 'mad proposition' to her (Ch. 30), Arthur writes to Hetty in the letter forced from him by Adam, 'I know you can never be happy except by marrying a man in your own station' (Ch. 32). Arthur values his position too much; he likes the power of patronage (to good ends) which it brings, as well as the popularity which he enjoys at many levels; he likes it too much for him to compromise it deliberately, but his thoughtlessness does it for him. The account of his return from Ireland, when he is on the verge of learning the truth, which is to cause 'violent convulsion in his whole frame', is the most powerful ironic passage in *Adam Bede*. Arthur's understandable pride in things as they are, or as he too conservatively thinks they are, is evidently coming before a fall. About to attend his grandfather's funeral and take charge of the Donnithorne estate, he relishes the 'English scene' with landowners' arms on inn-signs and fields which carry 'an agreeable suggestion of high rent'. When he arrives at Hayslope, which he sees 'sleeping on the hill, like a quiet old place as it was', he imagines his grandfather as he once was, 'coming into the estate, and making his plans. So the world goes round' (Ch. 44). Human stories do not go, however, 'round', even in Hayslope. Arthur's view of recurrent security and power providentially preserved for his family even extends to supposing neo-classically that good comes out of evil, such 'is the beautiful arrangement of things!' (Ch. 29) He means to do a lot for Hetty, outside of marriage, in the future, but news of her actions brings him the shock of a devastating disgrace. He returns from the war at the end, shattered by fever, 'altered and yet not altered' (Epilogue), a phrase of Adam's which neatly encapsulates the paradox of experience.[20]

Adam Bede piquantly exemplifies a balancing of moods of nostalgia for and dissatisfaction with the past and country life. Many of its most evocative descriptions combine warmth with misgivings. The Hall Farm itself was originally a Hall whose family, probably dwindling down to mere spinsterhood, 'got merged in the more territorial name of Donnithorne' (Ch. 6). The aristocratic mirror before which Hetty preens herself was a piece of second-hand genteel furniture probably bought 'at a sale' (Ch. 15). The note of uncertainty is not uncharacteristic. Such speculative explanations of origins imply that behind the apparent placidity of Hayslope lie chains of moral choices, often of unpredictable outcome,[21] some large, some small, which accumulate into historical process as perceived by classifying and generalising observers. The human attempt to impose pattern and structure on the irregularity of individuals in contact and interconnection with one another over time at once resists and re-emphasises movement and change. Habitual behaviour and recurrent festivals, like 'the custom of baptism' which Mr Irwine thinks more important than its doctrine, have the same ambiguous aspects. At the heir's birthday feast, the ha-ha separates the classes, yet is bridged 'for the passage of the visitors' (Ch. 25). The vista in this episode is made to extend most felicitously into the distant past and the far future, spanning almost a century, yet with a movingly uncynical comic stress on fallibility: old Martin Poyser tries to communicate with the ninety-year-old Jacob Taft, whom he remembers pursuing the Scottish rebels fifty miles on foot in 1746, but Taft has no response to make beyond a deferential greeting based on the perception that he is 'in company'. In the background the Benefit Club band plays, its banner proclaiming, 'Let brotherly love continue', the motto 'encircling a picture of a stone pit' (Ch. 22). Against this pricelessly funny and at the same time morally powerful image one can set Mrs Irwine's rosy prevision of her godson Arthur's life with a woman who can manage him; she adds, 'I suppose if I could live another fifty years, I should be blind to everything that wasn't out of other people's sight, like a man who stands in a well, and sees nothing but the stars' (Ch. 25). Few writers can match George Eliot for that special poignancy, where she admits that people's control of life, and by implication the novelist's of her material, is limited.

But she also has her feet firmly on the ground. *Adam Bede* is informed by a highly acute concern with economic matters right from the start. Adam's own advancement from foreman-joiner to part-owner of the Burge business is typical of the way power is at once devolved downwards and seized from below in a capitalist economy developing on a feudal base. Profits and savings can be turned into investments. Adam's success is supported by Arthur's promise of capital and facilitated by his experience as superintendent of the woods and overseer of the repairs on the Donnithorne estate. Such work is entered into the more willingly as it multiplies economic activity itself, 'for the sake of other people beside the owner' (Ch. 48). Property is not to be redistributed by a powerful bureaucracy, but diversified and extended gradually, which is a way forward that George Eliot approves. Socialist egalitarianism, on the other hand, is associated with the donkey-race in which, with everybody encouraging everybody else's donkey, 'the sorriest donkey' wins: the fact that the argument of sticks was needed for stimulation implies no high regard for the socialist state (Ch. 25). In the commentary, philanthropists and reformers of abuses come in for some sceptical scrutiny of their motives.

This caution on the scope and effect of political activity underlies much of the comedy over Hayslope's bucolic ignorance of great affairs. Though the Napoleonic War may affect everyone by keeping up prices, to the benefit of the farmers, it is not certain that it is being well managed. Mr Craig may well be right to blame 'them ministers' with their 'bad government' for doing more harm to the country than the 'furriners' (Ch. 53). There is no guarantee that people much better informed than the villagers have got politics right. Adam Bede is no 'proletaire with democratic ideas' and 'theories about setting the world to rights', but he is free-spoken on subjects which affect his known sphere of operation like 'ill-seasoned timber' and 'hasty contracts' (Ch. 16). He is certainly relieved to be able to pay, with a 'terrible sweep', from his savings, for Seth's substitute in the militia, thus securing his small business's immunity from disruptive state interference in war-time (Ch. 19). With Seth he plans a small furniture-making enterprise with designs ingenious enough to increase demand from women in 'orders from round about' (Ch. 20). Living in an area where there is 'plenty o' employ' (Ch. 2) and no scarcity, Adam is not socially demarcated from tenant farmers who own their own stock and equipment and are sustained by 'a latent sense of capital' (Ch. 9). He is on the 'way up' (Ch. 19) to becoming a 'master-man' (Ch. 20) in his own right. Bartle Massey's self-financing educational efforts are attuned to similar ends, to facilitate the prosperity of a dyer and a stone-sawyer, for example; he urges Adam to take his opportunities and 'get forward in the world'. The emphasis is not on profitability as such. Adam insists on charging 'the regular price' for his work, which he believes is the 'just' price (Ch. 21).[22] In this moral spirit, he admires Moses for having 'carried a hard business well through, and died when other folks were going to reap the fruits' (Ch. 50). It is the expansiveness of enterprise which appeals to Adam Bede, the long-term benefits; he has schemes for improving the roads 'that were so imperfect all through the country' (Ch. 38), which would involve the co-operation of the landowner. Not all the economic news is good news, of course. The narrator notes that some self-reliant artisans lack 'the art of getting rich', though 'the work of their brains has guided well the hands of other men' (Ch. 19). The most significant fact about economic relations is their numerousness, which brings diversity and complexity.

Snowfield, where Dinah works as a mill-hand, Stoniton, Treddleston, Oakbourne and other towns belong to a commercial environment which impinges only slowly and indirectly on the village life. But travel, difficult though not as hazardous as in, say, Scott's *Heart of Midlothian*, becomes more important in the later stages of the plot. The increase in population and improvement in trade brought by the Snowfield mill has led to the supplementation of coach-travel by the 'taxed cart' kept by the inn-keeper (Ch. 38), which the inveterate walker Adam eventually uses. But the labour which is sometimes 'turned off for a time' (Ch. 30) at the mill lacks the flexibility which efficient transport would allow. There is implicit criticism of a system of poor-relief, based on the parish, which inhibits mobility of labour. Lisbeth Bede approves the action of her 'old man' in leaving Stonyshire as a youth; 'he said as there was no wood there, an' it 'ud been a bad country for a carpenter'. Correspondingly, Lisbeth criticises Dinah for judging others by herself, who as a single woman with modest requirements had enjoyed economic self-sufficiency in Snowfield; 'the hungry folks had better leave th' hungry country. It makes less mouths for the scant cake' (Ch. 11). Such arguments touch on the disadvantage of rootedness, the need for adaptability and experiment. Even the farming life, so often invested with an aura of tranquillity, as when the sunshine is 'asleep itself on the moss-grown cow-shed' (Ch. 18), is analysed by Mrs Poyser as subject to vicissitudes and short on satisfaction. She is very much aware of the need to balance accounts and argues for allowances to cover expenditure on lime and gates. For insurance, she is careful to save 'against sickness' and lay by against a bad harvest. It is stressed that she shares responsibility for the farm-business with her husband, she looking after the dairy and he the crops, a common division of labour, which modifies our assumptions about the subservience of women in the past. She insists on contributing her own brain-power to the partnership and indeed has chosen a husband with brains, so as not to be 'tackled to a geck as everybody's a laughing at' (Ch. 9). Mr Poyser boasts of her 'discernment' on the 'matter of short-horns', which she disfavours for their low butter-yield. The narrator underlines the point: 'The woman who manages a dairy has a large part in making the rent, so she may well be allowed to have her opinion on stock and their "keep" – an exercise which strengthens her understanding so much that she finds herself able to give her husband advice on most other subjects' (Ch. 18). Mrs Poyser is not, then, just a pithily talkative character; her knowledge of practical economics gives her confidence and also a realistic assessment of her own power. She uses the limited right of free speech, which all the characters enjoy, to defend her legitimate interests,[23] an element in the situation that makes her discomfiture of the old Squire, when she 'has her say out', more than an example of 'irregular justice'. She is not likely to be surprised that its frequent repetition in the surrounding district as 'news' is relished more than reports of the Napoleonic War (Ch. 33); indeed local opinion is a factor she uses against the Squire, his name being 'no better than a brimstone match in everybody's nose'. Mrs Poyser's main argument is an economic one, however; her point is that the Squire's proposal for the Poysers' farm to specialise more in milk production ignores both the unpredictability of demand for milk products and the high overheads in managing a dairy, which makes it unlikely that Thurle, 'who is a man of some capital', would be prepared to risk it by investing in *two* farms. In calling the Squire's bluff, Mrs Poyser brings together two of the novel's themes, the futility of oppression and exploitation in a community where open criticism can be voiced, and the independence of individuals in a wage-economy if they can apply themselves intelligently. 'I tell you for once as we're not dumb creatures to be abused and made money on by them as ha' got the lash i' their hands, for lack o' knowin' how t' undo the tackle' (Ch. 32). The analogy with animals is now significantly abandoned, for Mrs Poyser has all her faculties awake. Undoing the tackle here means leaving the estate for another tenant-farm, a move which is not said to be economically impossible (labour was short on the land), though it would have been emotionally difficult. In staying on, the Poysers exercise free choice. Mrs Poyser does not think it their duty to submit to landowners beyond what 'flesh and blood will bear'. Fortunately, Arthur, through his delegate Mr Irwine, later eases their situation.[24] Mr Irwine had warned Arthur that plans to apply Arthur Young's theory of agricultural management might run into opposition on the ground, which it would prove costly to overcome by negotiation. But he is well aware that it is economic activity that maintains 'scholars – and rectors who appreciate scholars' (Ch. 16), so there is no doubt that under his guidance and with Adam Bede's assistance the repairs and improvements will be carried through. *Adam Bede*, therefore, endorses as the most realistic model for change the principle of economic growth under the leadership of people of capital and property with the consent of people of 'an honourable, independent spirit' (Ch. 48), who have to be bargained with and given a share in the profits under a tolerant flexible system of common law.[25] This idea is actually what Hayslope embodies.

No such explicit political commitment is, however, made by the narrator (whom I shall characterise as feminine) herself. Despite the air of confidential familiarity adopted, the narrational presentation is, in fact, extremely dense; there are more layers and angles than anyone could expect. The very setting in the past makes for indirectness; we are left questioning how far things *have* changed. When the narrator refers to Adam Bede's 'respectful demeanour' towards a gentleman as an obsolete characteristic, as the reader, addressed in the second person, 'must expect' (Ch. 16), our sense of objectivity slips. Both narrator and reader become fictionalised figures, and we are released to judge between them whether deference and gentlemanliness are desirable and whether the complex issues involved were different in 1798 from what they were in 1859 or what they are now. The narrator exercises a Protean elusivity, at points appearing as a 'judicious historian' who yet 'abstains from narrating precisely what ensued' (as though total factuality were possible), at other points appearing as a cautious observer, unable to predict what 'the chances are' about a character, yet assuming knowledge of his future by planting clues; 'we don't enquire too closely into character in the case of a handsome, generous young fellow, who . . . if he should happen to spoil a woman's existence for her, will make it up to her with expensive bon-bons' (Ch. 12). Since the novel partly does conduct a close inquiry into such a character, we feel again free to consider for ourselves what is the relation between privilege and responsibility, between sex and ruin, between publicity and emancipation. Clearly, then, we need not expect the narrator to preserve a consistency of gender; narrator and narratee can both be male, as when it is said, 'We are apt to be kinder to the brute that loves us than to the women that love us' (Ch. 4), and both be female, as when Hetty's desperate wanderings are contemplated; 'God preserve you and me from the beginners of such misery' (Ch. 37). The beginners being male, the present company must be female. It will be noted that here the narrator prays directly to God, whereas at another point man is said only to *need* 'a suffering God' (Ch. 35), a Feuerbachian gloss. Such unabashed shifts in the narrator's sex and ideas are matched by changes of tone, now garrulous, now coy, now analytic, now fanciful; at times she appears a connoisseur ('Paint me an angel, if you can, with a floating violet robe'), at times a homely raconteur, 'content to tell my simple story' (Ch. 17) and at times a linguist, pointing out that words themselves are unimposing and non-mimetic; 'it is only that they happen to be the signs of something' (Ch. 50). Although George Eliot's commentary may seem to carry more weight than the story (what is told as fact or event, what is recorded as dialogue or what is presented as characters' thoughts), it is hard to pin it down to anything authoritative. It more frequently abjures authority than insists on its privileged role as truth told in the voice of the writer.

The multiple focus of the narrator goes with an ambiguity of *status* which is even more bewildering, if taken too seriously. By status I mean relation to the characters in the novel. At times the narrator is clearly a writer with 'ink at the end of my pen' (Ch. 1), and, more specifically, 'an able novelist' capable of conceiving clergyman characters who are more representative than 'sublime abstracts of all clerical graces' (Ch. 17). At other times, the narrator is a talker *in* the novel, present in the fictional past, for whom 'imagination is a licensed trespasser', who can bring the reader

into the same world as the characters: 'Put your face to one of the
glass panes in the right-hand window: what do you see?' (Ch. 6). Yet
again, the narrator can actually participate in the dialogue of her
fictional world and extend it beyond the time-span of the narrative;
she has talked to Adam Bede in his old age about Mr Irwine's
successor, Mr Ryde, who was 'like a dose o' physic' (Ch. 17), was,
that is, after the novel has ended; she repeats one story as Adam
told it 'to his dying day' (Ch. 4) and she even clairvoyantly knows
what Adam remembered 'to the last moment of his life' (Ch. 20).
Such proleptic observations locate the narrator in the fictional
Loamshire, which seems confirmed when we learn that when she
is abroad she sees things which remind her that she is 'not in
Loamshire' (Ch. 35). Yet she is apparently a socialising city-dweller
too, to whom 'it would be a pleasant variety' to see country-dancing
sometimes instead of 'low dresses and large skirts' (Ch. 26). By
way of complete contrast, she also belongs to Shepperton, often
listening to the opinion of Mr Gedge, the landlord of the Royal Oak
there (Ch. 17). Now Shepperton is not only in a different district
from Loamshire: it is in another novel, *Scenes of Clerical Life*! Some
of this ubiquitousness can be reconciled with singleness of identity,
no doubt, but the main impression of the narrator we receive is one
of volatility.

  I doubt if any of this narrational uneasiness is accidental. George
Eliot is content to let her points be considered as they arise, using
the convention of the moment. She has no wish to be identified
with any overall didacticism. She explicitly dissociates herself from
'mental philosophers who are ready with the best receipts for avoiding all mistakes' (Ch. 33). Simple nostrums like 'correct principles
of education' (Ch. 49) leave her undeceived. She expects inconsistencies everywhere. She believes a wise man will place 'an ingenious
web of probability' as the 'surest screen between himself and the
truth' (Ch. 26). She reminds us 'how much of human speech is
mere purposeless impulse of habit' (Ch. 5) and accepts that human
converse 'is not rigidly sincere' (Ch. 17). These disclaimers are part
of a tactic to counteract a pretension to omniscient narration,[26]
which would widen the gap too much between George Eliot and
characters who, as objects of her dramatic irony, themselves often
know little of what is going on. The narrator's unique privilege of
looking into characters' minds, being in two places at once, living
in two periods of time simultaneously, is exercised discreetly, in
the manner of an investigator reconstructing events and motives

which led to some triumphant or catastrophic event, emphasising luck and plausibility. The handling of Arthur's missed opportunity of confiding in Mr Irvine, for example, is skilfully tentative; we are presented with what crosses their minds, the embarrassed looks, the underlying motives too complex for the narrator to 'dare' to assert that it was so or not so, except to mention the unacknowledged work done in mental business by 'unnoticed agents' (Ch. 16). The care with which the narrator plays with notions of limited truth and provisional wisdom gives *Adam Bede* its humorous expansiveness. The concern with the lovable essence of human nature, 'its deep pathos, its sublime mysteries' (Ch. 17), is in no danger of obsessiveness, because of the comic use of contrast and incongruity, which the narrator supports by constantly exposing and shifting her technique.

One further masterly example; again from the account of Arthur's hopefulness just before he reads the terrible news of Hetty's trial in Mr Irwine's letter. We anticipate with cruel excitement his well-deserved shock:

> The level rays of the low afternoon sun entered directly at the window, and as Arthur seated himself in his velvet chair with their pleasant warmth upon him, he was conscious of that quiet well being which perhaps you and I have felt on a sunny afternoon, when, in our brightest youth and health, life has opened a new vista for us, and long to-morrows of activity have stretched before us like a lovely plain which there was no need of hurrying to look at, because it was all our own. (Ch. 44)

The narrational dexterity in the one sentence, proceeding from historical objectivity, psychological description, tactful recruitment of the reader as experienced co-observer, evocation of imagery suggesting both impercipience and the power of ownership, on to the notice of the urgent superscription on the Rector's letter which follows, gives us just that right blend of painful recognition and enthralled superiority which novel-readers most enjoy. As Aeneas S. Dallas remarked in *The Times* contemporary review of *Adam Bede*, 'We have a pleasant sense of security in either laughing or crying with such a companion'.[27] The security comes, in the face of so much tending to insecurity, because of the dominating, flexible intelligence at work. George Eliot believes that an effective impact on people is likely to be made by writers with a secure psychological base in the presence of adversity. She does a great deal, therefore, to disturb and reassure both her conservative and her radical readers,[28] who are, of course, free to gloss her text in any direction, if they can escape being caught out in undue selectivity. Every detail merits close attention. Momentous comments are sometimes embedded in the statements of the most unlikely characters, like Lisbeth Bede. It is true that in *Adam Bede* there is no character who approaches the narrator in culture and versatility. In her next novel the writer would deal with a character more like her own younger self.

3

A Story of Nature:
The Mill on the Floss

The Mill on the Floss (1860) followed rapidly on *Adam Bede*, an altogether darker companion-piece, the characters being 'on a lower level generally, and the environment less romantic,'[1] as the author herself remarked.

Set thirty years on from her first novel, it leaves the fertile slopes of the Midland shires for the hazardous watery plains to the east, where the Ripple runs into the Floss south of the Mudport estuary, whose tide, 'the awful Eagre', checks the impetuous current, coming up against it in spring 'like a hungry monster' (I,5). The constant fear of the riparian population there is of drowning. Dependent on wharf, water-wheel and black boats, it takes risks and thrives, beaver-like, trading with its continental counterpart in Holland. The narrator, pronouncedly feminine this time, envying the ducks and 'in love with moistness' (I,1), introduces into this liquid destructive element her two adolescents, Tom and Maggie Tulliver, whose roles are to struggle and be immersed. The germ of the novel was the idea of an impending flood.[2] With the flooding goes feeling, feeling for young life swept away.[3] The first appearance of Maggie Tulliver is as a little girl in a 'chill damp' season, standing 'at the edge of the water', but, dreamt of, not seen, by the narrator, whose 'really benumbed' arms had seemed to be resting 'on the cold stone', an omen of death, surely, and of the tombstone at the end. Even after finishing the novel, George Eliot was glad to get away from thinking about Maggie and the mill, 'for she and her sorrows have clung to me painfully'.[4] She later admitted to 'having an unused stock of motherly tenderness, which sometimes overflows, but not without discrimination'.[5] So when in March 1860

Lewes told Herbert Spencer to go in and comfort George Eliot ('she is crying her eyes out over the death of her children')[6] he had no need to explain that the children in question were fictional. She was terminating *The Mill on the Floss*.

Some of the tears suggest deploring. This whole novel has a contentious air, with the disputants more than likely to topple and be engulfed, as happens literally to the reconciled brother and sister in 'The Last Conflict' (VII). There is a first conflict too, and many others. Families argue, generations quarrel, lovers separate, siblings nag, friends fight. There are feuds, boycotts, lawsuits, tiffs and hagglings. The seasons are divided, trees cloven, hills parted, bridges broken, dwellings ruined, dolls defaced, locks jaggedly snipped, and within the individual there are contending passions, contradictory impulses, split loyalties. If at the end the hero and heroine, like David and Jonathan, were not divided, in their life they increasingly were. As U. C. Knoepflmacher has noted,[7] *The Mill on the Floss* is founded upon 'Collision' which was the original title of Book V; he says, ' fragmentation is inherent' in its unstable world, which is pluralistic and puzzling (it has been, as is repeatedly said, 'too many' for Mr Tulliver, V,7, and really for nearly everyone in it). Observing the rifts, the narrator is less patient in tone that we might expect; her interventions are sometimes ominous, sometimes poignant, always problematic, and though ready to turn humorous at any moment, in fact *very* humorous, they are not I think, very good humoured.[8] Life is actually too sad, too short, too complicated for much of the posturing of the emmet-like inhabitants of St Ogg's, whose 'oppressive narrowness' irritates the narrator (IV, 1). In *The Mill on the Floss*, then, most of the comedy is satiric, supplied by the narrator, or when attempted by the characters not shared by those against whom it is directed. Umbrage is taken too quickly for that. On the other hand, there are no outright villains in the story. The negligence, casualness, pettiness and rigidity that reveal themselves are regarded by the narrator with an annoyance that can moderate into forbearance and understanding; she warns the reader who is inclined to be severe on the mistaken characters to 'remember that the responsibility of tolerance lies with those who have the wider vision' (VII, 3).

It is the river which leads the attention to the width of the environment; the Floss 'links the small pulse of the old English town with the beatings of the world's mighty heart' (IV,1). This Wordsworthian phrase does not, however, mean that for George

Eliot nature never does betray the heart that loves her.[9] The rich responses to nature in the descriptive passages of the novel are overshadowed by the more prominent recognition of the random-ness and destructiveness of life on earth. Much of man's productive experience is also violent; grinding, pulverising, crushing, sawing, hooking, burning, liquefying, all go on, some unintended. It is a world where accidents of all magnitudes will happen. The narrator, though not moody herself, is both amused and sobered by the moodiness of the characters and their underestimating of nature. The two main themes of the novel, growing up and falling in love, lend themselves to amusement, but it is stunted growth and frustrated love that are emphasised. In both long episodes, the first stretching, appropriately enough,[10] for five of the seven books into which *The Mill on the Floss* is divided, aspiration has to give way to disappointment, pleasure to suffering, excitement to dilemma; in both cases there are repeated small movements of this sort, before painful climaxes. It is an intricate, detailed kind of tragic development not dependent on any single moral flaw or initial error, but pervading all aspects of speech and thought, personal feelings and social relations, so that the final catastrophic drowning of the young hero and heroine cannot surprise us. The author's claim that she had looked forward to the concluding tragedy 'with much attention and premeditation from the beginning'[11] is borne out by even a cursory reading.

The mill itself in its constant motion is capable of a hypnotic effect, but that is deceptive. With its rushing water and booming, unresting wheel, 'like a great curtain of sound, shutting one out from the world beyond', it seems to belong to an order of things where time stands still and the imagination can recycle past experi-ence. It produces in the narrator a 'dreamy deafness', heightening peacefulness (I,1). To the child Maggie too the mill seems 'a little world apart', which engages her by its monotony: 'The resolute din, the unresting motion of the great stones, giving her a dim delicious awe as at the presence of an uncontrollable force – the meal for ever pouring, pouring – the fine white powder softening all surfaces' (I,4). Maggie is a story-teller, like the narrator, though not a writer; their longing for a different world with 'great spaces' seems sustained by their aesthetic response to steady material forces, like the river itself. But the world of normal consciousness with intimation of change and mortality inevitably obtrudes itself with a jolt that is both wry and sad. The mill is, after all, a lot more than

an adjunct to a picturesque rural house. It is an example of early
industry, a human artefact, which had replaced a half-timbered
building damaged in the floods three generations back and with
a malthouse added. Massively productive, it needs servicing and
could still be improved, 'especially if steam were applied' (VI,5).
It can also be badly damaged by the elements; at the end part of
it falls with the crash of trees and stones against it and hurries
down the flooding Ripple in the form of 'heavy fragments' (VII,5).
Though the mill can survive its disintegration, its rebuilding is
not a 'thorough repair' to those who have known it in the past.
The human present does not grow seamlessly from the past, but
is divided from it by change and loss.

   The mill is also, as a piece of working capital, the occasion of
human disputes and tensions. Mr Tulliver, a headstrong, emotional, prejudiced, ill-informed man, who is obstinately vindictive
to some and generous to others, is obsessed with his personal
ownership of the mill. Descended from one Ralph Tulliver, who
had reputedly 'ruined himself' (IV,2), Maggie's father is proudly
conscious that Dorlcote Mill has been in his family's hands for a
century 'and better' (II,2). Yet he is not keen to see it pass into
the control of his own son, Tom; 'he'd be expectin' to take to
the Mill an' the land, an' a-hinting at me as it was time for me
to lay by an' think o' my latter end. Nay, nay, I've seen enough o'
that wi' sons' (I,3). The implicit contradiction in this attitude to
inheritance is characteristic of Mr Tulliver's mentality. The mill,
situated near the sea and dependent on a lively tributary current
for its power, is affected by agricultural schemes upstream, dams,
weirs, 'dykes an' errigations' (II,2),[12] which could have brought
Mr Tulliver useful compensation, but which he resists more and
more uncompromisingly. His forays into litigation bring about
his bankrupcy. Closely involved with these hostilities is his decision not to train Tom as a miller, but instead to give him an
expensive secondary education which will qualify him to be 'a
help to me wi' these lawsuits' (I,2) as a surveyor, solicitor or
'smartish' entrepreneur, though in the last case it is to be in
a 'business as he can go into without capital' (I,7), whatever
that could be ('all profits and no outlay', he enviously suggests,
I,2). Such a groundless desideratum contradicts what Mr Tulliver
knows about agriculture, since he has lent his brother-in-law Mr
Moss, a tenant-farmer working poor soil, a capital sum without
interest, though his own property is already mortgaged for two

thousand pounds on the freehold, one half of which sum went to his sister on her marriage to Moss. Mr Tulliver believes, however, the general report about himself as a 'man of considerable substance' (I,8) and imprudently fails to pay off any of the capital on his mortgage. Instead he borrows from his wife's sister, Mrs Glegg, with whom he quarrels vehemently when she reminds him of the fact, eventually returning the money to her when she does not want it back. These details of Mr Tulliver's financial mismanagement emerge from the dialogue and commentary in the early chapters. As they are above the children's heads, though, given time, they would both have sorted things out more sensibly themselves, an atmosphere of menace overhangs the childhood scenes. Despite her father's kindness to Maggie when others criticise her, he is not the responsible parent she needs. His decision to spare his sister Mrs Moss the consequences of his financial embarrassments is certainly honourable and is upheld by Tom after his father is incapacitated; it derives from the father's fear that Maggie might one day be as dependent on someone's generosity as his sister now is. The risks he takes are too dangerous, given the number of his dependents. He does nothing to encourage Maggie towards any kind of independence.

It is not only Mr Tulliver's impecuniousness when he loses the main lawsuit that is so damaging; it is his totally vindictive, unforgiving attitude to his opponent's lawyer, Wakem, and to this man's crippled artist-son, Philip Wakem. Ironically by sending Tom to Stelling's for the education which turns out to be so useless for the practical-minded boy, the miller brings first Tom and then Maggie into close contact with Philip and sows the seeds of further unhappiness and animosity. Mr Tulliver has attributed devilish qualities to Wakem, believing that 'rats, weevils, and lawyers were created by Old Harry' (I,3). This combative theology, referred to mockingly by the narrator as 'rampant Manichaeism', is the 'form of Protestantism unknown to Bossuet', little different from Pagan revenge, which appears in a later chapter title: Mr Tulliver presented the Christian doctrine of mercy with a 'very unreceptive' surface, on which it could not find a nidus (IV,1). His feuding bent is itself an object of disapproval by his wife's family, the Dodsons, who regard it as a form of rigidity, not rectitude. For them it lacks both respectability and foresight; 'It 'ud be a fine deal better for some people . . . if they'd let the lawyers alone,' remarks Mrs Glegg, certain that the Tulliver family is 'going headlong to ruin' (I.7).

But Tom, unfortunately, tends to admire and later to replicate his father's inflexibility, with adverse effects on Maggie's personal life. He also adheres to Mr Tulliver's dying wish that he should try and get the Mill back again from Wakem whenever he could ('It was in his family for five generations', VI,6) and he finally works off the price. Tom's return to the mill in order to vindicate his father leads indirectly to the catastrophe, since it was to rescue him from there during the flood that Maggie, in spite of having been made aware of the danger of lethal collision in the confused currents, jeopardised and lost both their lives.

The series of mistakes and crises which spoil the Tulliver children's lives has another source, apart from ownerhship instinct, namely, sexism. Mr Tulliver, determined to be the boss in his own home, chose Bessy out of the Dodson sisters because 'she wasn't o'er cute . . . ; for I wasn't going to be told the rights o' things by my own fireside' (1.3). Mrs Tulliver's intellectual inferiority to her husband brings him unexpected disadvantages, however. She retains 'a facility of saying things which drove him in the opposite direction to the one she desired' (I,8); she piques his pride by getting her sister Mrs Pullet to intervene with Mrs Glegg about recalling her loan so that he now insists on repaying it when he can ill afford it, with the result that the family breach is made 'more difficult to mend' (I,13). Mr Tulliver also finds it convenient to deceive Mrs Tulliver on the bill of sale on their furniture, 'the possession of a wife conspicuously one's inferior in intellect' being like other high privileges 'attended with a few inconveniences' (III,1). Later, still more seriously, Mrs Tulliver quite off her own bat alerts Wakem inadvertently to the possibility that he might rub salt in her husband's wounds by acquiring the mill himself and employing Tulliver to run it. The imagery used in this episode, comparing Mrs Tulliver with a fly-fisher with unalluring bait or a hen unable to dissuade a farmer from wringing her neck, and then as Wakem's victim, with a man turned fortuitously into mincemeat by 'some fly-wheel or other' or a roach considered by a pike to be 'excellent good eating', is especially harsh and sardonic. The legal profession, as entrencher of male privilege, is given no quarter. Wakem is not above petty revenge when the opportunity offers, though he is no evil schemer; he merely 'always knew the stepping-stones that would carry him through very muddy bits of practice' (III,7). Mrs Tulliver too is ridiculed for her exaggeration of her own personal influence. The subservience forced on her by her husband and the law leaves her a fetishism over her household possessions, ornaments and clothes[13] as her main outlet.

The mismatch between the Tulliver parents does not only exacerbate family tension; it has direct genetic results, 'like as if the world was turned topsy-turvy' (I.13). Tom's relative slow wittedness and purposive honesty are attributed to his taking after his mother's side, whereas Maggie's high intelligence, darkness and impetuosity are seen as Tulliver traits. 'That's the worst on't wi' the crossing o' breeds: you can never justly calkilate what'll come out' (I,2). Maggie first enters the room, in the narrator's phrase, as 'this small mistake of nature'. It is the people around her who mistake her capacity rather than nature's mistaking it, of course, but it is true that some of her traits are unfortunate. Her dreaminess and forgetfulness sit ill with her sharpness of judgment and pride in her own erudition. Maggie would have benefited so much from a literary education that it is quite deplorable that one has to be bestowed fruitlessly on Tom, while she is left to fend culturally for herself. She is clearly handicapped unfairly by the prejudices of the older generation. Her father's belief that Maggie's cleverness will 'turn to trouble' (I,3) is self-fulfilling, enforced by the family's inhibitions about her upbringing. As a girl Maggie is not envisaged as having any vocation beyond being married or becoming Tom's housekeeper, for whom his caring for her will not exclude punishment, 'when she did wrong' (I,5). Tom, of course, perpetuates the unfairness into adulthood. The reasons for his growing alienation from his sister are intimately probed: they outlast the reconciliations brought about by affectionate feeling, shared memories and mutual distress. Maggie, deprived of the prospect of independence, becomes psychologically adrift, acting 'like a gypsy' (I,7), emotionally over-reliant on the males in her life and enthralled to a private world of fantasy in which her desire for harmony and self-fulfilment can find expression, closely linked to her intense aesthetic appreciation of sounds and sights. Many of Maggie's mistakes are obviously comic, like her pushing her head through Tom's kite 'all for nothing' (I,5), as are the stories she makes up, like the one about a young earwig that falls into a 'hot copper' (I,10), but their cumulative effect is quite sinister. The death of Tom's rabbits through her neglect is hardly pretty.

Tom continually asserts his superiority to Maggie in his boyish skills, as in building playing-cards into the 'wonderful pagoda', which she inadvertently upsets. Tom 'would never do anything cowardly' like hitting a girl (I,9), but Maggie has no code on which to found a similar restraint. When Tom, angry with her for spilling his cowslip wine, excludes her from the pleasures of the 'insurrectionary visit to the pond' (I,10), Maggie pushes the favoured Lucy into the cow-trodden mud. Such incidents, though lacking, as the narrator points out, the magnitude required of a tragic action by Aristotle, are bitter at the time and clearly antici- pate the rough treatment meted out by Maggie to Lucy in adult life, when she involves herself with Lucy's boy-friend without warning her. They derive, of course, from Maggie's sense of exclusion; there had been 'no room' for Maggie on the peninsula of dry grass where Lucy had been escorted by Tom. She is ever diffident about making room for herself. When incautiously or desperately she attempts it, as in her flight from her own shadow to the gypsies, the result invariably is to make matters worse. Maggie's capacity for shrewd observation and reasonable generalisation comes out delightfully in the conversations in which she is permitted to join as a child, yet she is always somehow snubbed. Tom, for example, when she notes that all women in her experience are crosser than men, reminds her that she will be a woman herself some day and probably a 'nasty conceited' one, whom everyone will hate for being 'disagreeable' (II,1). The requirement of compliance presses unfairly on Maggie.

Her view of older women as too prone to complain and disapprove is certainly borne out by the behaviour of her mother and aunts, the Dodson sisters. Though Æ. S. Dallas in *The Times* review of 1860 went too far in designating them a 'degraded species' of 'stingy, selfish wretches, who give no sympathy and require none',[14] their defensive narrowness is prominently displayed in that tone of saddened comedy which is perhaps George Eliot's single most felicitous effect. Aunt Pullet's whispered pride, for example, in possessing 'the best bonnet in Garum Church, let the next best be whose it would', combines conventional piety and materialistic bad taste in an enjoyable amalgam, but when her fascination with illness is adduced the effect is subtler. She regards Mrs Glegg's preference for home remedies (like 'chewing turkey rhubarb') to going to the doctor as dreadful, as 'flying' i' the face o' Providence; for what are doctors for if we arn't to call em in? And when folks have got money to pay for a doctor, it isn't respectable, as I've told Jane many a time. I'm ashamed of acquaintance knowing it' (I,9). This well-meaning illogicality has overtones of anxiety.[15] Critical candour within the

Dodson clan goes with a coolness to all those outside it, who seem to include in-laws.

The idea that families continually disperse and re-form themselves is too disturbing to be acknowledged by the Dodsons; mere cloning would seem more suitable to the childless Mrs Glegg, who criticises Mr Tulliver for spoiling Maggie: 'My father niver brought his children up so, else we should ha' been a different sort o' family to what we are.' That there might have been gain as well as loss is again too disturbing to be admitted; not that Mrs Glegg has not a lot of valuable advice to give. But it is given too unsparingly. Her warning that Tom is being educated above his fortune being rebuffed by Mr Tulliver, she turns on Mrs Tulliver, 'very much with the feeling of a cur that seizes the opportunity of diverting his bark towards the man who carries no stick. "It's poor work, talking o'almonds and raisins"' (I,7). Mrs Glegg is staking a claim for women's equal status in the discussion of serious affairs, yet at the same time weakening her case by her own ill-temper. She is determined to survive in the world she knows. When her husband accuses her of going on 'biting and snapping like a mad dog', Mrs Glegg is quick to pick up his hint about leaving her 'with everything provided for her'. She now takes a more conciliatory view of the future, the narrator adding wittily, 'For if people are to quarrel often, it follows as a corollary that their quarrels cannot be protracted beyond certain limits' (I,12). Though R. Ebbatson may be right to refer the finely balanced tone here to the cunning combination of the narrator's 'highly educated syntax and diction' with the Gleggs' 'ignorant ideas and colloquial diction',[16] Mrs Glegg, in spite of her quaint beliefs, does not lend herself easily to stereotyping. Constricted to the sphere of the small investor rather than that of the independent businesswoman, she feels both the 'pleasure of property' and the importance of a reliable network of kin-relationships. The pride she takes in having all her cousins with money 'out at use' or owning 'some houses of their own, at the very least' (I,12), is partly self-protective, but it is also related to impersonal principle, to the 'great fundamental fact of blood' (I, 13), which should ideally apply universally to all men and women, but is in provincial society limited to near-relatives. When Maggie all but loses her reputation, it is Mrs Glegg who insists on still attributing honour to her while she can, bursting forth in severe reproof of Tom's severity with, among others, the remark that 'fair-play was a jewel' (VII, 3). The narrator's analysis is especially cogent here; 'it was a case in which her hereditary rectitude and personal strength of character found a common channel along with her fundamental idea of clanship as they did in her life-long regard to equity in money matters'. The water-imagery suggests a positive, if confined, forward movement of limited benefit. The absence of irony is very noticeable.

Maggie's own conspicuous failure to get her act together in the more expansive conditions of her young adulthood is presented in terms of both blockage and uncontrolled impulse. Though she appears to be at one with the strong growths of nature, the branching ash, the dog-roses, the 'grand Scotch firs', Maggie's emotional involvement with the deformed artist, Philip Wakem, subjects her to all sorts of stress. One has a 'sense of opposing elements, of which a fierce collision is imminent', in observing her, as we are told. Her loyalty to Philip traps her into furtiveness, since the relationship, if known, would infuriate her father and, as it actually does, earn her brother's contempt. The 'urgent monotonous warning' voice of conscience comes athwart the harmonious voice of friendship (V,1). Philip sees himself as tending her mind, which is withering in its youth 'for want of the light and space it was formed to flourish in', but it must be said that he gives her little idea of equality or independence. His aim is to possess her by converting her 'sweet girlish tenderness' into eventual love. The 'certain dim background of relief' of which Maggie is conscious when Tom forces her separation from Philip probably, therefore, includes a suppressed repugnance to a personality which presses need without arousing a sexual response. The episode with Philip already belongs in its subtlety to the last part of the novel, which Joan Bennett sees as anticipating the 'new development'[17] of psychological fiction seen through the lens of an observer, since the narrator gives the required perspective in comments and hints. Philip's culpability is, of course, admitted, while not regarded as gross.

Maggie's ultimate trial, her affair with Stephen Guest, Lucy's acknowledged young man, gains its extraordinary power because of the contrast with its predecessor. Maggie's physical passion is now awake, and Stephen's accompanies it; the process of self-discovery is shown effectively on both sides. Unfortunately, traces of moral cowardice and deviousness, notably in dealings with Lucy, accumulate until an unresolvable dilemma is reached. Maggie drifts into the position where she has, in effect, eloped with Stephen, but refuses his proposal of marriage, because of her wish not to injure

Lucy and Philip. Even though the strong sexual attraction between Maggie and Stephen has invalidated the two relationships which it has supplanted, Maggie feels her honour would be compromised if she went on with Stephen. She is unlucky in giving her conduct the appearance of casualness without having the confidence to build on her own natural desire. It must be added that no one else is particularly helpful. The jealous Philip writes to Maggie that the strong attraction proceeded from only one side of her and Stephen's characters, 'belonging to that partial, divided action of our nature which makes half the tragedy of the human lot. I have felt the vibration of chords in your nature that I have continually felt the want of in his' (VII,3). It may be true that nature as well as culture divides people in the way Philip means, that some and not others have an inherent disposition to sensitivity and aesthetic pleasure: he assumes that a gradual union based on cultural affinity is superior to a tempestuous affair based on physical passion. Stephen is certainly shown at first as following intellectual tastes rather than searching out truth for himself, but he speaks respectfully of Dr Kenn's views on taxation at one point (VI,6) and matures rapidly under Maggie's influence. She is led by Stephen's devotion to doubt 'the justice of her own resolve' in renouncing him (VII,5); she has not the sense that she will succeed in her resolution without further falls and repentance. Philip's argument only adds to her confusion, making her doubt if her love for Stephen would have lasted.

Lucy, too, is less than perceptive when she spontaneously praises Maggie for her moral superiority in giving Stephen up (VII,4). And Dr Kenn, in approving Maggie's following her conscience in giving priority to remembered loyalties, shows her no way forward: he abstains from advising Maggie that an ultimate marriage with Stephen would be the least evil in a situation where 'each immediate step was clogged with evil' (VII,3). Each of these attitudes can be justified, but Tom's reaction is particularly forbidding. Limited in intelligence by nature and only superficially polished by his education, Tom feels hostility and repulsion, based on his observation of Maggie's past untrustworthiness, her habit of changing her perverse resolves into 'something equally perverse' (VI,12). Unlike his aunt Glegg, he assumes the worst of Maggie and refuses to have her under his roof. Prejudiced and coldly inflexible in his sense of family disgrace, he expresses a loathing of her character and conduct. Maggie's secrecy in her relations with Stephen, sustained partly to avoid injury to Lucy, but in fact increasing the chance of it, touches Tom's pride in his uprightness and blinds him to his own interest in the affair. With Stephen's affections elsewhere engaged, Lucy might have come to entertain Tom's long-cherished feeling for herself with favour: she is aware that 'he always had that pleasant smile' when he looked at her. But instead of counselling caution, Tom reinforces Maggie's guilt, so that 'it seemed as if every sensitive fibre in her were too entirely preoccupied by pain ever to vibrate again to another influence. Life stretched before her as one act of penitence' (VII,2). It is mainly this exclusion from her brother's forgiveness which turns Maggie's alienation into despair.

At times Tom's and Maggie's characters seem split from a single personality. Had they been united into one, his prudence and self-command and her sensibility would have produced an integrated personality. But divided, they tend to clash unpredictably, leaving both vulnerable to accident and sudden pressures. Maggie's emotionality is not by itself tragic, the narrator insists. Though she is caught in conflicts between 'inward impulse and outward fact' (IV, 2), internally her passionate sensibility can make 'her faults and virtues all merge in each other', giving to her impatience and vanity 'the poetry of ambition' (VI,6); left communing with herself alone in her 'bright aerial world again', Maggie is able to enjoy piano-playing and music-theory, where her romantic and idealising qualities, associated with tenderness, forgetfulness and gentle remorse, can express themselves without harmful consequences. The narrator questions, in this connection, Novalis's dictum that character is destiny. Had Hamlet's close relatives not impinged on his life, his destiny would have been normal. Even the passion for Stephen which shocks Maggie with its 'invisible influence' is not in itself dangerous. There is no inherent reason why Philip's dream of an 'awful crash' at the foot of 'a glistening, green, slimy channel of a waterfall' (VI,8) should ever actually befall Maggie. The arbitrary nature of the flood which drowns her is, then, part of the design. Where character comes in is in the tendency to renunciation and passivity followed by impulses of affectionate loyalty, which makes Maggie vulnerable to misfortune; liable, but not predestined. Unable to make 'a world outside' herself as men do, she forces herself back from the affair with Stephen into isolation, searching, as Philip reminds her, for 'a mode of renunciation that will be an escape from pain' (VI,7). The pain comes from her consciousness of the unhappiness and disapproval of others. It is in this state of restlessness that she is caught by the flood and reminded of her old home. She is impelled by an 'undefined sense of reconcilement with her brother'. His trust in her is likely to be restored by the 'primitive mortal needs' produced by the natural calamity. The dangerous mission of rescue is undertaken, then, in response to the emotional pull of home and family, and, when he is rescued by Maggie, Tom is duly awakened to a new sense of unsuspected 'depths in life' lying beyond his supposedly 'keen and clear' vision (VII,5). The depths include the value of memory, mutual support in times of emergency and spontaneous courage.[18] But under Maggie's temporary ascendancy as these influences are at play, Tom unquestioningly responds to Maggie's impulse to see Lucy, a highly risky undertaking with the cross-currents then at their fiercest.[19] Tom's agreement to row vigorously to Tofton, where Lucy should be, is conditioned by 'a certain awe and humiliation' which he feels in contemplating his sister's intensity of life and effort at this crisis. His old boyish plan to have a well-stocked ark ready for the floods is forgotten (I,6). Tom's habitual caution, checking the Tulliver impetuousness, is now in suspense under Maggie's imperious foolhardiness. The consequences are fatal, since she ignores the 'distinct idea of danger' that had pressed on her in an agony of dread a little earlier. The interaction of the two personalities, traced with intricate patterning, thus contributes to the circumstances which surround their deaths, without controlling them.

The Mill on the Floss has, then, a consistent tragic technique throughout. It avoids suicide and murder (Maggie arrests her father's arm before he can flog Wakem to death with his 'riding whip'; V,7), it displays frightening error and accident, and it investigates causation as being highly subtle and intricate. The repeated references to death by drowning and dangerous waters suggest an environment which can move on without people, since people do not fully understand and control it. Mr Tulliver's head-scratchings over old Harry's role in this puzzling world, where if you drove your wagon in a hurry you might 'light on an awkward corner' (I,3,), his wife's awareness that people will believe in a Providential judgement upon herself for her having done 'summat wicked' (I,4), Mrs Deane's view that trouble 'isn't sent without a cause' in an unpredictable world (III,3), or Luke's doctrine that God dislikes things 'out 'o natur' such as lop-eared rabbits (I,4), are all untrained attributions of purpose and meaning to an environment, the implication of which is that human mentality is unfit for the world in which it is placed. Proper use is not made of accumulated information.

In Mrs Glegg's day, the St Ogg's mind 'did not look extensively before or after. It inherited a long past without thinking of it'. Since there had been no floods recently, people thought that the next day would be like the last, 'and the giant forces that used to shake the earth were forever laid to sleep'. Such ignorance or complacency is in its way as disturbing as metaphysical certainty, though it was 'received with all the honours in very good society' (I,12). The narrator with her 'large vision of relations' speaks from a vantage point of scientific study, where 'every single object suggests a large sum of conditions' (IV,1) but there are still no easy answers to physical or moral problems. The young people in *The Mill on the Floss* rise towards the level of understanding of the narrator above 'the mental level' of the previous generations, to whom they are nevertheless tied by heart-felt memories, filial loyalty and confused respect. Familial ties effect a kind of moral pattern, but they can reinforce unnecessary constraints and weaken the vigilance required if one is to avoid rash moves and accidents. Maggie is, therefore, not ready for the affair with Stephen Guest, which throws her off her feet and involves her in concealment. The flood puts even that in perspective, being so much vaster and more dangerous. It alone can be used to make sense of the novel's title, when in the unpredictable movements of water the river comes to the mill, which is normally on the Ripple, not on the Floss. No one takes any precaution against the flood though several characters have riverside homes. Even the resourceful Bob Jakin, who has invested his savings in pleasure-boats for hire, is swept away helplessly in his own boat 'far past the meeting current'. The heavy rains which bring on the flood are a variation of nature not unknown to the inhabitants, yet are too rare and irregular to be expected, occurring more frequently, indeed incessantly, elsewhere, in 'the counties higher up the Floss'. To Maggie the flood is 'that awful visitation of God which her father used to talk of' (VII,5). The half-hearted recourse to theism, associating doctrine with the previous generation, highlights human vulnerability and ignorance in the face of a menacing environment, which is often deceptively calm. The flood can be aligned with innumerable other random events in the novel, major and minor,

central and peripheral, on and off-stage, such as the accident which
had crippled Philip Wakem 'in infancy' (II,3), the turn of the tide
which carries Maggie and Stephen past the point of no return at
Luckreth (VI,13), the fortuitous combination which goes to every
individual conception and birth, destructive fires of various sorts,
chance meetings and attractions, the lump in the throat which
destroys Jap the dog (II,6), the illness which takes off Mrs Deane,
the timing of Mr Tulliver's two strokes. In a world where cockatrices
and wolves have not 'ceased to bite' (VI,12), aggression, ailments,
coincidences and mistakes are interwoven in human experience.
Maggie's grandmother, whom she resembles 'as two peas', died
young, we are informed (III,9). The unhappy Jetsome, Wakem's
illegitimate son, is 'pitched off his horse in a drunken fit'. Mr Tilt
has 'got his mouth drawn all o' one side' (VI,12). Poor Gratton shot
his mother by accident (VI,2). Aunt Pullet's constant harping on
her own demise is a comically selfish version of the same theme of
insecurity: 'I may go off sudden when I get home to-day – there's
no telling' (III,3). Even her critics make similar assumptions. She
is rebuked by her sister Mrs Glegg for lamenting the dropsical Mrs
Sutton's death as much as if their cousin Abbott 'had died sudden
without making his will ' (I,7).

Less neurotic or calculating in her reaction to personal misfortune is the mill-hand Luke's mother, who fought sore against
'shortness o' breath when it fust come on', but afterwards 'made
friends wi't' (III,8). That seems to be the best course when one
of the 'thousand natural shocks that flesh is heir to' arrives, to
try to get used to it. Special effort may be needed when larger
adversity strikes, as when 'the rowers pulled anew' when the vision
of St Ogg was seen during ancient floods, and yet there are no
guarantees of security in the known world; the records of the
past are themselves subject to mischance and misinterpretation.
The narrator inclines to the briefest manuscript versions of the St
Ogg legend since it is 'likely to contain the least falsehood' (I,12).
Human motives are mixed and often casual, running parallel to the
myriad coincidences of teeming natural life.

The Mill on the Floss seems especially concerned with tiny prolific
life, especially insects; the entomological allusions seem to be questioning the significance while also asserting the claims of individual
young people like Tom and Maggie Tulliver. Mr Glegg, inexhaust-
ibly occupied with the caterpillars, slugs and insects in his garden,
may be ridiculous in noticing 'remarkable coincidences between

these zoological phenomenena and the great events of that time', such as the burning of York Minster (I,12). But the question of the scale of events, the interconnection between large and small, the vastness of the universe which dwarfs human concerns, both wittily and gloomily preoccupies the narrator. The flood which 'swept as sudden death over all smaller living things' threatens the novel's characters too, by this token. In nature's enormity, minute threats may be as important as huge ones, and similarly in social life. When Riley recommends Stelling to Mr Tulliver as Tom's tutor, with all the incalculable, bad consequences which the novel traces, the ingredients that go to the advice are not delicate scruples, but 'little dim ideas and complacencies' which make up the auctioneer's consciousness; the narrator explains ironically, 'One cannot be good-natured all round. Nature herself occasionally quarters an inconvenient parasite on an animal to whom she has otherwise no ill-will. What then? We admire her care for the parasite' (I,3). The personification of nature as a caring but inconsistent female is itself sharply ironic. Nature has evidently no will as such at all and cannot reasonably be admired in the way a caring person may be. We know that the parasite is as subject to adversity as the animal to irritation from the parasite. The 'superannuated bluebottle' which Tom punishes instead of Maggie, like the toad he tickles and cockchafers he desires to master, is an inferior creature subject to arbitrary torment; it is noticed 'exposing its imbecility in the Spring sunshine, clearly against the views of Nature, who had provided Tom and the peas for the speedy destruction of this weak individual' (I,9). The erudite wit here not only mocks the boy's search for excuses, but also questions simplistic biological metaphysics. Nothing in the way of views or a destructive purpose can be attributed to nature. The relation of the bluebottle to the boy's aimless frustration is random. It is Tom's father's fault to 'interpret any chance-shot that grazed him as an attempt on his life' (III,7). All such rationalisations lead to confusion; every case must be examined sceptically on its merits; otherwise it will be misread like the indeterminately featured human faces which nature turns off 'by the gross' only to conceal the 'rigid, inflexible purposes' which underlie them, thus refuting simple people's 'confident prophecies' (I,5). Despite the overwhelming, pervasive stream of allusions to the dangers of nature in *The Mill on the Floss,* the narrator's own superb, intelligent, knowledgeable voice, embracing, in beautiful studied prose, geography, history, science, the arts and philosophy, by its even, patient, amused, female tone counteracts the pessimism with an implicit claim to advancement and survival.

The importance of education as a theme in the novel appertains to this narrator's voice; Maggie clearly could have become as learned, if not as astute, as the speaker. Why did she not? How far did she get? The novel continually poses these questions. The fact that she is excluded from the classical education provided for Tom is, as I have indicated, especially poignant, for she would have made a lot of it, perhaps even improved it. That type of education is itself rigid and unadapted. Indeed the Revd Stelling's educational practices resemble the automatic behaviour of animals which human intelligence is supposed to have superseded; like that of a beaver 'understood to be under the immediate teaching of nature', who instinctively builds a dam, even in captivity; 'the absence of water or of possible progeny was an accident for which he was not accountable' (II,1). This statement is ironically attributed to a beaver, but the unaccountability of people in the face of accidents is a theme of the novel. Stelling applies Euclidian geometry and Latin grammar to Tom, irrespective of Tom's circumstances and aptitude. He is compared (as a teacher) with an 'animal endowed with a power of boring a hole through a rock' (II,4). To Tom lessons provide a 'mill-like medium of uninteresting ideas' (II,7); he can no more understand their justification than 'an innocent shrew-mouse imprisoned in the split trunk of an ash-tree in order to cure lameness in cattle' can understand superstition (II,1). The torturer of small animals is now himself like a tortured small animal. George Eliot's powerful satire here does not exclude the idea that it may be difficult to tailor educational reform to individual needs like Tom's (Philip seems to have made more of Stelling's offerings), but it gains a special thrust from her acute awareness of the injustice suffered by girls in schooling. If education generally in those days 'was almost entirely a matter of luck – usually of ill-luck', with a father having no more certainty of selecting the right school for his son than someone taking a 'dice box' in his hands (II,4), for girls it was much worse. They came out of school untrained for life, with no other part of their 'inherited share in the hard-won treasure of thought . . . than shreds and patches of feeble literature and false history' (IV,3). Maggie is thus ignorant of psychology and science, and of morality too in its deepest sense. Scott and Byron are not subtle and modern enough for her, not as regards women's problems certainly. Her mind withers in a 'vulgar level' of culture (V,3). Not being 'a thoroughly well-educated young lady with a perfectly balanced mind' (VI,3), Maggie has no framework of reference in which to find her bearings during her emotional entanglements with Philip and Stephen. The narrator's irony concerning contemporary perfectibility in female education (a bid for sympathy with her heroine) does not invalidate the point that Maggie is culturally disadvantaged. What strikes us most in her encounters with Stephen is her vulnerability. His fine bass voice and 'well-marked horizontal eyebrows' make her glance vibrate (the appeal of his masculinity is unmistakable), but she is unaware that he sings in 'a provincial amateur fashion'. The deficiencies in Stephen's culture are clearer to the reader than to Maggie. His easy exposition of one of the *Bridgewater Treaties on the Power, Wisdom, and Goodness of God, as manifested in the Creation* (1833–6) shows sincerity and a concern for topicality, but not the painful intellectual honesty of which Maggie is capable. By the time she has refused to elope with him, Stephen has learned the hard way that Providence is unreliable, though he persists against the odds in trying to make the best of a bad job. Maggie is too demoralised to match him here and languishes in a bewilderment not altogether unlike her father's, faced by a puzzling world. Her soul goes out to the 'Unseen Pity that would be with her to the end' (VII,5), a prevision of enduring religious consolation, which is ironic in view of the actual imminence of her end.

Maggie's end gives rise to mixed feelings precisely because it would be so natural for her to pray for it, given her state of self-despair, yet she does not. In some ways Tom's death is the more tragic of the two, since he had learned already what his capacities were and at the very end was beginning to learn about his limitations too. Tom picks up his business skills as he goes, helped by his uncle Deane, to whom a formal education such as Tom had received from Stelling is a 'raw material in which he had had no experience' (III,5). He picks up his investment skills from the packman Bob Jakin, who, if a bit of luck turns up, is always 'thinking if I can let Mr Tom have a pull at it'. Jakin's friendly support for his Tulliver friends is more than sentimentality; it is part of a general philosophy of observing the signs, recovering from adversity, insuring against loss, profiting from unexpected windfalls, which humanity needs if it is to progress. The untutored Jakin made his original nest-egg as a reward for his sharpness in dousing a fire at Torry's mill. Bob's opportunism includes the ability to take advantage of the presence of accidentally damaged goods and persuade others to overlook what may be superficial or negligible chance flaws. It is in this way that Aunt Glegg learns the 'breadth of his thumb.' Moth-holes and mildew, the effects of insects and dampness, two phenomena to which the novel continually draws our attention, are, in Bob Jakin's view, 'sent by Providence' to foster his trade in cheap woollen kerchiefs: 'it's took me a deal o' study to know the vally o' such articles' (V,2). Such un-ideal but useful commerce is regarded as comically benign by the narrator, who extends the metaphors from cloth-making, moisture and animal vitality into her accounts of Maggie's emotional experience, where there is no corresponding sense of confidence and ingenuity. Maggie's daily life is a woof, absorbing a 'tissue of vague dreams' and 'threads of thought and emotion', but here imperfections can have abysmal results. There are times when feeling can overwhelm restraints, 'can rise and leave flood-marks' never reached again; at such times speech is both 'sincere and deceptive' (V,4). The perception that language itself is not to be trusted as the expression of some inner truth, that consciousness is not necessarily coherent, but grabs at chance associations, presenting them as analogies, is a further, deeper scepticism present in *The Mill on the Floss*. At one point the narrator challenges Aristotle on this issue, regretting the fact that 'intelligence so rarely shows itself in speech without a metaphor – that we can so seldom declare what a thing is, except by saying it is something else' (II,1). Changing the metaphor not only alters one's conception of a thing (the metaphor here being the classics as culture or ploughing); it is a sign that human intelligence is frequently arbitrary and unreliable even at its most prestigious and committed.

To regard the flood and drowning as inevitable or conclusive or, conversely, to discover that they do not necessarily follow from the characters' actions is, therefore, to miss the point of *The Mill on the Floss* completely. Such a drastic use of nature to symbolise culpability or irresponsibility would have been regarded by George Eliot as fallacious. In a reported conversation with a Russian interviewer, who inquired how Maggie Tulliver would have dealt with her powerful passions had she not drowned, George Eliot replied, 'Have you not found that life, itself, often provides unexpected possibilities and resolutions through death? Indeed, for me it has often been the certitude of death that has given me the courage to live.'[20] This Darwinian view of death as a means to more highly organised life does not diminish the tragedy of the loss of individuals, particularly of young, gifted individuals, whom we have come to know in detail in an extended work of fiction. But it shows death as a condition of Maggie's and Tom's lives (in a context of acknowledgement that such things occur) which is what *The Mill on the Floss* presents to us as at once terrible and possible.

It is a work in which hopes are successively dashed and memories of the 'primitive fellowship of kindred' (II,2) revived to sustain a complex response to life's uncertainties. The supreme moment in which Tom and Maggie 'in an embrace never to be parted' live through again 'the days when they had clasped their little hands in love' (VII,5) is not, then, sentimental melodrama,[21] but an assertion of the need for human mutual support, in spite of prejudice and error, in the face of nature itself. The finale, read with bated breath by generations of readers, seems to me properly integrated with the novel as a whole.

4

George Eliot's Shorter Fiction, including *Silas Marner*

Of George Eliot's six shorter prose-tales only *Silas Marner* is developed into a full novella with a double plot. The others conform to Henry James's notion of the short story as anecdote, where a single situation is carefully elaborated.[1] They all contain interesting narrative effects, like the two dialogue scenes run into the one chapter (Ch. 3) in 'Amos Barton', the rendering of Dempster's consciousness in a state of delirium tremens in 'Janet's Repentance' (Ch. 23) or the large time gaps in *Silas Marner*. In none of these tales do the chapters have titles or mottoes in aid of contemplation. If narrative haste is scarcely a quality to be associated with George Eliot, since she gives over so much space to narratorial comment, yet she can also use unexpected deaths and brief, suspenseful chapter-endings like Dunsey Cass's exit, 'So he stepped forward into the darkness' (*Silas Marner*, Ch. 4), to cut the content, though not the substance, of her stories. But what distinguishes each one of her shorter works is the impression given of a strong theme delicately handled. Behind the presentational cover of sympathy for commonplace people experiencing unromantic incidents in average communities set in ordinary landscapes, where there is 'nothing to break the flowerless monotony of grass and hedgerow but an occasional oak or elm, and a few cows sprinkled here and there' ('Janet's Repentance', Ch. 26), there is a nudging towards implicit radical analyses of complex and sensitive issues. The humorous and emotional side-effects cannot obscure the seriousness of the implications. Admittedly, 'The Lifted Veil' is exceptional in respect of several of these points made about George Eliot's shorter fiction, yet it too bears a very distinct mark, its fantasy content.

George Eliot's first published story, 'The Sad Fortunes of the Reverend Amos Barton' (1857), is a good example of a disturbing text, with a problem beneath its innocuously mild exterior. The effect is less surprising perhaps when we read that the subject came to the author when she was lying in bed one summer morning in a dreamy doze.[2] But what is the subject of 'Amos Barton'? Ostensibly it is the only one of the three *Scenes of Clerical Life* (1858) that lives up to the collective title. Here the clerical portrait is prominent. The awkward clergyman is followed in his avocations, visiting his parishioners, preaching to the poor, meeting with fellow parsons, consulting the squire. In these contacts Barton makes a poor showing, reflecting on them as disagreeable duties. The tone is satirical in a way that suggests Trollope,[3] with Martin Cleves, 'the true parish priest, the pastor beloved, consulted, relied on by his flock', set against the Reverend Archibald Duke, who thought 'the immense sale of the "Pickwick Papers", recently completed, one of the strongest proofs of original sin'; and the clergy's talk about their bishop left unspecified, 'lest we should happen to overhear remarks unsuited to the lay understanding, and perhaps dangerous to our repose of mind' (Ch. 6). The narrator's lay understanding is less inhibited near the end when we learn of 'some bitter feeling' aroused by the vicar's use of a pretext to remove Barton from his curacy so that the vicar might ultimately give it 'to his own brother-in-law' (Ch. 9). But the questioning of the ecclesiastical system is by now felt as a background concern in the tale.

The main misfortune of Amos Barton has already occurred at this juncture, the loss of his wife Milly after childbirth. Weakened by domestic labour and worries, she has had six children and is considered to be delicate: 'she won't stand havin' many more children' (Ch. 5). The narrator explicitly addresses the problems of the Barton household in economic terms: 'By what process of division can the sum of eighty pounds per annum be made to yield a quotient which will cover that man's weekly expenses?' But implicitly the problem is left as personal. In his pressing situation the only consolation for Barton must be sexual pleasure with his wife. Milly, it is emphasized, is a lovely woman who blushes tremulously and 'makes sunshine and a soft pillow' for Amos. 'The flowing lines of her tall figure made the limpest dress look graceful, and her old frayed black silk seemed to repose on her bust and limbs with a placid elegance' (Ch. 2). Her physical attractiveness to the ungainly but energetic Barton in his 'tight pantaloons' is unmistakable.[4]

To support this reading, the narrator associates the irregular, picturesque world of Shepperton with a careless fertility, with his own 'nurse', the 'school-children's gallery', 'the penetralia of private life' (this in a cancelled passage),[5] the 'pleasant rhythm' of the milk falling from 'the udders of the large sleek beasts', Barton in his sermons floundering about 'like a sheep as has cast itself' (Ch. 1), not to mention the workhouse rebel, Miss Fodge, who 'had contributed to the perpetration of the Fodge characteristics in the person of a small boy' (Ch. 2). Even a negative joke, like the reference to the unsympathetic cook to whom Mr Bridmain's man-servant 'did *not* make love' (Ch. 3), keeps up the atmosphere. The scandal surrounding the visit of the Countess Czerlaski, a former governess and widow of a dancing-teaching, is therefore predictable. When her brother decides to marry her maid, the Countess leaves in indignation and takes up residence with the Bartons, so that in the neighbourhood 'new surmises of a very evil kind were added to the old rumours' (Ch. 5). It is believed that Amos has taken her as a mistress during his wife's last months of pregnancy. The doctor surmises that Barton 'may have attractions we don't know of', and the Rector suggests that he may have 'some philtre or other to make himself charming' (Ch. 6). Such ribaldry, however unfair to Barton, is only a distortion of the truth, that he is a demandingly passionate husband, affectionate 'in his way' (Ch. 2). Milly's deathbed words, if the rash of dashes is cleared from them, 'You-have-made-me-very-happy' (Ch. 8), are not likely to refer to intellectual companionship! Indeed on his last visit to Milly's grave Amos confesses, 'I wasn't tender enough to thee – I think of it all now' (Ch. 10). The implication, that sexual problems do not disappear in marriage, but can have tragic consequences, comes subtly across to us. It is obvious that Barton had no knowledge of contraception; he who had gone through the 'Eleusinian mysteries of a university education' without being able to master English spelling and syntax (Ch. 2) was hardly the man to acquire advanced opinions or unprejudiced information on a taboo topic. But the sharp irony has its effect. If 'Amos Barton' succeeds in its purpose of stirring sympathy with 'commonplace troubles . . . in very ordinary decent apparel' (Ch. 7) it does so because it deals not only with the details of a tiring life, Milly's 'assiduous unrest' of mending and so on (Ch. 2), but also most understandingly with 'unspoken sorrows' (Ch. 5), which its characters are not able to articulate. It is notable, as Dianne F. Sadoff has pointed out,[6] that as a widower Barton still needs a woman to make 'the evening sunshine of his life'; it is the elder daughter Patty, who, aged about thirty with 'some premature lines round the mouth and eyes', fills that surrogate role at his side (Conclusion). The pathos, then, has a hard core.

'Mr. Gilfil's Love-Story' (1857) is altogether more candid, which it can afford to be since its theme of fostering and snobbery is less controversial. Set just before the French Revolution in Cheverel Manor, a castellated house which would have made a charming picture had 'some English Watteau' existed to paint it (Ch. 2), it has something of the trappings of a historical romance. The clerical element adheres mainly to the frame of the tale. The frame concerns the Reverend Maynard Gilfil's later life as a hunting and farming parson, preaching undoctrinal sermons and sipping gin and water in solitude, apart from the 'mutual understanding' he enjoys with his old brown setter. Gilfil has carried widowhood into the introspection of old age, keeping his long-dead wife's chamber intact with its 'blinds and thick curtains' drawn. Even in the 'antecedent romance' of his courtship of Lady Cheverel's musical protégée Tina, Gilfil cuts an everyday figure, giving earnest advice: 'Time and absence, and trying to do what is right, are the only cures' (Ch. 9), he tells Tina, who is passionately and hopelessly in love with the heir to the estate, Captain Wybrow. Though the worthy Gilfil at one point feels painfully that he has 'lost the being who was bound up with his power of loving' (Ch. 19), he wins her hand after all, once Wybrow has died unexpectedly, only to lose her again finally in her 'struggle to put forth a blossom' (Ch. 21). Gilfil has enough solidity to function effectively as the character who is on the receiving end of the incidents in the plot, but the principal interest is elsewhere.[7]

In 'Mr. Gilfil's Love-Story' George Eliot develops a tense situation between the Italian-born Tina and the English aristocratic set in which she is bred. Some of the dialogue has the touch of Jane Austen at her most serious, as when Miss Asher, the thin-lipped beauty to whom Captain Wybrow is betrothed, tells him, 'An honourable man will not be placed in circumstances which he cannot explain to the woman he seeks to make his wife' (Ch. 9). The narrator's explanation of this lady's gracious condescension to Tina as 'the malicious anger that assumes the tone of compassion' (Ch. 13) is psychologically acute, as is the ironic account of Wybrow's own divided feelings; he 'always did the thing easiest and most agreeable to him from a sense of duty' (Ch. 5). The interplay of dangerous personal relations in the great house is managed with wit, suspense and economy in twenty brief chapters. Sir Christopher's architectural passion, his dislike of 'insipid' Palladianism (Ch. 4) and his quarrel with his sister, both adequately sketched, play a part in tangling the circumstances surrounding Tina in her equivocal position. The decor is appropriately delicate, featuring pretty flowers, tender operatic arias, ornamental pictures, the gardener's turf and gravel, the willow-fringed pool 'laughing with sparkles' (Ch. 17), but the stately Lady Cheverel finds that her world is too complacent. Her idea of grafting 'as much English fruit as possible on the Italian stem' (Ch. 3), without properly adopting Tina, is superficial and predictably fails. The talented girl, torn between gratitude, resentment and guilt over the secret affair with the weak Wybrow, eventually contemplates murder. Rushing noiselessly and looking 'like the incarnation of a fierce purpose' (Ch. 13), she clenches a dagger, believing she will plunge it into her false lover's heart. Though the rather dull Gilfil exculpates the heroine by arguing that she could not *in fact* have brought herself to do what she admittedly meant to do, when she was prevented by Wybrow's death, which came as a result of a heart attack, yet we are forced to reflect that Tina was very lucky not to be put to the test. The narrator's ironic technique has made violence seem perfectly plausible.

A large contribution is made by the animal imagery. Tina's single parent, her father, who is Lady Cheverel's music-copyist in Milan, already refers to her as 'the marmoset' when he leaves her at his landlady's 'on the floor with her legs in a heap of peas' (Ch. 3). The narrator next compares her humorously with a kitten. Later in the narrative Tina's father dies, and she is taken, still in infancy, to England to be brought up as a useful companion to the childless Lady Cheverel; the idea that she is different from the family is constantly reinforced by the link with animals. Sir Christopher is always calling her familiarly his 'little monkey', 'the black-eyed monkey', 'you silly monkey', even when she is seventeen or eighteen years old. The diminutive and attractive Tina would seem naturally to suggest various small animals to characters and narrator alike. They bring in, apart from monkeys, a humming bird, a frog, a puppy, a linnet, a duck, a leveret, a grasshopper, a mouse, a waterfowl and even, when she is on her mission of hatred, a tigress, thus neatly combining condescension with a certain Darwinian apprehension of an instinctively fighting tenaciousness in Tina, the object of so much jealousy, affection and pity.

But the allusions to the animals and human–animal relationships do not function reductively. George Eliot assumes both an emotional value and a need for responsibility in humanity's dealings with animals. Much, for example, in the introductory chapter of 'Mr. Gilfil's Love-Story', is made of the clergyman's concern for Dame Tripp, whose attitude to her pet pig involves a comic assumption of equality. She will not have the pig slaughtered for bacon, because she appreciates its company: 'I do not mind doin' wi'out to gi' him summat. A bit o' company's meat an' drink too, an' he follers me about, an' grunts when I spake to 'un, just like a Christian.' Gilfil is sufficiently moved to make Dame Tripp a gift from his own store of bacon, even though she hardly ever attends his church (she is a leech-gatherer by profession, though not gravely Wordsworthian). Her need for company curiously prefigures Lady Cheverel's for Tina's, and is actually more understanding. At various points in the tale the narrator emphasises the gap between human and animal intelligence ('Animals are such agreeable friends – they ask no questions, they pass no criticisms', Ch. 7). No such gap exists, of course between Tina and the aristocratic circle in which she finds herself; the barrier set up by patronage, however benevolent it may be, frustrates her sexual passion and nearly causes a catastrophe. Tina recovers, however, at Foxholm Parsonage amid the 'unsentimental cheeriness of pullets, sheepdogs and carthorses' (Ch. 20), for long enough to give Gilfil a few months of happiness. In an impressive passage the narrator describes life as a 'mighty torrent, rushing from one awful unknown to another', mentioning the stars, the tides, human invention, commerce and politics, compared with all of which Tina's trouble is lighter 'than the smallest centre of quivering life in the water-drop' or the anguish of a bird that has found its 'nest torn and empty' (Ch. 5). But 'Mr. Gilfil's Love-Story' is carefully worded throughout to make the scale of high and low, large and small, in life seem only relative, leaving us with a sense of 'nature's social union', such as informs Burns's poem 'To a Mouse'.[8]

'Janet's Repentance' (1857) is the most ambitious of the *Clerical Scenes*. Longer by a third than its predecessor, it returns to the period which George Eliot could recollect from childhood. There is a gallery of local townsfolk, involved in sectarian disputes. In the climactic set-piece, an Evangelical clergyman, Mr Tryan, has to run the gauntlet of mockery from the High-and-Dry Church party. Here a crudely satirical play-bill, representing the 'keenest edge of Milby wit' (Ch. 9), is quoted in full.[9] This religious strife forms an unpleasant back-drop to the main centre of interest, Janet Dempster's alcoholism, her sufferings as a battered wife and her recovery under the guidance of the despised Tryan. The story has a single main thrust, Janet's demoralisation, her escape from marriage and her regaining of self-command. Her husband's reckless self-destruction and the consumptive clergyman's fatal self-sacrifice are contributory elements only. 'Janet's Repentance' has an underlying optimism, a trust in corrective nature, a belief in the dignity of woman and a respect for the purposive individual.

The theme of drink is handled tactfully, with humour and sympathy, as might be expected, but also with due regard for the grimmer aspects, the causes, danger-points, consequences. The narrator indicates that it is a problem which has not gone away; the prosperous Milby of the Victorian present, where ladies who take too much upon themselves 'are never known to take too much in any other way', is ironically contrasted with the dull Milby of more than a generation back, where 'many of the middle-aged inhabitants, male and female, often found it impossible to keep up their spirits without a very abundant supply of stimulants' (Ch. 2). Such passages, while offering a reason for apparent changes in behaviour, also question the extent of the changes.[10] Drink, directly or indirectly, affects all the characters in Janet's Repentance', from the dissenting Reverend Horner, 'given to tippling and quarrelling' (Ch. 2), to the doctor who puts his feet up in the Red Lion, having already 'been in the sunshine' while on his rounds (Ch. 1). Dempster the lawyer is proud of his ability to hold his drink, but it proves a habit which loses him his money, his wife and his life. Janet has her fear of his violent temper to excuse her own weakness; 'it's enough to make her drink something to blunt her feelings', as the understanding Mrs Pettifer remarks, 'and no children either, to keep her from it' (Ch. 3). But by loosening restraints on emotions drink makes the situation worse for all concerned. Dempster's chronic aggressiveness towards man and beast is only compounded by drink; Janet's retorts and gestures of despair, emboldened by drink also, whet his hatred. He is castigated by the narrator as 'an unloving, tyrannous, brutal man', moved by love of power and 'lust of torture', who 'needs no motive to prompt his cruelty; he needs only the perpetual presence of a woman he can call his own' (Ch. 13). The complex psychological and social factors seem to be producing an atmosphere of hopelessness. The influence of alcoholism is intelligently contextualised. The nadir is reached when Janet, driven from her home at night, but taken in by Mrs Pettifer, feels utterly helpless, her over-excited brain shaping the future in misery as 'a dreary vacant flat, where there was nothing to strive after, nothing to long for' (Ch. 16). She quite lacks the courage to attempt to live independently. There is, however, a structure of negatives and positives built into this tale. Nature is said to provide love over and above human justice, giving us 'fruit from no planting of ours' (Ch. 5). Milby is not only a dingy town, but one where in spring the roofs and chimneys can be clothed by rainbows 'in a strange transfiguring beauty'. It contains different mixtures, of 'purity, gentleness, and unselfishness' as well as 'griping worldliness, vanity, ostrich-feathers and the fumes of brandy' (Ch. 2). The biblical vocabulary intruded into such vivid accounts suggests a humanised Christian ethic rather than the pietism to be found in temperance tracts. And Mr Tryan's ministry to Janet, which is crucial to her cure, depends not on other-worldly doctrine, but on fellow-feeling. He confides to her that he too has something on his conscience: the suicide of a young girl, Lucy, who had left her father's home for him at College and then gone off 'with a gentleman' while he himself was on vacation (Ch. 18).[11] He has managed to live with his guilt by working to rescue others of life's failures, of whom Janet is clearly one. The narrator stresses the importance of personal contact in the steadying of Janet's character: when ideas are 'clothed in a living human soul with all its conflicts . . . and shake us like a passion . . . we are drawn after them with gentle compulsion, as flame is drawn to flame' (Ch. 19). The fire imagery, used again after Janet overcomes the temptation to relapse, when Tryan's prayer sustains her, 'as the broad tongue of flame carries upwards in its vigorous leap the little flickering fire that could hardly keep alight by itself' (Ch. 25), connotes here human warmth and supportiveness, which are accorded in this story a kind of mysterious energy. If the tone of 'Janet's Repentance' seems sometimes too earnest, it is no doubt because of the sensitivity of the subject and the difficulties of identifying the appropriate therapy.

In a brisker narrative Janet might have married her rescuer, but, as it is, with both Tryan and Dempster dead, she has to cope on her own, consolidating her self-conquest by adopting one of her husband's relatives as her daughter, who eventually brings her grandchildren, so filling the 'fatal blank' which childlessness had made in Janet's life. These particulars of her case are recorded in the tale rather as the 'large store' of neighbours' personal details are noted down by old Mr Jerome, the wealthy non-polemical Dissenter. Jerome, the possessor of a paradisiacal garden, carefully targets his charity on the actual needs of individuals, such as a horse or a mangle, and this helps them to stand on their own feet, without becoming dependent on parish welfare. Jerome's view of poor relief is that 'the parish shillins turn it sour'; and his to Janet, we are told, are 'truthful lips' (Ch. 26). It is precisely the sight of Jerome with his granddaughter that turns Janet's own thoughts to adoption, so there can be little doubt that his social role as operator of an informed benevolence is presented as exemplary, its principles even being applied by the heroine herself.

'The Lifted Veil' (published anonymously in 1859) is framed, on the other hand, as a warning. It presents a terrifying situation, in which there is no trust at all to fill up 'the margin of ignorance which surrounds all our knowledge' ('Janet's Repentance', Ch. 22). Instead there is unnatural mistrust; there are thought-readings, second sight, visions of the future and revivification of the dead by blood-transfusion, all revealing horrible truths, all pessimistic prophecies of the self-fulfilling kind. George Eliot herself called it 'a slight story of an outré kind – not a *jeu d'esprit*, but a *jeu de melancholie*'.[12] Written in the first person, it maintains throughout its two chapters the confessional note. The narrator, Latimer, is of a sensitive, unpractical nature, educated yet neither a scientist nor a poet; he has 'the poet's sensibility without his voice' (Ch. 1). We might feel that his supernatural insight into the future and into other people's minds aligns him more with the novelist than the poet, but, with a physique formed for passive suffering, he lacks the energy to write anything down, except for his last-minute apologia, which is the tale.

To add to his misfortune, Latimer falls in love with an even harder egoist than himself, Bertha, his brother's fiancée. Conscious of her negative nature, he foresees that she would prove a malevolent wife, but still marries her. He completely lacks religion, hope or sympathy, being conscious that other people's spoken words are

George Eliot

'like leaflets covering a fermenting heap' of frivolities, puerilities, meanness, caprices and 'indolent makeshift thoughts' (Ch. 1). Eventually he loses his telepathic gift, living instead 'continually in my own solitary failure' and fearful of the presence of 'something unknown and pitiless' (Ch. 2). That this intimation refers to his wife's intention to poison him has to be supplied by the reader, for the experiment of the talking corpse which leads to Bertha's exposure would have been unnecessary had Latimer foreseen it. The morbidity of 'The Lifted Veil' may have been a necessary release in which George Eliot could briefly explore a world where her usual moral aspirations are denied, but it also affords evidence of her willingness to evoke horrified curiosity over possibilities on the frontiers of science, and is not without entertainment value. She did not acknowledge it as her own until 1877 when it appeared in the Cabinet edition of her works.

'Brother Jacob' (written in 1860, published in 1864) is overtly comical in a sardonic way. Henry James called its central character, David Faux 'an admirable picture of unromantic malfeasance'.[13] This rogue, who prospers for some time under another identity after stealing his mother's money, takes on a particularly ludicrous persona in becoming a confectioner, skilled in fleecing his customers. He is, in fact, so unscrupulous and disloyal as to earn the narrator's contempt for his poor spelling, sallow complexion and self-congratulatory 'active mind' (Ch. 1). Nemesis for David takes the unexpected form of his idiot brother Jacob, a genuine 'innocent', representing that incalculable element in human relations which schemers and cheats are liable to ignore. Jacob helps to expose David's real background just when he is about to marry into respectable Grimworth society. Since he has violated the sanctities of family life by robbing his mother, manipulating his handicapped brother and disappearing abroad without sending them a word until he has a chance to claim a legacy, he can hardly make excuses; 'he smiled a ghastly smile' (Ch. 3). The contradictions in David Faux's other role as a genteel suitor give rise to some of George Eliot's most comical writing: 'His views on marriage were not entirely sentimental but were as duly mingled with considerations of what would be advantageous to a man in his position as if he had had a very large amount of money spent on his education'. The piquancy extends to the analysis of the confectioner's progress in business. A 'special commercial organ' is developed for the production of mince pies, which takes that work out of the hands of 'maids and matrons in private families', where it had traditionally flourished in primitive simplicity. This introduction of 'neck-and-neck trading' into Grimworth, a town not used to 'small profits and quick returns', does not bring the immediate general benefit that some economists might have predicted. The women are not set free 'to add to the wealth of society in some other way', but remain idle, constrained by lack of alternative training and, it goes without saying, by social prejudice against women as entrepreneurs. The confectioner is almost the sole beneficiary; the specialisation does not function as 'the inevitable course of civilization, division of labour, and so forth' (Ch. 2). Rarely does George Eliot write as caustically of greed and its ramifications as in this short story.

Silas Marner (1861) is in some ways mellower, yet certain of the pre-occupations of 'Brother Jacob' are carried over into it: theft, deception, exile and prejudice, for example. It was included with 'The Lifted Veil' and 'Brother Jacob' in a single volume in 1877, and, though longer than them, definitely falls into the category of short fiction. Many of its scenes are treated very economically; there are only a few didactic asides. We know it was very rapidly composed.[14] Even where the narrative pace is leisurely, as with the Rainbow Inn scene (Ch. 6), suspense is heightened by leaving Silas Marner at the bar door at the end of the previous chapter, about to make a shattering announcement, which does not occur until chapter 7, a technique also found in Scott. The narrative soon hurries on, conveying us to the next morning with the whole village already 'excited by the story of the robbery' (Ch. 8). The varied speed with which these strange events are covered, occurring among slow-thinking, untutored inhabitants of obscure places in old times, is curiously skilful.

The narrator also deliberately evokes the primitive and the legendary. Weaving was, in fact, an 'indispensable' trade at that period, but weavers, 'alien-looking men', bent under mysterious burdens and resembling 'the remnants of a disinherited race', are invested with a quality of weirdness.[15] Silas Marner himself, his 'dreadful stare' and 'pale face' associated with his liability to cataleptic fits (Ch. 1), has a dimension of grotesquerie which he never entirely loses. His looks remain against him. His has been a 'strange history', dependent on luck, even when things have gone well for him. The crucial event is the replacement of the stolen gold with the golden-haired infant girl, whom he is able

to adopt. The naivety of the characters helps to mediate the sense
of the marvellous. Education has no role to play in *Silas Marner*.
Even the philosophic narrator, who can point out, for example,
that the unwept death of Eppie's mother, 'which, to the general
lot, seemed as trivial as the summer-shed leaf, was charged with
the force of destiny to certain human lives' (Ch. 14), often effaces
herself to let the quaint minds of the story learn and teach their
own lessons, which are moral and humble.

Silas Marner and his village friend Dolly Winthrop agree that the
proper deduction from their experiences is that they should trust
in the unseen good which in due course brings out 'the rights' of
things and secures for people the gift of family loyalty: 'Since the
time the child was sent to me and I've come to love her as myself,
I've had light enough to trusten by' (Ch. 21). This belief in a Providence which caters for loving relations is a kind of Wordsworthian
wise passiveness, and suffices too for Nancy Cass, who accepts that
there must be some 'high reason' for her childlessness (Ch. 17),
as also for the trusting marital relationship which she enjoys with
Godfrey; she advises her husband to resign himself 'to the lot
that's been given us' (Ch. 20). Such limited understanding is
again observed to be sufficient for personal happiness in the
matter of Silas's refusal to improve his domestic conveniences by
the addition of a grate and oven; 'he loved the old brick hearth
as he had loved his brown pot – and was it not there when he had
found Eppie? The gods of the hearth exist for us still; and let all
new faith be tolerant of that fetishism, lest it bruise its own roots'
(Ch. 16). But to be tolerant of beliefs which express a generally
defensive optimism is not to endorse them as explanatory myths.[16]
Nancy Cass's refusal to adopt children and, more unobtrusively,
Silas Marner's disinclination to marry are unendorsed.

A faith of which the narrator of *Silas Marner* is disapproving is reliance on luck or the taking or risks by gambling on an undeserved
stroke of good fortune. The Cass family in the first part of the tale
is particularly prone to this form of pretentiousness. The father's
interest in cock-fighting doubtless depends on the excitement of
betting; the uncle's disgust when the luck turns against him at cards
extends to a world 'where such things could happen' (Ch. 13); the
son Dunsey's reliance on his own luck ('you must keep me by you
for your crooked sixpence') lands him literally in the pit, dead; and
his elder brother Godfrey's preference for trusting to 'casualties'
rather than to 'his own resolve' (Ch. 13) results in his missing his

one chance of the love of a child of his own. Favourable chance *may*, of course, resolve difficulties which have been occasioned by shirking and shortcomings, but to 'worship' it is to invite disaster (Ch. 9). Life contains both laws of consequences and random events. Marner's cataleptic fits occur unpredictably, allowing, for example, William Dane to cheat him with impunity, but also the infant child to reach the shelter of his house. Molly's death was predictable, but its location near Silas's cottage, was not. The coincidence enabled Godfrey to conceal his first marriage from Nancy and Silas to gain a new purpose for living. Events may seem to turn out right in the end, but the poetic justice felt by some readers as gratuitous[17] is actually not total. Nancy could be wished better luck than a childless marriage, as her sister Priscilla indicates fairly (Conclusion), and William Dane deserved to be tracked down and exposed. Life's complexities appear in these ragged edges which the formula of the neatly-ended plot cannot contain.

Though the story of *Silas Marner* encompasses both pathos and sentiment, the tone can be unsparing when it comes to the faults of our 'rural forefathers', those flushed and dull-eyed people without the 'higher sensibility that accompanies higher culture' (Ch. 13). There is a radical undertone in the presentation of the squirearchy and the backward pre-industrial village which brings the story closer to Crabbe than to George Eliot's favourite Goldsmith. Henry James's admiration for the display of the 'grossly material life of agriculture England' in the days of 'full-orbed Toryism' in *Silas Marner* is justified.[18] Even Dolly Winthrop, with her refusal to 'speak ill o' this world' in case she offends the powers above, lets slip that 'if there is any good to be got, we've need on it i' this world – that we have' and adds 'what wi' the drink, and the quarrelling, and the bad illnesses, and the hard dying, as I've seen times and times , one's thankful to hear of a better' (Ch. 10). The story cannot, therefore, be truly said to be 'comfortably'[19] set among squires and weavers in the 'rich central plain' of England; it is set rather in 'what we are pleased to call Merry England' (Ch. 1), and that includes places characterised by inefficient farming and social immobility.

The exercise of authority based on land-ownership is noted with much harsher sarcasm in *Silas Marner* than in *Adam Bede*. The whole Cass family is sharply portrayed. The men's weaknesses are traced to an inner and outer cause, the lack of a presiding female presence at the Red House and their unchallenged assumption of superiority, with resulting casualness, indecisiveness and treachery.

The New Year dance scene brings a shift of perspective. It is the first scene presented through a female consciousness, that of Nancy Lammeter. We are drawn to Nancy through her concern for her less pretty sister and through the malice of the two town-bred Miss Gunns, who regard her dialectal speech as vulgar and her dispensing with servants as a form of ignorance. When the narrator tell us that Nancy 'had the essential attributes of a lady, high veracity, delicate honour in her dealings, deference to others, and refined personal habits' (Ch. 11), she is successfully protecting the character's virtue against snobbery, that of the Miss Gunns. But Godfrey Cass cannot be protected from the snobbery to which he himself contributes. The class barrier thus erected proves too high for Godfrey to cross at the end. Yet the 'hereditary ease and dignity' of the Cass family is for Godfrey 'a sort of reason for living' (Ch. 3); and Dunsey Cass, whose dull mind is stimulated only by cupidity, is still to be thought of as a 'young gentleman', to whom walking is a bewilderingly unwanted 'mode of locomotion' (Ch. 4). Snobbery is perhaps hardly the word for the unquestioning arrogance of these Cass men, who are used to 'parish homage' (Ch. 9). The squire believes he has 'the hereditary duty of being noisily jovial' (Ch. 11), yet despite his self-possession and authoritativeness of voice, he is indecisive in handling his sons, following faulty indulgence with 'sudden fits of unrelentingness' (Ch. 8). In view of Godfrey's own moral weakness in not acknowledging his child when it turns up ('he had only conscience and heart enough to make him for ever uneasy under the weakness that forbade the renunication', Ch. 13, the renunciation of Nancy Lammeter, that is), his emergence sixteen years later as squire himself, one of Silas Marner's 'betters', those 'tall, powerful, florid men, seen chiefly on horseback', is highly ironic. His daughter's preference for 'working folks, and their houses, and their ways' (Ch. 19) strikes us as perfectly understandable after what we have read,[20] quite apart from her affection for Aaron. Godfrey Cass's view of what is good for his daughter is vitiated by his sense of social superiority; he has the unjustifiable impression 'that deep affections can hardly go along with callous palms and scant means' (Ch. 17). His punishment is to fear that Eppie thinks him worse than he is; she may suspect him of having acted unjustly towards her mother (Ch. 20). But Eppie, wishing to hold to her own, is not critical of class deference as such. The 'charter of Raveloe' which the New Year's Eve dance at the Red House seems to renew, confirming the social hierarchy –

'what everyone had been used to' (Ch. 11) – is not to be challenged by her. The character who comes nearest to questioning the system of hereditary privilege is Aaron. When Eppie baulks at having lavender in her planned garden for the characteristic reason that lavender is to be found only in 'gentlefolks' gardens', Aaron points out that cut slips of it are just thrown away, a fact which sets him thinking about the more equal distribution of goods in society; 'there need nobody run short o' victuals if the land was made the most on, and there was never a morsel but what could find its way to a mouth' (Ch. 16). At a time when communications were so poor, such radical thought remains 'untravelled' (Ch. 1), left in the air, as it were. The possibility of organised political protest is perhaps glanced at in the sight of men and women streaming from a large factory 'for their mid-day meal' which meets Silas and Eppie instead of the old Lantern Yard chapel and its familiar surroundings, now 'all swept away', when they visit the northern manufacturing town years after he had left it. But the main point is still the uninformed state of rural people: we recall that 'those were not days of active inquiry and wide report' (Ch. 13). Poor communications leave Raveloe in its ravelled, tangled state.

But despite its fixed responses and hostility to strangers, the rural community *is* able to offer the disillusioned immigrant Marner a stability which is not available in the town. Significantly, he is able to exercise economic independence in Raveloe, since he is no longer working for a wholesaler-dealer. Too honest to drive 'a profitable trade in charms' and herbal remedies (Ch. 2), he accumulates wealth almost automatically and remains unpersecuted, though at first isolated. The local inability to explain his peculiarities or to suggest a context in which they could have arisen gives him a kind of negative protection, the robbery notwithstanding. When Eppie's needs furnish him with a purpose for earning, he begins to respond more positively to his human surroundings.

Marner's salvation through parenthood is by no means a simple matter, however. His repressed, self-doubting personality retains much of its surprising quality throughout the tale. The special closeness of his friendship with William Dane, which led to the Lantern Yard brethren calling them David and Jonathan may be a clue; it prepares us for his reluctance to attempt to win his fiancée's 'belief in his innocence' (Ch. 1) after the lots point to his supposed guilt. Under the shock of betrayal by his friend, Marner retreats from women into impulsive industriousness as the weaver

of Raveloe. In comparing him with the spider at his unrelenting
work George Eliot is able to impress us with the *harmlessness* of a
figure usually associated with miserliness, with its harmlessness but
not exactly with its innocence. He draws out the gold coins 'to enjoy
their companionship', bathing his hands in them, and thinks of the
half-earned ones 'as if they had been unborn children' (Ch. 2).
The gold has fashioned him into correspondence with itself by
its 'hard isolation'. The sexual implications of his obsession are
specially detectable when he discovers the loss of his gold; he
passes 'his trembling hand all about the hole' and shakes 'so
violently' that he lets fall his candle (Ch. 5). The point is clinched
in the corresponding scene where he fingers the foundling; with
his heart beating violently he touches, not 'hard coin with the
familiar resisting outline', but 'soft warm curls' (Ch. 12). Marner's
insistence that he keep the child comes from a need deep within
himself and represents self-recognition. Uttered abruptly 'under a
strong sudden impulse', unintended, but like a revelation, the claim
refers to himself, a 'lone thing', as he says, partly 'mayed', but able
now to relate to another 'lone thing'. The scene in which Godfrey
Cass, the real father, watches Silas as he lulls the child combines
a Wordsworthian width of view with a psychological force that is
George Eliot's own; the child is soothed:

> into that wide gazing calm which makes us older human beings,
> with our inward turmoil, feel a certain awe in the presence of
> a little child, such as we feel before some quiet majesty or
> beauty in the earth or sky – before a steady-glowing planet, or
> a full-flowered eglantine, or the bending trees over a silent path-
> way. The wide open blue eyes looked up at Godfrey's without
> any uneasiness or sign of recognition: the child could make no
> visible, audible claim on its father, and the father felt a strange
> mixture of feelings, a conflict of regret and joy, that the pulse
> of that little heart had no response for the half-jealous yearning
> in his own, when the blue eyes turned away from him slowly, and
> fixed themselves on the weaver's queer face, which was bent low
> to look at them, while the small hand began to pull Marner's
> withered cheek with loving disfiguration. (Ch. 13)

The final oxymoron in this passage not only secures the scene from
an excess of sensibility, but also establishes the peculiarity of the
new situation which is taking shape, the one-parent family with the

stepfather in the female role. There are many tactful, supportive touches for Silas Marner's determination to maintain this (for him) liberating role. Dolly Winthrop, for instance, admits, 'I've seen men as are wonderful handy wi' children'. Silas insists on taking full responsibility, on learning the ways of rearing and fending for them both; 'she 'll be *my* litle un'. Though Eppie's development brings him new links with his neighbours, with nature, 'with the whole world', it also reinforces his individuality. The reasons why Marner takes Eppie with him on most of his journeys to the farmhouses is not to make new ties, but to keep her out of Dolly's hands; he does not always adhere to Dolly's welcome suggestions. Eppie is brought up on Silas' own system of 'downy patience', not punishment. He bears the burden of her misdeeds 'vicariously' (Ch. 14), a humanist version of the atonement doctrine which allows for indications of the man's psychological satisfaction, but first he even tries to teach her by himself before sending her to a dame school. He does not conceal from Eppie that she is an orphan and adopted, but rears her 'in almost inseparable companionship with himself', a process which yet allows her transfer to the protection of another (Aaron) when time weakens the father's earning capacity: 'I like to think as you'd have somebody else besides me' (Ch. 16). Marner's sincerity here is the proof of his intensity. And Eppie responds in kind, she can own nobody nearer than him: 'We've been used to be happy together every day, and I can't think o' no happiness wi'out him' (Ch. 19). Aaron seems to enter this symbiotic world mainly to see it through to its logical end. The tale ends with 'a peculiar sort of family marriage'[21] in which Dolly stands in temporarily as a partner for Silas to make up 'the four united people' before returning to her actual husband, the wheelwright. Silas has not so much given Eppie away as gained his 'larger family', to accommodate which his property has been improved at Godfrey Cass's expense (Conclusion). The story thus contrives to combine a universally acceptable moral of pure, healing love with a penetrating and tolerant study of a rather unusual character, Silas Marner.

5

Europe and Beyond: *Romola, Daniel Deronda*

George Eliot's international outlook soon strikes the reader. She can take a world-look while dwelling on very provincial matters. Though she never travelled outside Europe, her narrator's allusions in the novels often roam through Europe and other areas, especially the Middle East. After her first trip abroad in 1849, she revisited the Continent as many as sixteen times in a quarter of a century, sometimes for several months at a time. Her total time spent in Germany and Austria was two years.[1] These journeys were part of her study of English culture in its wider context. Her reading in the classics, in Jewish and Christian writings, in post-Renaissance literature and philosophy in the principal modern European languages, gave her a deep insight into both geography and history. She was, of course, particularly concerned about the progress of democratic and nationalist politics in nineteenth-century Europe. Without quite foreseeing the disastrous turns these movements would take in the next century, George Eliot treated them soberly. She devoted two novels to such problems, one set in Renaissance Italy, the other in the mid-Victorian present with the future of Europe's Jews as a major concern.

For a long time until recently neither *Romola* nor *Daniel Deronda* found much favour with some readers. Their unfamiliar subjects and out-of-the-way learning could be off-putting. But the truth now is that so much of George Eliot requires rare knowledge that there is no longer a special objection to these two works. In fact the glosses which George Eliot adds to an Italian word or so are now regarded not as pedantic distraction but as a help to editors. George Eliot saw herself as a scholarly author in the tradition of Chaucer, Shakespeare, Milton and Scott and would have been delighted to join them as an object of purposeful erudition.

Romola (1863) is actually George Eliot's most ambitious novel. Though centring on a few years in the late fifteenth century in Florence, it has a quite comprehensive sweep, covering the classics, the Middle Ages and the early modern world. It explores themes that are still relevant, like the responsibilities of women, the power of sexuality, the relation of religion and psychology, the application of learning to life, the scope for rational politics in small states based on market economies, and the possibility of international stability. What most impresses is George Eliot's ability to reflect these issues in innumerable small patterns in the texture of the novel without simplifying them. It is a work where we feel the presence of a steady, but not a heavy, hand.

It originated when Lewes suggested Savonarola, the pre-Reformation reformer, to George Eliot as a topic for fiction, while they were in Florence in 1860. They inspected paintings of Savonarola's execution and a manuscript written in his own hand. George Eliot soon reported that 'Florence, for its relation to the history of modern art, has stimulated me to entertain rather an ambitious project'.[2] Having made the link between the development of aesthetic humanism and Savonarola's challenge to autocracy, she began work on *Romola*. She and Lewes returned to Florence in 1861 to study old books and buildings. They attended a ceremony in Santa Croce in support of a free, united Italy, a political ideal of special importance to George Eliot. Back in England, she planned the whole novel anxiously. She linked the Tito material (the adopted son's ingratitude towards his benefactor) to the political and cultural context by focusing on the outrage which can be provoked when power and expediency accompany physical charm and elegant manners.[3] Vindicating to R. H. Hutton integrated interrelatedness in the novel, she wrote that there was 'scarcely a phrase, an incident, an allusion, that did not gather its value to me from its supposed subservience to my main artistic objects . . . It is the habit of my imagination to strive after as full a vision of the medium in which a character moves as of the character itself'.[4] Such comments should not mislead us, however, into seeing *Romola* as all historical realism.

It is difficult not to take the main character as symbolic. Romola is a classical scholar's daughter; she marries an untrustworthy but

handsome Greek and turns to a Christian leader for guidance.
Her name suggests a women of destiny (Romulus was a founder
of Rome). Though childless, she is an exemplary figure, whose
suffering leads to self-reliance and an unusual understanding of
the tendencies of things around her. This role of her heroine was
essential to George Eliot's conception of Romola; she told Sara
Hennell that the scenes in which Romola drifts away and then sets
to work among disease-ridden Jewish refugees were adopted by her
at the earliest stage 'by deliberate forecast . . . as romantic and sym-
bolical elements'.[5] The historical novel, then, for George Eliot, is
not merely reconstructive, but allows for exceptional actions which
are significant for the future. The bravery involved, though more to
do with rescue, healing and protest than battles and pursuits, may
even recall the old epics.

Such scenes are included in *Romola*, not just as picturesque
illustrations, but as pragmatic indicators. Both characters and
readers are assumed to be living in a period of crisis in which
old models of authority are being modified or replaced by new
ones which themselves are only temporary and imperfect. No doubt
such crises are really continuous throughout history, but they seem
especially perceptible when a meteoric individual like Savonarola
both speeds up change and destroys himself in the process. In
Romola dramatic relevance is provided by the heroine's respectful
questioning of Savonarola's principles and motives. There are two
dimensions to Savonarola in the novel; he is both a historical product of ascetic monasticism (including the unreliable habit of seeing
visions) and an object of psychological and moral scepticism. This
duality of explanation and criticism gives the text its materialistic
confidence.

Florence, it is made clear, is in an advantageous position for progressive experiments like Savonarola's because of its commercial
prosperity. The business activity of 'this mercantile city' (Ch. 30)
normally thrives, though it is at risk from international tensions. It
is one of those places seen by the angel of the dawn in the Poem,
whose domes and spires rise 'by the river-sides'. The centre of the
city is the old market, regulated by the Signoria to ensure fair
trading, the site of an ancient provision-market where probably
'the Fesulean ancestors of the Florentines descended from their
high fastness to traffic with the rustic population of the valley'; it
was celebrated by the fourteenth-century poet Pucci as 'a market
that, in his esteem, eclipsed the markets of all the earth beside'

(Ch. 1); and George Eliot enjoys describing its operations with vivid humour. In the fifteenth century Florence's wealth was based on the clothing trade; it was the 'city that half-clothed the well-dressed world' (Ch. 8), so that the references to contemporary dress in *Romola* have a significance that overrides the trappings of costume-drama. It was the textile industry which gave the *florin* its influence in the European treasuries. Florence is in no sense provincial; 'one may never lose sight of the Cupola and yet know the world, I hope' (Ch. 1), is a comment that comes early in the text. Florins could hire armies, which had given Florence its disputed hold on Pisa with its outlet to the sea. Through Pisa comes 'the wool from England' without which trade would languish (Ch. 63). The narrator's general approval of Florence's enterprises appears in a detail like the fact that among the companies of disciplined tradespeople in the city's processions the Frati Umiliati have the 'glorious tradition of being the earliest workers in the wool-trade' (Ch. 43). Usually the approval is guarded, however, because of people's liability to mistakes and misunderstanding.

The Bardi family, for example, from whom Romola springs, had been at one time like Christian Rothschilds, receiving revenues in wool from Edward III of England in return for furnishing 'specie' for his wars, which duly brought them bankruptcy. The Bardo of the story, Romola's blind father, lives over a jewelry warehouse, believing that he has forsaken 'the vulgar pursuit of wealth in commerce' (Ch. 5) in order to collect classical texts and ancient art and leave his library to the public. Nevertheless he is forced to endure a system of patronage without copyright which he admits is no better than licensed robbery. Romola admires her father's hostility to all injustice and meanness, but suffers under his prejudice against female scholarship. Bardo has also run into debt through educating his son Dino, who disappoints him by turning to the monastic life. Bardo's idealistic but imprudent character is contrasted with the vindictive and calculating character of another scholar Baldassarre, who is also let down by a son, the adopted Tito Melema. Tito uses the wealth entrusted to him by Baldassarre to further his own career instead of ransoming his father from slavery. Their deadly game of hide-and-seek ends with them both dead on the river bank, to be discovered by a stone-carter, peacefully pursuing his trade, who carries their bodies in his wagon to the grand Piazza, 'that notice might be given to the Eight' (Ch. 67). The rudimentary tradesman properly and openly disposes of the remains of two superior but secretive men locked in enmity. The irony is not lost on the reader.

The business of life in the Florence of *Romola* involves exchange of information, from the top to the bottom of society and from near to far. The importance of communication is recurrently stressed through the character of the pedlar Bratti,[6] who remarks that 'a Florentine doesn't mind bidding a fair price for news' (Ch. 1). It is Bratti who gets a purchaser for Tito's ring, sold anxiously because it brings recognition. Though the pedlar will sell virtually anything for a small profit, including red crosses to please Savonarola's supporters ('better buy a blessing', Ch. 51), he is not corrupt. His heart is 'too tender for a trader's' (Ch. 70), and for a small consideration he gives Romola vital directions for finding Tessa and the children after Tito's death. Another centre of news is the shop of Nello the barber, where men of different parties and talents exchange views. Nello himself does much of the talking, which consists of retailing 'yesterday's crop of gossip' (Ch. 16). Proud of his part in enhancing Tito's fine appearance, Nello puts him in touch with people who can help him in his secretarial career. It is above the barber's shop that Tito takes lodgings, from where he can spot friends and foes. From here he can observe the public displays and festivities, symbols in which, according to the younger Cennini, 'the great bond' of the republic expresses itself, enabling the people to rise above their petty wants 'to the sense of community in religion and law. There has been no great people without processions' (Ch. 8). These orderly civic spectacles, including the money-changers and dealers in foreign cloth, preceded by the representatives of England, Germany, Milan and Venice, link the network of commerce and communications to the authority of the state with its power to enforce obligations. The 'bond' can of course, be threatened by ambitious groups aided by unscrupulous individuals like Tito, who is willing even to support treachery if the rewards are high enough to guarantee him the easy life. But he too is watched and noted, and in the end destroyed.

The European context which the repeated references to trade and travel suggest in *Romola* bears directly upon the political issues. With the Pope's authority damaged, the Italian states have to shuffle their alliances to take into account the influence of France and Germany. The Florentine characters in the novel find themselves sharply affected by international disputes and suffer unpredictable hardships without being able to alter events as they would wish.

When in 1493 Milan invites France to break the alliance between Medicean Florence, Naples and the Pope, Savonarola and the church reformers welcome the French army of occupation into Florence, hoping for the reconquest of Pisa. It was a time when 'the spirit of the Republic had recovered some of its old fire' (Ch. 21). The image of fire indicates the danger as well as the energy of political upheaval. The rival parties within Florence tend to have narrow aims, some violently vindictive and predatory, others undoctrinally simplistic. None is prepared to move to responsible representative government, though Savonarola's idea of reviving the Grand Council of 3000 seems the most promising. His followers, however, include fanatics who threaten non-conformists and pursue their high-principled opponents even to execution. When Savonarola's youthful supporters collect people's adornments to be burned on the Bonfire of Vanities, Romola accepts that he disapproves of such excesses; 'he would have such things given up freely' (Ch. 50). But when he refuses to intervene to save her uncle from execution, she fears that mercy and justice are being sacrificed to party expediency; 'what he called perplexity seemed to her sophistry and doubleness' (Ch. 59). George Eliot is very successful in using Romola, brought up on classical history, to confront Savonarola in tense, dramatic scenes which clarify the conflicts of the day. What had appealed to Romola in his speeches was the denunciation of tyranny, the demand for the expression of the public will, the 'special care for liberty and purity of government' (Ch. 44), and not only in Florence.[7] Savonarola proposed to stir up the European powers to summon a general Council to reform the Church and 'depose' the Pope, who had abused his office. Savonarola's ambition extends to new forms of international co-operation and intervention to improve the 'moral welfare of men' (Ch. 71). Romola's mixed feelings of disappointment and veneration, in his case, are fully justified and vividly rendered.

Alongside the inexperienced Romola, George Eliot boldly brings into *Romola,* as a political commentator the young Machiavelli, who historically was later to analyse Renaissance *Realpolitik* in *The Prince*. Machiavelli represents more cautious but very perceptive views; he sees that, despite the pull of his oratory, Savonarola cannot in the short term outdo the power of a Pope who opposes the spread of popular government, yet time is on the side of the supporters of church reform for all that; Machiavelli thinks that but for his 'half-way severities' (Ch. 60) and unwise pledges and predictions Savonarola 'might have done something great' (Ch. 65). Machiavelli's qualified tribute to Savonarola sets in relief the unscrupulous cynicism of Tito Melema, with whom he often discusses political affairs. Tito sees the political world as a chaos of inconsistencies to be exploited for his own material gain. Yet at his point of deepest moral degradation, when he betrays Savonarola by having his letter for the French King conveyed into his enemies' hands, Tito is made to compliment the reformer hypocritically in a way that almost carries conviction: 'religious enthusiasm, as I conceive, is not necessary in order to appreciate the grandeur and justice of your views concerning the government of nations and the Church' (Ch. 64). The imaginative authenticity of this scene, in which the spy is forced, in spite of his character, to be sincere, is enhanced by the narrator's reference to Savonarola's 'own minute and exquisite handwriting, still to be seen covering the margins of his Bible', which touchingly reminds us of the value of the novelist's own scholarship. Romola herself is proof against her husband's insistence that there is no place for heroism in the politics of Florence. Though Tito alarms her affection and arrests her intellect 'by hanging before it the idea of a hopeless complexity in affairs which defied any moral judgment' (Ch. 44), the narrator later counters that the 'mixed condition' of political life is not a sign of 'hopeless confusion, but of struggling order' (Ch. 57), a belief which Romola learns to hold for herself.[8] The historical novelist's technique of bringing historical figures into contact with fictional ones, supported by authorial commentary, itself dispels any pessimistic feeling that history is meaningless.

Tito does not, of course, *begin* as a Judas-figure; in the opening chapters of *Romola*, when he is newly arrived in Florence, a Greek but educated in Italy, he seems a promising type. The tracing of the stages of deterioration in his character is at once fascinating and perturbing. Keener to avoid pain than to seek sensual delight, and even averse to causing pain to others, Tito simply chooses 'to make life easy for himself' (Ch. 23), but cannot escape being affected by habit, fear and forgetfulness; an unmoody, good-humoured nature always decides that it owes something to itself. He feels it natural to put his own claims above those of his benefactor, Baldassarre, but miscalculates the strength of the consequent resentment. Tito is genuinely surprised by moral feeling. His relationship with Tessa, which develops alongside his courtship of Romola, inevitably involving him in deception and hypocrisy, is almost like innocent drifting, since it takes a protective form. Tessa is a country girl, submissive and unsuspicious, basically lazy ('I don't like much work', Ch. 33), but without jealousy, well suited to sexual acceptance and child-bearing. Tito rescues her from a teasing conjuror with a firm moral argument – what right has the conjuror to hold her against her will? And then Tito may be said to give her what the conjuror obscenely calls the 'better confetti at hand' (Ch. 10) than the lapful *he* can promise. The conjuror with his 'imperfect acolyth', the monkey, fidgeting with a small taper, which falls 'more or less aslant' (Ch. 14), belongs to a world of lust and high spirits from which Romola is excluded, but to which the frightened Tessa is reconciled through the mock marriage ceremony. Elements of kindness and self-indulgence are hard to separate in Tito's soft-natured attitude to Tessa. He needs a little ease, 'a little repose from self-control', and from Romola's noble moral judgments (Ch. 34).[9] Tessa keeps open Tito's 'fountains of kindness', as George Eliot felicitously phrases it, and with her he achieves a fulfilment which no one else in the novel gets. His springing affection for Tessa and the children is termed 'pure, and breathing purity' (Ch. 50). When he thinks of leaving Florence, he never thinks of leaving them behind. Yet it is the same man who in his role as political dealer can speak contemptuously of wool-beaters' bad breath and a postman's soiled appearance (Ch. 43), as he prides himself on his fine air as a serviceable diplomat.

What underlines the treatment of Tito's changing character is George Eliot's insistence on his good looks. Totally avoiding extenuation in her account of his moral thinking, she is able to describe his perfect masculinity with virtually uninhibited gusto. He is surely the most vibrant male in English fiction before Lawrence. Ruling out crude narcissism, George Eliot gives most of the evidence of Tito's attractiveness to other characters. In a note Baldassarre describes Tito as *'aged twenty-three, with a dark, beautiful face, long dark curls, the brightest smile'* (Ch. 10). Piero de Cosimo the artist sees the face as one on which vice can write no marks, it being 'informed with rich young blood' (Ch. 4); the blind Bardo feels the long curls again and again, 'as if their spiral resistance made his inward vision clearer'; and the unflattering Bernardo mentions the 'lithe sleekness' of this 'pretty Greek' (Ch. 6). Romola's view of her lover provides the climax. Her first surprise at his appearance 'could hardly have been greater if the stranger had worn a panther-skin and carried a thyrsus', and she responds with a blush to his unassuming, gently beseeching and admiring glance, which the narrator says is 'perhaps the only atonement a man can make for being too handsome' (Ch. 6). Romola's own looks, with her reddish-gold hair and sincere hazel eyes, match his soft-coated animal quality in attractiveness; after their declaration of love his dark curls mingle with her rippling gold ones as rapidly 'as the irreversible mingling of water' (Ch. 12).[10] The high point occurs when Tito kisses 'the thick golden ripples on her neck' and she sees his sunlit image:

> the rich dark beauty which seemed to gather round it all images of joy – purple vines festooned between the elms, the strong corn perfecting itself under the vibrating heat, bright winged creatures hurrying and resting among the flowers, round limbs beating the earth in gladness with cymbals held aloft, light melodies chanted to the thrilling rhythm of strings – all objects and all sounds that tell of nature revelling in her force. (Ch. 17)

The combination of Greek, Renaissance and Wordsworthian allusions helps George Eliot to bring off a celebration of masculinity that quite lacks embarrassment or prudery. The relaxed sensuality of Tito, nurtured in his favourite Southern Italy, where thought, he says, is broken only by 'delicious languors' (Ch. 17), is figured in the triptych, his betrothal gift to Romola, where he is portrayed by Piero de Cosimo as Bacchus with his 'purple clusters' (Ch. 20). In the reception-room next to where it is unveiled is a model of a flute-playing Faun by Michelangelo, whose later paintings of young men may lie behind George Eliot's description of Tito.

The convincingness of this evocative technique makes Romola's later disillusionment all the more dramatic. The first shock comes when Romola's arm, laid on Tito's chest, feels his protective chain-armour; it is as if a fiend had changed his 'sensitive human skin into a hard shell' (Ch. 27). Subsequently the hardness in Tito's conduct towards her, when he disposes of her father's library, destroys her delight in his touch and earns her contempt as he leans there 'in his loathsome beauty' (Ch. 32). Their alienation reaches a point where there can be no recovery of her effusiveness. His face becomes altered by 'a hidden muscular tension'; he has as little inclination to genuine confession 'as a leopard has to lap milk when its teeth are grown' (Ch. 48). His selfish political stratagems not only repel Romola, but give the envious Ser Ceccone the opportunity to destroy him. Tito evades the mob only by plunging into the Arno, which rushes him into the avenging hands of Baldassarre. George Eliot expresses regret for the destruction of the physical man as she pursues the necessary punishment of the habitual betrayer. Her account of the still unforgettable figure in its 'strong prime' visible in the river, the square forehead with 'the long lustrous agate-like eyes' and 'the blue veins distended on the temple', anticipates the image of Tito's corpse, with the father's knuckles pressed 'against the round throat' (Ch. 67). George Eliot achieves a supremely horrifying relation of a murder, not by piling on the agony, but by preserving to the last the sense of a man's beauty, an effect comparable with those in Wilfred Owen's war poems. She could, though, hardly have done it except in a continental setting.

That the problems posed by an amoral character like Tito are not easily set aside is emphasised through the characterisation of his son Lillo, whose features are a coarser version of his father's. Lillo wants to achieve success in life by doing something that would not hinder him 'from having a good deal of pleasure'. Romola warns him against equivocation through the unidentified example of a man whose preference for pleasure and safety led him into baseness: 'he betrayed every trust that was reposed in him, that he might keep himself safe and get rich and prosperous' (Epilogue). This summary is unfair to Tito (he did not ultimately betray the trust placed in him by Tessa), and the unsteadiness of voice with which Romola makes it betrays a regret which her strictness does not cover. The fact that no one could replace Tito physically for her comes across clearly enough. Romola herself is left in a mentor-like role in a very restricted sphere, tending a humanistic altar to Savonarola, a statesman whom she admits many people disliked.

In some ways Romola is *too* perfect a heroine. She never ma¹es a culpable mistake and is always ready to reverse course vl en she recognises advice as valid. Certainly her striving for rationality and independence is admirable. Yet she remains an unfulfilled woman, with no second chance of personal happiness.[11] A ense of oppression overhangs Romola. She is largely untouched by the superstitions of the age, having been influenced by her father's contempt for her brother Dino, who had taken up religious practices 'befitting men who know of no past older than the missal and the crucifix'. Dino's warning vision about her future husband she rejects[12] as derived from 'the shadowy regions where human souls seek wisdom, apart from the human sympathies which are the very life and substance of our wisdom' (Ch. 15). Here Romola's humanism leads her into a trap of incaution as does the futile classicism of her blind father. It is only in the 'supreme fellowship with suffering' which Savonarola evokes that she can find a key to life, though no radiant angel comes 'across the gloom with a clear message for her' (Ch. 36). In the beleaguered Florence of 1496 Romola finds work in 'tending the sick and relieving the hungry' (Ch. 42), seeming a visible Madonna, sustained by the praise and thanks of the suffering people, but with 'no innate taste' for the work of charity, no deluded aspirations to sainthood (Ch. 44). She is drawn to severity, committing a mental injustice 'against merriment', as she carries in her heart the thought of her childlessness, 'woman's heaviest disappointment' (Ch. 49), and she is liable to fall again into apathy, as when she drifts away to sea, thinking of human fellowship as 'mere unfairness and exclusiveness' (Ch. 61). The politics of the city-state, which she has experienced at first hand in her dealings with her husband, her uncle and her mentor, Savonarola, are dominated by jostling for power among self-interested groups,[13] from which she turns away. Romola believes in individual rights under the law, and Savonarola's scheme for a Christian system, for all its good points, is too narrow for her. It is notable that Romola regains her moral poise when she begins to work among a non-Christian group, Jewish refugees from Spain or Portugal, 'compelled to abandon their homes by the Inquisition' (Ch. 68). It was one such of 'those dogs of hell' (Ch. 1) for whom Tito was half-mistaken by Bratti at the beginning of the novel. Working among the plague-stricken victims of prejudice, Romola views 'all objects from a new position' (Ch. 69), sharing her life with those around her at the level of individual organisation of a relief effort. Her support of the widowed Tessa and the children represents a similar, longer-term commitment. She remains the type of detached, advanced woman, who *adapts* a relationship to her own time, based on her own judgment, looking forward to others like herself born before their time, throughout subsequent history.

If *Romola* focuses on an episode in Europe's past, *Daniel Deronda* (1876) can be regarded as a remarkably prescient guess at the future. Written after the Franco-Prussian War about the period just preceding it, it shows a much altered but still dangerous Europe. Many of the problems of communication encountered in *Romola* may have been overcome by science; telegrams flash from country to country and trains and ships steam about, but the political world remains very unsettled. England's insularity gives no sense of security. The last rumblings of the movement towards Italian unity are heard in the background of the story as when Deronda visits Genoa, where 'the very air seemed to carry the consciousness that war had been declared against Austria'. The main issue in the novel, the possibility of founding a national home for Europe's Jews, has ancient roots; in fact there is an echo from *Romola* in the Genoa scene, when Deronda, rowing about in the harbour, has historic memories of Spanish Jews driven to Italy, overspreading the quay 'with a pall of famine and plague . . . like groups from a hundred Hunger-towers turned out beneath the mid-day sun' (Ch. 50). George Eliot's image is strong enough to foreshadow the Holocaust.

The incipient Zionist cause could attract in the 1860s a critical consciousness like Deronda's. He specifically defends the Jewish nationalist Mordecai by comparing him with the Italian nationalist Mazzini. But *Daniel Deronda* foresees no easy passage to the establishment of a free Israel. Not only is Deronda made aware of the tradition of hatred for the Jews in Germany ('Our youth fell on evil days', Kalonymos tells him, recalling the wholesale slaughter of Jews in Mainz, Ch. 60), but also he himself points to the probable resurgence of Arab nationalism: 'We may live to see a great outburst of force in the Arabs, who are being inspired with a new zeal'. Mordecai welcomes the prospect without seeing it as in conflict with his plans to establish a Jewish land and polity in Palestine. He admits there will be difficulties, but sees Israel as a neutral state like Belgium, set up on land purchased from the Turks, whom he calls 'debauched and pampered conquerors' (Ch. 42).

Mordecai sees Israel as belonging, along with Britain and America, to a court of nations, to which outraged individuals or groups may appeal for defence. These far-seeing ideals undoubtedly look forward to the United Nations. Mordecai, never having carried out his intention to travel to the Levant, lacks the first-hand experience of the region which would have enabled him to 'speak with a fuller vision' (Ch. 43). But the novel makes several references to Arab culture; for example, some of the documents in Deronda's grandfather's chest, are, he thinks, 'in Arabic' (Ch. 63); so that when Deronda and Mirah finally leave with the 'idea of restoring a political existence' to the Jews, his initial intention in the East,

which is 'to become better acquainted with the condition of my
race in the various countries there' (Ch. 69), implicitly takes
in the Arab provinces, where we know he expects a national
revival. Deronda's future progress, then, is into a painful world
of conflicting claims.[14]

The Jews in the novel vary widely in background and character,
perhaps the worst being Lapidoth, who is presented almost as a
piece of human flotsam: he takes his son's preaching 'as a man
finding shelter from hail in an open cathedral might take a little
religious howling that happened to be going on there. Lapidoth
was not born with this sort of callousness: he had achieved it'
(Ch. 66). George Eliot's own sharp style contrasts with the awkward
volubility of Mordecai, which, though it fails to impress Lapidoth,
his father, imposes on Deronda 'a certain awe' (Ch. 34). The
intensity of Mordecai's fixation upon Deronda as his disciple, partly
explained by his tubercular condition and his long immersion in
prophetic literature, can be positively embarrassing; 'I am only
another prayer – which you will fulfil' (Ch. 46). Mrs Meyrick has
a point when she doubts whether Mordecai's Jewish pertinacity is
not that of 'a man whose conversation would not be more modern
and encouraging than that of Scott's Covenanters' (Ch. 46). But
she accepts Deronda's view that Mordecai is an enthusiast rather
than a fanatic. Given Deronda's suspicion of his own illegitimacy,
his hesitant but cordial response to what he sees as Mordecai's
'impressive distinction' is understandable (Ch. 47). He takes up
only 'some of Mordecai's ideas' (Ch. 67); no doubt the idea that
'women are specially framed for the love which feels possession
in renouncing', an idea which is spiritedly challenged by Mirah
(Ch. 61), is one of those that Deronda does not take up. But
Mordecai's larger views, which associate the founding of Israel with
the earlier founding of America and with 'the better future of the
world' (Ch. 42), genuinely inspire Deronda with the vision of a
liberal international order. Hence the 'precious seeing', produced
by 'a loving reverential emotion' (Ch. 47), which Deronda fears
others, even Mirah, may not share. George Eliot herself feared
that readers would dislike this part of *Daniel Deronda*. Mentioning
the disgraceful English arrogance 'towards all Oriental people'
as an example of the stupidity which she hoped to combat, she
expected the novel to 'create much stronger resistance and even
repulsion' than it actually did.[15] The width of culture evident
in the whole novel provides many points of reference against

which Mordecai's optimistic form of Zionism can be assessed. Both he and Deronda have travelled widely in Europe: Deronda had done a Rhineland tour before going to Cambridge and got a good 'grip of French and German' (Ch. 16), while Mordecai had studied in Germany, visited Holland and Bohemia and written in Hebrew. Mordecai's reason for declining to publish his writings is significant. He distrusts his own command of English eloquence, 'as one who beats a board' having 'an ear to hear the faults' of his own speech (Ch. 40). Many readers would be willing to take Mordecai at his word here, were it not that George Eliot makes him go on so.[16] It may be a failure in narrative tact, but it is more probable that the linguistic ineffectuality inbuilt into Mordecai's character is meant as a sign of the Jewish dispersal among diverse European cultures and of the Jews' lack of a modern means of communication such as was available to German or Italian nationalists. Mordecai rejects 'the rote-learned language of a system, that gives you the spelling of things, sure of its alphabet covering them all'; he speaks in a metaphoric, archaic style, which, though consistently based on traditional imagery, is inevitably vague:

> Man finds his pathways: at first they were foot-tracks, as those of the beast in the wilderness; now they are swift and invisible: his thought dives through the ocean, and his wishes thread the air: has he found all the pathways yet? What reaches him, stays with him, rules him: he must accept it, not knowing its pathway. (Ch. 40)

The paradox of a style which fails to communicate, except on a very private plane, yet deals with matters of modern communications and political evolution so pressingly, highlights Mordecai's dilemma. His message is grounded on the earth (literal and symbolic pathways criss-cross *Daniel Deronda*), but the medium is too airy. Essentially, Mordecai needs Deronda to reassure him that he is in touch with reality; the presence of a young fellow who will continue the struggle and is sufficiently educated, travelled and determined to begin organising things, makes the difference.

If the pathways on which Mordecai sets Deronda are to lead to the purchase and settlement of land by Jews in Palestine,[17] then that sheds an ironic light on the story Gwendolen and her friends, set among landowners and politicians in England. Deronda informs Gwendolen that his aim is to devote his life to giving the Jews 'a

national centre, such as the English have' (Ch. 69). That the advantages of such historical achievements always come in a very mixed
form is just what can be deduced from the novel's English side.
Deronda gives up his life in England; Gwendolen, from a rootless
beginning, survives agonising vicissitudes to make the best of an
English home. *Daniel Deronda*, with its alien title, perhaps surprises
its readers with its fond evocations of the landscape of southern
England, the area which Orwell in later troubled times was to
call 'probably the sleekest landscape in the world'.[18] The country
homes in which the action is set are given names, Offendene,
Brackenshaw, Ryelands, Cardell, Firs, Diplow and so on, redolent
of the land, its surface and vegetation. Though the legal and moral
entitlement of landowning is a vexed question, the love of the land
with its historical associations is an important value. Sir Hugo
Mallinger of Topping Abbey, Deronda's guardian, can trace his
ancestry back to a Norman 'who came in with the Conqueror', but is
constrained by the conditions of an entail through which the estate
at Diplow can be inherited by Grandcourt. Deronda, however,
appreciates the privileges of his social position not proprietorially,
but culturally and aesthetically. His favourite retreat at the Abbey
had been a window-seat with a view of 'a great reach of the park,
where the old oaks stood apart from each other, and the border-
ing wood was pierced with a green glade which met the eastern
sky' (Ch. 16). Again, 'the capitals of the cloister taught him to
observe, and delight in, the structure of leaves' (Ch. 35). Deronda
recalls his privileged environment and education affectionately (its
effects can 'never die out', Ch. 53), but the discovery of his racial
difference[19] transfers his commitment to the promised land under
the eastern sky, on which, as it happened, he had had his eyes
as a youth. Gwendolen lacks his rooted upbringing; her tender
years had been spent 'roving from one foreign watering-place or
Parisian apartment to another' (Ch. 3). She despised the dullness
of the 'ill-plenished lives' of poor English people abroad (Ch. 21).
The narrator regrets the fact that Offendene with its glimpse of
'grand steadfast forms played over by the changing days' had not
been Gwendolen's childhood home. The passage is justly famous:

> A human life, I think, should be well rooted in some spot of a
> native land, where it may get the love of tender kinship for the
> face of earth, for the labours men go forth to, for the sounds
> and accents that haunt it, for whatever will give that early home

a familiar unmistakable difference amidst the future widening of knowledge. (Ch. 3)

The influence of Wordsworth on such passages is clear, but there is also a hint of the conservative Coleridge: the country around has dairy farms looking 'much as they did in the days of our forefathers – where peace and permanence seemed to find a home away from the busy change that sent the railway train flying in the distance' (Ch. 13). The wilful Gwendolen belongs to the world of speed and change. The restlessness of her unsatisfied personality is brilliantly caught in the opening gambling scene. In between her impetuous blind dashes there is a kind of inertia or boredom. But the Romantic pull of country life, mediated through Deronda's calming advice, eventually returns her to Offendene, which she is able to rent with the proceeds of the property left to her by Grandcourt. She now thinks of this place with its 'shadowy plantations with rutted lanes where the barked timber lay for a wayside seat', as 'a restful escape, a station where she found the breath of morning and the unreproaching voice of birds' (Ch. 64). The vocabulary, suggesting settlement and agriculture, links Gwendolen's retreat with Deronda's scheme.

Gwendolen's final proximity to her cousin Rex suggests to one friendly character, Hans Meyrick, that those two might start up their old romance again. He thinks that Rex's resolve to remain a bachelor is a 'green' one (Ch. 69). Though the novel is determinedly open-ended on this point Rex is a significant English figure in *Daniel Deronda*, representing an honest, undandified, professional type whose background is closely influenced by the land. A product of the same educational background as Deronda's, Rex comes across as a decent, fresh-hearted youth. Had Gwendolen been less nervous, superficial and socially ambitious, he might have suited her as a partner. The narrator is tempted to a 'futile sort of wishing – if only things could have been a little otherwise then', but regards goodness as a harvest from a crop germinating underground, where each stage has its peculiar blight, such as being choked by an 'action of foul land' or 'damage brought by foulness afar'. At the same time the morning scene, 'the grassy borders of the lanes, the hedgerows sprinkled with red berries and haunted with low twitterings, the purple bareness of the elms, the rich brown of the furrows' (Ch. 7), suggests the joyful potential of Rex's and Gwendolen's young lives. Gwendolen's rebuff proves only a temporary psychological setback to Rex. Roused by the sight of a timber waggon, he determines on a pioneer's life in Canada, but is persuaded by his father to resume his law studies. Mr Gascoigne's pride in his son's integrity and sense of vocation (he regards him as 'superior to himself') is admirable in itself: when the novel returns to the pleasant Pennicote Rectory, where human experience appertains mainly 'to that quiet recurrence of the familiar, which has no other epoch than those of hunger and the heavens', the rural values of growth, permanence and quietness reassert themselves. Rex pleases his father by justifying the activities of the legal profession as involving the scrutiny of evidence and cases in 'an orderly way'; he even aspires to having 'something to do with making the laws' (Ch. 58). The sane, reforming spirit embodied in Rex shows a promising strain in English country society.

His father is, of course, the object of much satire. Mr Gascoigne's unquestioning respect for established social conventions ('he had taken orders and a diphthong but shortly before his engagement to Miss Armyn', Ch. 3) and his imperceptive prudentiality bring him some deserved shocks.[20] The limitations of the Wessex 'society' in which he plays his role are sharply ridiculed in the scenes where Gwendolen feels so impatient in her yearning for some vague distinction. At this early stage in the story all the characters are, as the narrator confirms ironically, 'on visiting terms with persons of rank' (Ch. 9). There are several barbed references to the exclusivity of this select circle, where worldly advantages are 'taken with that high-bred depreciation which follows from being accustomed to them' (Ch. 14). These characters' dim consciousness of current affairs ('the results of the American war' do not excite them, Ch. 9) makes their concern with gossip, money, marriage and inheritance seem particularly petty: they are 'busy with a small social drama almost as little penetrated by a feeling of wider relations as if it had been a puppet-show' (Ch. 14). It is, of course, the business of the novel to fill in the wider relations.

When someone like Miss Arrowpoint does challenge the complacency of this gentry-set by insisting on marrying the German-Jewish pianist Klesmer, the resulting clashes bring the whole complex theme of the novel into clearer focus. Klesmer defends his artistic achievement as being on a higher plane than mere inherited privilege and points to the philistinism of those who would refer to him as a mere musician. He criticises English politicians for their lack of idealism, for allowing 'the need of a market' to determine 'all mutuality between distant races', and even excuses the Crusades for having had a 'banner of sentiment round which generous feelings could rally'. English insensitivity is personified in Bult, the rival suitor for Miss Arrowpoint's hand, described as having 'the general solidity and suffusive pinkness of a healthy Briton on the central table-land of life'. The allusions to lands and wars reverberate in the reader's mind. Bult suspects Klesmer of being a Pan-Slavist, 'a Pole, or a Czech, or something of that fermenting sort'. The text skims closely over that ground which was already breeding the causes of the First World War which occurred half a century in the future. Klesmer calls Bult a 'political platitudinarian', though it must be said that his own Shelleyan claim for artists as helping 'to rule the nations . . . on level benches with legislators' is impracticably vague. Miss Arrowpoint's choice of Klesmer is given a heroic touch by her defiant attack on her parents' belief in social immobility. She rejects her father's argument that as 'head of estates' her husband ought to be a gentleman. Urged to 'think of the nation and the public good', Miss Arrowpoint points out that their property had originally been 'gained in trade' and might, if sold, 'pass into the hands of some foreign merchant'. Klesmer denies that he values the property as such, but it is doubtful if he is as independent of moneyed patrons as he thinks (Ch. 22). He is, in fact, soon accepted at Quetcham Park as son-in-law and prospective steward of the estates. Lady Pentreath calls it 'a troubadour story'; she regards the Arrowpoints' snobbery as ridiculous since she good-humouredly accepts the English tradition of recruiting upwards into the aristocracy (Ch. 35), a position which, in practice, is not far from Miss Arrowpoint's view that it is a public evil to confine property to a certain class.

The narrator's position on politics seems close to Deronda's. He is 'fervently democratic in his feeling for the multitude, and yet, through his affections and imagination, intensely conservative' (Ch. 32). But Deronda's contempt for party politicians is properly criticised by Sir Hugo Mallinger as impracticable. Sir Hugo can tolerate and admire a dissenting view, but he thinks there can be too idealistic a view of politics; government could never be carried on 'if everybody looked at politics as if they were a prophecy' (Ch. 33). Deronda, on his way to meet Mordecai, finds this conversation jarring. But there is a sense in which the wheel will come full circle. In due course Israeli politics can be expected to look not unlike English politics, with interests representing the land, commerce and bureaucracy in competition and religious ideas influential. Such developments can be inferred from the text of this novel. Meanwhile Deronda can fix his 'practically energetic sentiment' (Ch. 32) on the feasibility of a Jewish settlement of Palestine, while Sir Hugo achieves satisfaction in securing the Diplow estates after all. The narrator, conscious of the privilege thus confirmed, accepts that 'we must have some comradeship with imperfection': it would be churlish not to rejoice in someone else's joy 'unless it were in agreement with our theory of righteous distribution and our highest ideal of human good', an ideal, incidentally, to which 'our own possessions and desires would not exactly adjust themselves' (Ch. 59). Here the irony is at the expense of egalitarianism. Are property rights to be challenged?[21] Nevertheless there is a frightening element in *Daniel Deronda*, the portrayal of Grandcourt, a person who relishes power based on land-owning in a personal way, while being indifferent to public duty. Quite lacking in 'self-consciousness or anxiety', Grandcourt's bearing inclines to the flaccid. The combination of boredom with a fitful taste for brutal pleasures (he had had a season or two 'tiger-hunting or pig-sticking' in the East) makes him a sinister figure: he has both 'cold and distinguished manners' (Ch. 11). With his assistant Lush, a former don, still with 'an odour of departed learning' about him, Grandcourt illustrates the corruption to which members of a leisured class are prone. He felt, for example, 'that he might kick Lush if he chose – only he never did choose to kick any animal, because the act of kicking is a compromising attitude, and a gentleman's dogs should be kicked for him' (Ch. 12). George Eliot's prose is at its most flexible as she captures Grandcourt's way of talking ('I don't care a toss where you are, so that you keep out of sight', Ch. 28) and analyses his way of thinking, full of convenient omissions and intimidating implications. Gwendolen rouses him by her very trickiness: 'He meant to be master of a woman who would have liked to master him, and who perhaps would have been capable of mastering another man' (Ch. 28). The piquancy of his despotism is especially felt as he controls his wife in her tedium and moral repulsion on their aimless Mediterranean cruise on his private yacht, a voyage which parodies Deronda's trip to Geneva to discover his origins. Grandcourt's crew suits such an elegant toy as this 'tiny plank-island of a yacht', 'one of them having even ringlets, as well as a bronze complexion and fine teeth' (Ch. 54), perhaps a shadow of Deronda himself. Grandcourt prides himself on a life-style, appropriate, as he thinks, to his status. His riches, mostly borrowed on the strength of his expectations, serve his indolence. Much bitter amusement arises from Mr Gascoigne's hopes for Grandcourt's political future; he tries to get Gwendolen to persuade him to enter Parliament, but the narrator sees Grandcourt's importance as 'of the grandly passive kind which consists in the inheritance of land. Political and social movements touched him only through the wire of his rental' (Ch. 48). He acts throughout in a totally mean way. He is a villain by negation; he is never outgoing, never enters into conversation unless it suits him, never shows any interest in the arts and learning which fill up the intellectual background of *Daniel Deronda*, never displays a hint of compassion. His name, with its connotations of Renaissance nobility, is an appalling mockery.

The women in *Daniel Deronda* are often shown in conditions of material uncertainty or psychological insecurity, sometimes both. The figure of the humiliated or abandoned women, like Grandcourt's former mistress, Mrs Glasher, 'the Medusa-apparition' (Ch. 48), is a motif in the novel. Even the one totally independent woman in the story, Deronda's mother, the opera singer Alcharisi, finds herself baffled by age and disease. The Meyrick girls, who aim at a modest self-reliance through teaching and embroidery, are more hopeful, but cannot count on much of a future. Catherine Arrowpoint's role as Klesmer's wife seems anticlimactic, confined, at least externally, to effecting social introductions.

These examples of failures and limitations are there to impress on us that Gwendolen does what she does with her eyes open. Since she marries Grandcourt in spite of what she knows about him, she betrays herself. Her motive of helping her mother cannot alter that, so that when Grandcourt is drowned after she has held back from throwing him the rope, Gwendolen instinctively punishes him with death for having destroyed her integrity. The horror of her experience, with its nightmares, curses, weeping and temptations to violence, leading to her final guilt and near despair, does not, however, mean that Gwendolen is placed in a world where lessons cannot be learned. Gwendolen's narrowness of outlook contributes to the catastrophe. She is implicitly rebuked by the narrator for her indifference to current affairs, to the American Civil War and the issue of abolishing slavery, in aid of which British people willingly

accepted economic sacrifice; 'when women on the other side of the
world would not mourn for husbands and sons who died bravely
in a common cause, and men stinted of bread on our side of
the world heard of that willing loss and were patient' (Ch. 11).
From this perspective Gwendolen's 'small inferences' and 'blind
visions' of her own pleasures seem crass, but beside her 'inborn
energy of egoistic desire' Gwendolen has a contrary tendency to
remorse and fear of wrong-doing in the area of personal relations:
'her feeling would have made her place any deliberate injury of
another in the region of guilt' (Ch. 27). It is on this small 'treasure
of human affections' (Ch. 11) that her personality can eventually
be rebuilt. Even then she has to bear the loss of Deronda as a
potential partner because of the racial factor which leads him to
obligations elsewhere. When she hears of his purposes in the East
it is like an earthquake to her, as when the great movements of
the world enter people's lives 'when the slow urgency of growing
generations turns into the tread of an invading army or the dire
clash of civil war, and grey fathers know nothing to seek for but
the corpses of their blooming sons, and girls forget all vanity
to make lint and bandages which may serve for the shattered
limbs of their betrothed husbands' (Ch. 69). The imagery of
earthquake, invasion and armed conflict is no longer felt to be
out of scale with Gwendolen's predicament. She returns to her
English ground, shaken, but no longer in want of those ideas
and sympathies which 'make a larger home' for her passion than
the narrow round of personal desires (Ch. 36). Deronda, whose
name in Spanish means a 'watchful patrol', but may echo sonally
Wordsworth's reference to 'earth's diurnal round',[22] raises her
horizon to the world beyond the individual self and then leaves
her to become part of it. The whole linguistic texture, therefore,
and the thematic design of *Daniel Deronda* are concerned with the
earth, the way it is portioned between individuals and groups and
the developing conflicts to which that gives rise, so that the future,
unknown in 1876, to which it points has to be faced, then as now,
with anxious responsibility. As a novel it has a unique sense of
place, extending even to the possibility of a place elsewhere, to
adapt Larkin, that underwrites existence.[23]

6

Political Change and the Home View: *Felix Holt, Middlemarch*

George Eliot's own political stance was guarded rather than committed. Her writings provide much both of comfort and of discomfort for those of opposing political views. She is quick to point out the inconsistencies of the politically active while coming down equally hard on the politically apathetic. Acutely conscious of the moral complexity of contentious issues, she has an evolutionist's patience when it comes to reform. She finds humour in the inadequacies of political debate, and tends to judge political failure as deserved. Always tolerant, however, and searching for the positive she offends very few in this area, disappoints some and genuinely amuses most of her readers.

During the second half of the 1860s, when the extension of the franchise was again the burning issue, George Eliot was drawn for material for fiction to the period prior to the 1832 Reform Act, which had been the first step in modern British democratic advances. She had personal memories of election riots at Nuneaton when she was at school there. She studied newspapers of those years and read histories and memoirs.[1] A novel with English politics as much to the fore as Italian politics had been in *Romola* was the result.

Certainly *Felix Holt the Radical* (1866), to give it its full title, confronts the political aspirations of people in the early nineteenth century in a way that *Silas Marner, the Weaver of Raveloe,* virtually avoids. Nearly all the characters in *Felix Holt* are politically opinionated; they even include candidates for Parliament and their agents. The hero's radicalism is peculiar to himself, however, and pleases no one but the heroine, Esther Lyon. The main plot, which climaxes in Esther's rejection of the life of the great house to which, as it turns out, she is entitled by birth, in favour of a lover closer to the ethos of the father who has brought her up, is almost identical with that of Part 2 of *Silas Marner*. The difference is that now the setting is urban, the moral ambience nonconformist and the life-style lower middle class. In *Felix Holt* the aristocratic life centred on Transome Court is especially bleak and guilt-ridden. The tragic figure of Mrs Transome, 'an Eve gone gray' (Ch. 49), despised and used by those she had loved,[2] is daunting enough, but the surrounding figures, her imbecile husband, her former lover (the corrupt lawyer Jermyn), their complacent son, well-meaning but sadly imperceptive (he is quite unaware of his illegitimacy), his own unpleasant child, whose mother had been a Greek slave, and the born servant Denner, hard-headed and 'godless' (Ch. 1), comprise an unprepossessing set if ever there was one, likely to turn anybody off the refined life; and Esther duly renounces it. She fears its mediocre delights where poetry, instead of being a rhetoric of moral effort, is 'only literature' (Ch. 44). Esther prefers the high, clear air of Felix Holt's companionship. She renders him homage as one whose great resolutions come 'from his kind feelings towards others' (Ch. 46).

George Eliot tries very hard with her hero Felix Holt, a radical sceptical of constitutional reform. His moment comes when he takes the lead of a rioting election mob with the risky purpose of deflecting it from worse violence than it actually commits. The problem with Felix is that, though he appears romantically liberated and energetic, with his open neck and shaggy hair, his actions, apart from the one already mentioned, are on a very small scale, confined to watch-making and private tutoring, while his attitudes as Esther's lover are timid beyond belief. Felix values Esther as the kind of partner whose beauty would make a great task 'easier' to a man (Ch. 27), but even from this patronising standpoint he holds back; her love was dear to him, he feels unpromisingly, 'as the beloved dead are dear' (Ch. 32). When after many vicissitudes they come together it is with angelic looks, with hands 'pressed together as children hold them up in prayer' and with trust that they are working together towards 'some great good' (Ch. 45), even though they can hope for no more actually than a minimal influence on things. Admittedly Esther's inner 'evolutionary struggle' (Ch. 49) is interestingly rendered: she slowly alters from being a socially ambitious 'prim Miss', a 'sort of spun glass, a fine lady affair' (Ch. 5), whom Felix wants to shame, to being the later 'rather wise' woman of twenty-two, 'struggling to relieve herself from the oppression of unintelligible feelings' (Ch. 40). The change is scrupulously traced shift by shift. But the note of elevated admiration for Felix seems strained. During his trial, ardour burns in Esther's bosom over his moral nobility ('She felt that he bore the outward stamp of a distinguished nature. Forgive her if she needed this satisfaction'). Her absorption in 'supreme feelings' is presented so uncritically as to cloy: 'In this, at least, her woman's lot was perfect: that the man she loved was her hero; that her woman's passion and her reverence for rarest goodness rushed together in an undivided current' (Ch. 40). Echoes of the more mixed emotions of Maggie Tulliver in *The Mill on the Floss* incline us to question these simple certainties, endorsed by a narrator whose tone can become fulsome.

Because of the adulation of the hero, *Felix Holt* depends crucially on the quality of his contributions to the debate on politics. Felix's campaign against the corruption of election agents and his active dislike of violence tell strongly in his favour. Nevertheless he has an air of specious virtue; he is a Radical without a party. His caution (he insists on linking political progress with scientific education and the prevalence of moral sobriety) seems to disqualify him from engaging in fiery oratory at all. In his High Street speech Felix dismisses the democracy which the Radicals of the day have on offer as providing 'the sort of power that ignorant numbers have', which 'comes in the end to the same thing as wicked power; it makes misery' (Ch. 30). He has no conception of politics as a process of experiment and correction which can in practice itself be learned if the issues are fully aired. The novel shows that the free political tradition is well-rooted in England and that fear of extending the franchise is exaggerated. Even the Tories' rather quaint discussion at the Marquis's dinner shows support for checks in the abuse of power. Joyce, the young farmer, points out that the result of reform may in practice be to replace one prerogative, the royal prerogative, with another: 'They want us to be governed by delegates from the trades-unions, who are to dictate to everybody, and make everything square to their mastery'. From another position, Baruch Nolan, a retired Jewish hosier, is prompted to defend the regulated free market: 'a country can't have too much trade, if it's properly managed . . . Trade makes property, my good

sir . . . . It's all one web, sir. The prosperity of the country is all one
web' (Ch. 20). Such political points, made by only partly informed
enthusiasts, are left by the narrator to be tested one against the
other. The novel grants a platform to yet another viewpoint in
the nomination day scene, where a fluent speaker, attacking the
monopoly of power by a land-owning minority, argues persuasively
about the need to give everyone a 'freeman's share' in what goes
on in life, that is 'to think and speak and ask about what concerns
us all', and attacks the Anglican church for purveying 'a religion
that gives us working men heaven and nothing else' (Ch. 30). It is
surprising that George Eliot does not place Felix's withdrawal from
such public controversy in a more ironic light.[3] But her plan was to
have him as the alternative to Esther's rich suitor. Felix therefore
prefers to live in a way which prevents 'any one from classing him
according to his education and mental refinement' (Ch. 22). He
is too scrupulous to commit himself to striving for an influential
position in a system where affairs are morally tangled: 'I do choose
to withdraw myself from the push and the scramble for money and
position' (Ch. 27). Felix's gesture might have more impact if he
were allowed to be a writer. He speaks like one, too much like one,
I think. As it is, the novel itself, by taking up the opportunity of
intervening, however tentatively and impersonally, in the political
debate which he renounces tends to contradict its own emotional
validation of its hero.

   Middlemarch (1871–2), though covering almost the same ground
historically and geographically as *Felix Holt*, leaves no such sense
of dissatisfaction. On the contrary, it has long had, and deservedly
so, the best press of any novel in English. An amalgam of two
planned pieces of fiction, one entitled 'Miss Brooke', the other
a study of professional life in a provincial town and its envi-
rons, *Middlemarch* spreads its interest widely. It avoids idealising
the heroine, who, like Esther Lyon, moves from an intellectually
restricted background to one that is more intellectually progressive. Dorothea Brooke's county milieu is spirited, vigorous and
humorous, however, not bitterly riven, so that she brings certain
advantages to her partnership with a London-based journalist and
politician, Will Ladislaw. The network of secondary plots centred
on the Vincy family in Middlemarch facilitates links across strata
of classes upwards, downwards and obliquely (one of the Vincy
connections turns out to be remotely related to Dorothea's lover).
Such is the density of the topical themes that George Eliot is able to

attach to this frame, including medical advances, electoral reform, agricultural improvements, the transport revolution, evangelical expansion, women's education, inheritance law and many minor matters, that the novel lives up to its subtitle, 'A Study of Provincial Life.' The significance of its central construct, 'Middlemarch', is extended beyond the describable appearance of a Midland town, vaguely based on Coventry in the 1830s, to encompass national social trends.[4] Middlemarch becomes the symbol of a huge, slowly irregular movement, a mass altering like a complex biological phenomenon under the influence of external forces.

Attempts to characterise the overall effect of reading *Middlemarch* often end in paradox; alongside the sense of admiration and amusement goes a definite sobriety. Many of the characters in the novel come to regard themselves as failures, or, if they succeed, as moral convalescents. Worry, disappointments, losses, cruel lessons, frustrations seem common experiences which ought to elicit, and frequently do elicit, mutual sympathy among them. Nearly all the sexual partnerships in this novel undergo painful readjustments. The narrator's voice is not, however, pessimistic; sceptical in places, undoubtedly, but implicitly unperturbed. There is progress of a sort in Middlemarch. It is much less than had been hoped (the New Hospital project founders), but seems to go on impersonally, unexpectedly, or is only deferred. Middlemarch seems located far away from the scenes of catastrophic flooding in *The Mill on the Floss*, nor is there prophesying of war as in *Daniel Deronda* (let alone air-raids such as ruined the real Coventry only seventy years after *Middlemarch* was being written). The town, though an industrial centre with rent-a-mob facilities, has an atmosphere closer to that of Mrs Gaskell's *Cranford* (1853) than to the raucous Milby and Treby of George Eliot's earlier north-Warwickshire stories. Middlemarch is no mirage, but it is distanced from definition, and the reason is that it is being envisaged not through a medium of vivid reminiscence or contemporary observation, but sociologically. It thus manages to be provincial without being regional. Middlemarch takes shape through a social medium of acquaintance and contact, cause and effect, circumstance and reaction, which connects and disperses individuals and groups of characters, depending on their assumptions of position, of belonging and of change.

That is not to say that actual dramatic scenes are not rendered adequately and visually in *Middlemarch*. But the upshot for the

reader is usually not only illuminating images and memorable
speeches, but also a shift along interconnecting currents. Old
Featherstone's funeral is a good example; the chill morning wind
that blows the May blossoms 'from the surrounding gardens on to
the green mounds of Lowick churchyard' is neatly described, as
are the swift clouds that 'only now and then allowed a gleam to
light up any object, whether ugly or beautiful, that happened to
stand within its golden shower'. But the account gives only glimpses
and is weighted towards symbolism, atmosphere and varying views;
the objects lit up soon turn out to be people to whom 'news' had
spread that it was to be a 'big burying'. Different types of discourse,
popular, comic, analytic, succeed one another rapidly; the narrator
challenges anyone who 'will here contend that there must have
been traits of goodness in old Featherstone', which leads to a wry
generalisation on the 'modest nature' of goodness. Dorothea and
the gentry only *observe* Featherstone's funeral from the Rectory of
Lowick, a name which suggests that the Anglican Establishment has
grown intellectually dim. Dorothea, looking down uneasily from
'a rarefied social air', finds 'something alien' in the scene, which
she associates in a 'dream-like' way with 'the deepest secrets of her
experience'. The narrator links past, present and future *for* her:

> Scenes which mark vital changes in our neighbours' lot are but
> the background of our own, yet, like a particular aspect of the
> fields and trees, they become associated for us with the epochs
> of our own history, and make a part of that unity which lies in
> the selection of our keenest consciousness. (Ch. 34)

The typical George Eliot *caveat* implied here, that unity is not found
in the world, but imposed on it by the selective mind, qualifies
the other implicit *desideratum*, that social disconnection should
be overcome. We have come a long way from blossoms blown
by the wind, yet the *aspect* of 'fields and trees' suggests also the
relative changes of observed and observer. The mention of 'vital
changes' experienced by neighbours leads us to anticipate future
events in the novel; the changes are to have both an economic and
a sexual dimension, since the contents of Featherstone's will are to
bring Raffles on the scene to reveal Bulstrode's shady past and to
force Fred Vincy to seek the kind of work which Mary Garth can
endorse as suitable prior to marrying him. In both developments
women are to support the men in crises. The margin of difference

made to Middlemarch as a whole or to Dorothea in particular
(through Lydgate's involvement) is hard to predict or calculate.
Middlemarch is a non-utilitarian work, though it honours Dorothea's
Radical impulses and condemns injustice. The reader's mind is kept
constantly on the move, in a second reading of the novel even
more so.

Despite her youth and privileged position outside the provincial
town, Dorothea's feelings remain the main touchstone for the
developments which George Eliot charts. She is the heroine of
the 'home epic' (the story of 'marriage', Finale) in much the same
way that St Theresa, the foundress of a religious community, might
be the subject of a saint's life. She suffers her share of defeats and
surprises, and in the end leaves for London, but she has several
victories in the sphere of personal influence. Dorothea is, of course,
the victim of restrictive conventions and traditional ideas which
confine women to dependency and inferior roles; ideas such as
appear in the pronouncement of her uncle, 'I cannot let young
ladies meddle with my documents. Young ladies are too flighty'
(Ch. 2). Mr Brooke does, however, allow Dorothea to choose her
own husband when she is evidently too inexperienced to do it
sensibly. Liberalism, as well as prejudice, can be irresponsible. The
novel, by its balanced treatment of both sexes and their relevant
attitudes, encourages us to reject sexual discrimination in any form.
The point about the unlimited variability of 'feminine incompetence', made ironically in the 'Prelude', applies equally to male
incompetence or competence, of course.[5] Dorothea's potential as
an instigator of reforms is not so much a matter of competence as
of opportunity. Limited by her Puritan upbringing and her pride
in being a lady, 'living in a quiet country-house' and practising
'well-bred economy' (Ch. 1), she yearns to overstep the strata of
her social life. She has 'an active conscience and a great mental
need', her nature being 'altogether ardent, theoretic, and intellectually consequent' (Ch. 3). She has set going an infant school
in the village; she speaks out in favour of practical science, what
she calls 'performing experiments for the good of all' (Ch. 2),
such as would increase crop-yield, and she plans model cottages
for farm labourers. Even her greatest blunder, her acceptance
of the reactionary scholar Casaubon's hand in marriage, is an
attempt to recruit a generous ally in the cause of progress. This
youthful misreading of character soon brings home to Dorothea
the need for humility. But she does not rest in self-criticism or

simply acquiesce in the sharp comments of her conventional sister, Celia. Dorothea not only learns patience, but applies it to others; she sees its relevance to waiting for people to find a vocation to which they are suited, as in the case of Ladislaw; 'Perhaps he has conscientious scruples founded on his own unfitness . . . law and medicine should be very serious professions to undertake, should they not? People's lives and fortunes depend on them' (Ch. 9). Patience is the overriding imperative of *Middlemarch*. In a world where informed intelligence is hard to find and eager moves forward lead to unforeseen mishaps, threatening disillusionment and cynicism, patience is required above all for hope to be realistically sustained.

Dorothea has had in the end a more satisfactory life than the man she so much admires, the young doctor, Lydgate, who was so sure of his vocation and began his career in Middlemarch with such high hopes of scientific discovery and the reform of medical practice. Yet another man whom she helps, Farebrother, reads the omens about Lydgate right, though Farebrother seems to have missed his own vocation. An unconventional vicar, with three female relatives to support, he gambles at cards and spends his winnings partly on his hobby, insect-collecting. But when these two discuss the future it is Farebrother who has the advantage; he knows the drawbacks of Middlemarch, its prejudices, factions, vested interests. Lydgate argues that he is less likely to meet 'empty bigwiggism' in the provinces; local people, being less pretentious than the London élite, 'affect one's *amour propre* less'. He scorns their mutual friend Trawley, who was once an idealist, 'hot on the French social systems', but now, married to a rich patient, practises at a German bath. Lydgate wants to reform the medical profession from within, not from the metropolitan power-base. Farebrother, however, points out that Lydgate's plan of reform on the ground is a good deal more difficult to carry through than Trawley's idea of a Pythagorean community: 'You have not only got the old Adam in yourself against you, but you have got all those descendants of the original Adam who form the society around you' (Ch. 17). He cautions Lydgate against being overconfident of keeping his independence. Farebrother's point, expressed in terms of Christian belief in Original Sin, could by implication be taken to favour national legislation on medical matters, but he does not go so far.

Farebrother's warning proves all too prescient, and Lydgate ends up (not unlike Trawley) husband of Rosamond Vincy and author of a treatise on gout, 'a disease which has a good deal of wealth on its side' (Finale). Lydgate preserves his respect for scientific principles, but his devotion to the scientific life is impaired. He genuinely believes that 'Science is properly more scrupulous than dogma. Dogma gives a charter to mistake but the very breath of science is a contest with mistake, and must keep the conscience alive'. In this sense of a 'contest with mistake' the morality of *Middlemarch* itself is a scientific one, hypothetical, experimental and provisional. But in his social life Lydgate suspends scientific caution for impulse. The entanglements and debts into which he falls mainly as a result of his wife's extravagance not only put him off scientific research itself, but deflect him from the moral principles he derives from it. Lydgate descends from 'the supremacy of the intellectual life' to the 'absorbing soul – wasting struggle with worldly annoyances' (Ch. 73). He compromises himself as a medical practitioner in his association with Bulstrode, who had supported him with a loan of money and was not above willing the death of the blackmailer Raffles. The complicated mutual disgrace of Lydgate and Bulstrode finally kills off their New Hospital project; all that is left of that is Lydgate's valuable case register, which he will send to 'a man who will make use of it'. Dorothea cannot help there; her operative sphere is limited. She does, however, lend Lydgate crucial psychological support at this juncture. Her belief in his integrity, stronger than Farebrother's, is important to him. Her generous influence allows him to see things again 'in their larger, quieter masses' (Ch. 76), even though he still has to leave the town. He relies on Dorothea to clear his name locally. Dorothea's beneficial nature is very effective in personal relations. In this way the prospect of her life, so 'full of motiveless ease' (Ch. 54), lightens, and her patience is rewarded. Her home view proves its value.

   The positive factor, which might in the long run make a differ-ence to Dorothea's 'unhistoric acts' (Finale) and raise them to the level of, say, Wilberforce's 'work at philanthropy' (Ch. 2), is publicity. *Middlemarch* shows a provincial England on the brink of an expansion of journalism. George Eliot herself rose from lower middle-class status to become the *de facto* editor of the radical *Westminster Review*. None of the young people in the novel, ten years older than herself, follows that exact path, but there is much discussion of publications; some feel the pull to get into print. The mediocrity of unpublished opinion in Middlemarch, especially on

medical matters, is a recurrent source of comedy. Even political
reform turns up on Dagley's lips as the 'Rinform', a distortion
with a possible allusion to the German *Rind* or ox, suggesting the
bovine benightedness of Middlemarch country types. Yet Dagley's
notion, picked up locally, that 'Rinform' is something for sending
landlords 'a-scuttlin'; an' wi' pretty strong-smellin' things too', is
not so far from the truth, since the 1832 Act did remove political
power from the more or less exclusive hands of the landowners.
As Mr Brooke's tenant-farmer, Dagley hits out strongly, indicating
'these primises, as you woon't give a stick tow'rt mending. Go to
Middlemarch to ax for your charrikter' (Ch. 39). Freedom of
speech brings advantages, since Brooke is shamed by Dagley's
accusations, but even more so by the denunciation in the Tory
campaign newspaper, *The Trumpet*, where Keck the editor has him
as a retrogressive man who 'shrieks at corruption, and keeps his
farms at rack-rent: who roars himself red at rotten boroughs, and
does not mind if every field on his farms has a rotten gate' (Ch. 38).
Brooke is at last pushed into doing something for his tenants. Keck's
outburst had been provoked by Ladislaw's writing on behalf of
Reform in *The Pioneer*, where he gives subjects 'a kind of turn'
(Ch. 34), as Mr Brooke, the owner, puts it. Brooke's employment
of Ladislaw as campaign manager and journalist is presented as a
happy opening for the hitherto dilettantish young man. Ladislaw
had been at ease in the commerce of ideas, in current controversies
and intellectual reading, but it took Dorothea to point out to him
that to be a poet he needed more than a sensitive, knowledgeable
mind: 'But you leave out the poems . . . I think they are wanted
to complete the poet' (Ch. 22). In fact, Ladislaw has to settle
for something prosaic but worthwhile: 'political writing, political
speaking, would get a higher value now public life was going to be
wider and more national' (Ch. 51). When he returns from building
up this career in journalism in London to complete his tortuous
wooing of Dorothea, Ladislaw's success is already signalled; there
had been a 'flattering reception (in dim corners) of his new hand in
leading articles' (Ch. 82). He eventually becomes 'an ardent public
man' and an MP, with Dorothea 'absorbed' in his life (Finale).

   In complete contrast with the mercurial, communicative Ladislaw is his guardian, Casaubon, a scholar so pathologically slow to
get his researches into print that he feels ultimately secure only
with himself. Lonely among his rows of notebooks, Casaubon
feels a vaporous pressure from that 'chilling ideal audience which

crowded his laborious uncreative hours' (Ch. 10). His brief ven-
tures into publication prove unrewarding, the audience is still
'cold, shadowy, unapplausive', and his wife, whom he had envisaged as an assistant, now seems suspiciously like its personification
(Ch. 20). Casaubon's problem, however, is not just his shrinking
from debate with fellow experts, deaf as he is to contemporary
'historical enquiries' by German scholars (Ch. 21); it is his mental bias towards an ambitious world-view. *Middlemarch* is critical
of those seduced by the false lure of simplistic order-systems.
Casaubon's life-project, his 'Key to all Mythologies', is a vindi-
cation of such an illusory phlogiston. Casaubon wants to force a
Christian interpretation on anthropological data, which he believes
are corrupt myths into which an early Revelation had degenerated.
It is a view that is prejudiced, holistic, unhistorical, 'free from
interruption', and Dorothea comes to realise that her husband
had 'risked all his egoism' on 'a theory which was already withered
in the birth like an elfin child' (Ch. 48). While pitying him
in his sense of impotence and isolation, she learns to connect
his secrecy with his exorbitant claims for himself. Dominance in
personal relations accompanies an ambitious world-outlook. An
added dimension is Casaubon's habit of projecting his private
history on to a generalised plane as the workings of a Divine
Providence. In his letter proposing marriage he refers to the
prospect of becoming Dorothea's earthly guardian as 'the highest
of providential gifts' (Ch. 5). Self-deception goes with commitment
to a myth of universal explanation.

These fundamental issues are discussed both lightly and passionately at various points in the novel. For instance, Godwin's human
perfectibility theory covering the moral and political sphere gets a
humorous knock from Mr Brooke when he comments that 'human
reason may carry you a little too far – over the hedge, in fact'. Again,
Humphry Davy's *Elements of Agricultural Chemistry* (1813), based on
dubious ideas like electrifying the land, represents the kind of
science which Mr Brooke says 'would not do. It leads to everything;
you can let nothing alone' (Ch. 2). The treatise that Fred Vincy
writes on the 'Cultivation of Green Crops and the Economy of
Cattle-Feeding', which wins him applause at agricultural meetings,
even though Middlemarch opinion wrongly attributes its author-
ship to his wife (Finale), is a different matter, since it is based
on practical experience gained by working with Caleb Garth.
Similarly in the field of pastoral religion the ministrations of

the unpretentious Farebrother are to be preferred to those of Bulstrode's protégé, the theologically argumentative Tyke, who blackmails his parishioners, like Griffin and his wife, by saying 'they should have no more coals' if they came to hear Farebrother preach (Ch. 17). Bulstrode's own case is another one where a lust for total explanation fuels a determination to have power over others. His position as a banker is based on the acquisition of a fortune by deception, but there is a characteristic combination of secrecy, faith in a favouring Providence, intellectual aggression and pleasure in the exercise of personal dominance. Bulstrode enjoys sectarian advantage ('recognised supremacy') as a patron of municipal improvements and selector of personnel for appointments. When, reminded by Raffles of his guilty past, Bulstrode seeks for excuses, even though he is still locked in 'the train of causes', the narrator comments explicity, 'There is no general doctrine which is not capable of eating out our morality if unchecked by the deep-seated habit of fellow-feeling with individual fellow-men' (Ch. 61). Such risk of hypocrisy affects everyone to some extent, but it is particularly relevant to those who rely on 'wide phrases', Evangelical or other. This theme runs right through *Middlemarch*.

Bulstrode's fall is mitigated by the support that he receives from his wife. She is willing to share in his humiliation, though a full exchange of confidences between them over his actions is impossible.[6] They shrink from words in their crisis. She too, as an 'imperfectly taught woman, whose phrases and beliefs were an odd patchwork', has been influenced by the Evangelical tradition, but she is sufficiently moved by loyalty, compassion and tenderness towards the man with whom she has shared her life to tell him, 'Look up, Nicholas'. Mrs Bulstrode is left with a 'maimed consciousness', but that may not be so bad. Her world-view lacks the overdetermined holism that characterises power-seeking theorists; her home view triumphs – the precedence she gives to personal relations rescues her husband from despair.

Lydgate, though a much more sensitive and positive personality than Casaubon or the Bulstrodes, runs up against a major problem which is also caused by his adherence to a too rigid framework of interpretation. The difficulty does not appertain to his profession; his scientific interest is presented favourably. Even if in his research he puts the question 'not quite in the way required by the awaiting answer' (Ch. 15), it is not implied that his studies are pointless or would never have produced any results. Lydgate's limitations

show up in his treatment of women. Hailing from an aristocratic
Northumberland family, Lydgate mixes on easy terms with stimu-
lating companions from the higher middle classes, carrying his
superiority round with him in the form of style, manners, accent
and deportment. But his attitude to the relations between the
sexes reveals a deep cultural flaw; not only in himself, of course.
A fault in European culture going back through mediaeval to
classical times, manifesting itself in the nineteenth century as a
male preference for an intellectually subservient though physically
pretty female partner, affects Lydgate. He makes a misjudgement
when he devalues Dorothea as a potential partner in preference for
Rosamond. The narrator terms it commonness; Lydgate's 'spots of
commonness lay in the complexion of his prejudices' (Ch. 15), a
desire for the best style of woman as to appearance, which would go
alongside the best style in furniture, in clothes, in other possessions,
without too much thought about the cost. Lydgate is unscientific in
his estimation of Rosamond. Checking and self-correction are in
abeyance. Her person demonstrates for him the mental qualities he
wants her to have, docility, for instance, and refinement, exclusive
of 'the need for other evidence'. He classes her radiant womanhood
with flowers and with music, as a beauty virtuous by its nature,
'being moulded only for pure and delicate joys' (Ch. 16). Lydgate
is confused about music as well as women, but essentially it is a
moral incaution that is being expressed here. The idea of his
commonness returns with a sad echo when near the end he is
grateful to Dorothea for standing by him when Rosamond did not;
it was for something 'too good for common thanks' (Ch. 81).

The scenes of crisis in the marriage of Rosamond and Lydgate
are (it can be fairly argued) unsurpassed in fiction in English;
indeed in any language apart from Russian. From the early stages
of *Middlemarch* George Eliot makes it clear that Rosamond is made
of tougher stuff than Lydgate; her course is steered 'by a wary grace
and propriety'. In an excellent parable, her egotism is likened
to a candle which arranges what are actually only indiscriminate
scratches on a pier-glass into 'concentric circles'. She had the idea
of becoming engaged to the socially superior Lydgate whereas he
at first had the opposite idea. But she had the advantage: 'Circumstance was almost sure to be on the side of Rosamond's idea,
which had a shaping activity and looked through watchful blue eyes,
whereas Lydgate's lay blind and unconscious as a jelly-fish which
gets melted without knowing it' (Ch. 27). Rosamond's attunement

to social conditions gives her a power comparable to forces in natural history, though it is in essence a combination of the sexual and the cultural. She is not a sordid plotter like Becky Sharp in Thackeray's *Vanity Fair* (1848). We are warned by the narrator not to be unfair to her. She is clever enough to manipulate Lydgate to get her way and rise in the world. She thinks that as an aristocrat he is stooping to be a professional, but she knows that her path, that of a middle-class accomplished lady, meets his. She also thinks it wrong to be concerned, even as a married woman, too much about money, and here her cleverness stops. The moment comes when Lydgate has to put her in the picture about the debt which he has piled up and the need for them to economise completely in their way of living:

> As she came towards him in her drapery of transparant faintly-tinted muslin, her slim yet round figure never looked more graceful; as she sat down by him and laid one hand on the elbow of his chair, at last looking at him and meeting his eyes, her delicate neck and cheek and purely-cut lips never had more of that untarnished beauty which touches us in spring-time and infancy and all sweet freshness. It touched Lydgate now, and mingled the early moments of his love for her with all the other memories which were stirred in this crisis of deep trouble. He laid his ample hand softly on hers, saying –
>
> "Dear!" with the lingering utterance which affection gives to the word. Rosamond too was still under the power of that same past, and her husband was still in part the Lydgate whose approval had stirred delight. She put his hair lightly away from his forehead, then laid her other hand on his, and was conscious of forgiving him.
>
> "I am obliged to tell you what will hurt you, Rosy. But there are things which husband and wife must think of together. I daresay it has occurred to you already that I am short of money".
>
> Lydgate paused; but Rosamond turned her neck and looked at a vase on the mantelpiece.
>
> "I was not able to pay for all the things we had to get before we were married, and there have been expenses since which I have been obliged to meet. The consequence is, there is a large debt at Brassing – three hundred and eighty pounds – which has been pressing on me a good while, and in fact we

are getting deeper every day, for people don't pay me the faster because others want the money. I took pains to keep it from you while you were not well; but now we must think together about it, and you must help me."

"What can *I* do, Tertius?" said Rosamond, turning her eyes on him again. That little speech of four words, like so many others in all languages, is capable by varied vocal inflexions of expressing all states of mind from helpless dimness to exhaustive, argumentative perception, from the completest self-devoting fellowship to the most neutral aloofness. Rosamond's thin utterance threw into the words "What can *I* do?" as much neutrality as they could hold. They fell like a mortal chill on Lydgate's roused tenderness. He did not storm in indignation – he felt too sad a sinking of the heart. And when he spoke again it was more in the tone of a man who forces himself to fulfil a task.

"It is necessary for you to know, because I have to give security for a time, and a man must come to make an inventory of the furniture."

Rosamond coloured deeply. "Have you not asked papa for money?" She said, as soon as she could speak.

"No."

"Then I must ask him!" she said, releasing her hands from Lydgate's, and rising to stand at two yards' distance from him.

"No, Rosy," said Lydgate, decisively. "It is too late to do that. The inventory will be begun to-morrow. Remember it is a mere security: it will make no difference: it is a temporary affair. I insist upon it that your father shall not know, unless I choose to tell him," added Lydgate, with a more peremptory emphasis.

This certainly was unkind, but Rosamond had thrown him back on evil expectation as to what she would do in the way of quiet steady disobedience. The unkindness seemed unpardonable to her: she was not given to weeping and disliked it, but now her chin and lips began to tremble and the tears welled up. Perhaps it was not possible for Lydgate, under the double stress of outward material difficulty and of his own proud resistance to humiliating consequences, to imagine fully what this sudden trial was to a young creature who had known nothing but indulgence, and whose dreams had all been of new indulgence, more exactly to her taste. But he did wish to spare her as much as he could, and her tears cut him to the heart. (Ch. 58)

The tension in such writing builds slowly, with the narrator's scrupulous psychological analysis and sensitive selection of physical detail[7] giving a sense of complete concentration without any distractions; every word counts (consider, for example, 'roused tenderness'). The speech, the action, the feeling, the subtleties in the whole changing relationship, are sensitively imagined with outward drama and inner thought classically balanced. If the narrator's discourse is privileged it is in a tone of modesty ('Perhaps'); the commentary focuses on the difficulties of communication. More trouble is anticipated. Rosamond is still confident of the favour of her own private Providence, and makes a number of mistakes. The worst is her attempt to keep Ladislaw in thrall as a flirtatious admirer. It takes Dorothea to teach her the lesson never to risk such misunderstandings again. Moved by Dorothea's generous assurance of Lydgate's probity in the Raffles affair, Rosamond is 'taken hold of by an emotion stronger than her own' (Ch. 81). She returns good deed with good deed, convincing Dorothea that Ladislaw loves her and not herself. Rosamond is in any case prevented from leaving Lydgate by her inherited middle-class dislike for the condition of the married woman gone back to live with her parents. She adapts to his more limited career prospects, sharing in his worldly success.

Her brother Fred, who also enjoys the Vincy characteristic of good looks, is a much more open-hearted type. He is destined for a worthy partnershp with his childhood sweetheart, the plain but lively Mary Garth. Fred has to extricate himself from his father's ambition for him to become a university-educated clergyman. He does, at first, share his sister's respect for a superior style of life; his part in the 'higher education of the country . . . had exalted his views of rank and income' (Ch. 14). Fred winces under 'the idea of being looked down upon', believing in the mystery of luck which will bring about agreeable issues 'such as are consistent with our good taste in costume, and our general preference for the best style of thing' (Ch. 23). The reliance on luck, however, brings disappointments and debts. It is Mary Garth's strictly conditional approval which sets him on the road to recovery. Preferring genuinely to 'have to do with outdoor things' like land and cattle, Fred takes up employment as Caleb Garth's assistant (estates manager).

In a key scene he insists to Mr Vincy that he is not going 'down a step in life' in pursuing that career; 'I think I can be quite as much of a gentleman at the work I have undertaken, as if I had been a curate' (Ch. 56). Gentlemanliness, in this context, is an achieved habit of good manners and moral dealing rather than a mark of rank, reminding us of Nancy Lammeter's ladylike quality in *Silas Marner.* Fred Vincy shows strength of character in taking charge of his life to suit his own talents and to meet the realistic aspirations of Mary Garth, with her 'dreadfully secular mind', whom he consistently loves. She, in turn, gently declines the advances of Farebrother; visions of 'new dignities and an acknowledged value' (Ch. 57) as the clergyman's wife do not tempt her, with Fred excluded from them.[8] The story of the loyal love of Fred and Mary gravitates steadily to the very centre of *Middlemarch.* Appropriately, it provides the last but one scene in the novel, with Mary as the bringer of good news, still teasingly conveyed, but with good-humoured, sensible allusions to economising and saving, while the narrator mentions, briefly but not perfunctorily, the 'strong feeling' involved and the 'spirit of joy' (Ch. 86).

The strong characterisation of Mary's father, Caleb Garth, adds further weight to this strand of the novel. In both the personal and practical spheres Caleb's plans and interventions are always constructive and encouraging. He embodies the virtues of the higher artisan class of the time, preserving a deferential attitude to those with inherited wealth, but not respectful unless their responsibilities are fulfilled, with opportunities provided for gainful earning. Clumsy of speech, and deeply distrustful of financial speculation, Caleb Garth is liked and admired by everyone whose opinion matters. His philosophy is patiently optimistic, founded on his observation of that interconnection between people's aptitudes and actions which gives scope both for practical innovations and a broader general contentment; 'his prince of darkness was a slack workman. But there was no spirit of denial in Caleb' (Ch. 24). It is highly significant that Caleb Garth has a mutual understanding with Dorothea. He quotes her approvingly on land improvement, noting that 'she sees into things in that way' (Ch. 56). His view that to get 'a bit of the country into good fettle' is 'a great gift of God' goes beyond the Puritan work ethic to a quasi-religious sense of a community and its environment. When he says, 'Things hang together', he is being theologically vague (no drawback, of course, in *Middlemarch*), but perceptive as to connections. He means that people set good and bad examples, which may have very wide repercussions. As for his distrust of politics ('What people do who go into politics I can't think: it drives me almost mad to see mismanagement over only a few hundred acres', Ch. 40), it is more concerned wth efficacy than principle and should not be regarded as total. Nevertheless it elevates the home-view over the world-view. Caleb Garth's regard for the next generation is the most appealing feature of his personality. His secret satisfaction when Fred Vincy is at last to be given the chance to farm at Stone Court, which he had hoped in vain to inherit from Peter Featherstone, affects the reader directly. He is 'elated with his hope of this "neat turn" being given to things' (Ch. 68), a phrase felicitously suggestive both of workmanship and of poetic justice, yet drawn unobtrusively by George Eliot from ordinary speech. It is an important moment in *Middlemarch* when Caleb Garth resumes the agency of the Tipton property of Mr Brooke after a twelve years' interval. This earlier 'neat turn' occurs as a result of pressure from Dorothea, Sir James Chettam and several other parties upon Mr Brooke: it may seem in some ways a conjunction of opposites, because Dorothea's uncle is as volubly indecisive as Garth is laconically determined.

Yet the constant comedy occasioned by Mr Brooke's wavering reformism is as necessary to the lively surface of the novel as Garth's solid conservatism is to its depth. A landowner of 'acquiescent temper, miscellaneous opinions, and uncertain vote' (Ch. 1), Mr Brooke is one of those beautifully judged fictional constructs which unfailingly amuse the reader, while occasioning justifiable irritation to the characters in contact with them, even to those most affectionately disposed towards them. During Mr Brooke's many appearances George Eliot never puts a foot wrong. He is superbly well characterised with his 'neutral leisurely air', his leg stretched out towards the wood fire, offering no check to his tendency to repeat himself ('This fundamental principle of human speech was markedly exhibited in Mr Brooke'). His comment on Casaubon's proposal of marriage to Dorothea ('I thought it better to tell you, my dear') and his expression of guarded permissiveness ('People should have their own way in marriage, and that sort of thing – up to a certain point, you know') are fatuously obvious, vaguely muddled, endearingly considerate and maddeningly unhelpful at the same time, yet seem to sum up much of human experience in the face of dilemmas about discipline and independence (Ch. 4). Mr Brooke's tolerance, fairness and indecisiveness provide a parody of liberal well-meaningness. In reaction against his early radical enthusiasms, he now favours theory only in small amounts. He drops names as readily as he drops the threads of his arguments. He can be exasperatingly inconsistent, as when the narrator comments sharply that it is one thing to make a Radical speech against the high income of bishops and another to think with pleasure of one's niece's husband's large ecclesiastical income: 'it is a narrow mind which cannot look at a subject from various points of view' (Ch. 7). Mr Brooke is certainly not let off lightly,[9] particularly at the hustings, where, as the independent Radical nominee for the Parliamentary candidature, he is mocked by an effigy of himself, a Punch-like voice in echo and a hail of eggs. It is a scene of ridicule no less nightmarish for being non-violent; a serious assault, we are told, would have had 'perhaps more consolations attached to it'. But despite this humiliation, which realises vividly for the reader the fear of unpopularity which is always attendant upon the love of publicity, Mr Brooke preserves a basic decency in all his inconsistencies. He is lenient with felons and does not force his tenants to pay their arrears of rent. The narrator notes that the setback to the cause of Reform occasioned by Mr Brooke's discomfiture in Middlemarch's market place could be put down to the 'entanglement of things' (Ch. 51). Mr Brooke's failure to connect is preferable to others' forcing of unwanted connections, and is closer to the narrator's tentative attempts to indicate connections in things than to any merely received general opinion. He does eventually accept that 'there's something singular in things' (Ch. 84), when supporting Dorothea's decision to marry Ladislaw. In the discussion of Ladislaw's lack of vocation it is, significantly, Mr Brooke who sympathises with the young man's reported desire that some geographical mysteries be kept untouched either by exploration or by science, 'some unknown regions preserved' (Ch. 9); and when Ladislaw later argues that the most viable wisdom is 'the wisdom of balancing claims' (Ch. 46), Mr Brooke's somewhat paralysed impartiality begins to look intellectually respectable even. Indeed when Dorothea and Ladislaw end up as political workers in campaigns that are no longer crusades they are in a political position not so far from Mr Brooke's as they would like to think they were: 'We must keep the reins. I have never let myself be run away with; I always pulled up' (Ch. 39). The symbolism of his name connotes shallowness and chattering fluency, but also a genial contribution to the river of life, in terms of which Dorothea's nature too 'spent itself in channels which had no great name on the earth' (Finale).

Such natural imagery plays a notable part in *Middlemarch*. The novel's title may suggest a central border or march, a Rubicon over which a provincial body has to cross in some shape or other. George Eliot uses many striking biological analogies to underline this idea of irregular development. The image of Dorothea as a cygnet which, reared uneasily among ducklings, never finds 'the living stream in fellowship with its own oary-footed kind' (Prelude), suggests misplacement but also a surprisingly powerful growth. Odd bird behaviour recurs frequently in *Middlemarch*, shattering any pre-conceived pictures of domestic animals living in cyclic harmony. There are, for example, the cannibalistic chickens owned by Mr Brooke's lodgekeeper, Mrs Fitchett. These 'wicked Spanish fowls' have 'ta'en to eating their own eggs', giving their owner 'no peace o' mind with 'em at all', a quite different Iberian product from that of the Theresan convent, clearly. Mrs Cadwallader's advice to Mrs Fitchett to sell them not only illustrates the 'socially uniting' effect of her free-spokenness, but touches on a breeding selectivity which it is decidedly not possible to emulate in the human context (Ch. 6), desirable as something like it might fleetingly seem, say, to Ladislaw, who, sensitive as to his own Polish blood, regards the Middlemarch middle class as 'a breed very much in need of crossing' (Ch. 62). The novel contains no outright atrocity, though Bulstrode's treatment of his first wife's daughter, the actress-mother of Ladislaw, is wicked enough. Dorothea is not disillusioned to learn of it; she had lost her unsuspectingness once before at least, when as a child her illusions about 'the gratitude of wasps and the susceptibility of sparrows' had been removed by evidence of their baseness (Ch. 22). She is still, of course, short-sighted; yet her blindness to things outside 'her own pure purpose' can carry her 'safely by the side of precipices where vision would have been perilous with fear' (Ch. 37), so that a physical and psychological peculiarity, like the luckiest of evolutionary mutations, can have an unexpected survival value. This complex unpredictability applies in particular to Ladislaw, who sees his own career, too gloomily, as a long incubation producing no chick, the world being full of 'handsome dubious eggs called possibilities'. The repeated notion of masked development, of the effective shapes that 'may be disguised in helpless embryos' (Ch. 10), suggests undercurrents in *Middlemarch* that cannot be plotted, or which are there to qualify

the concept of plotting itself. Characters' behaviour is correspondingly far from straightforward. For instance, Ladislaw's passionate
rebellion against the 'inherited blot' (Ch. 61) of the Bulstrode
connection brings him back for a *second* farewell to Dorothea,
which 'lends an opening to comedy' and leads Sir James Chettam,
looking for evidence of Ladislaw's volatility, to be 'so far unlike
himself' (Ch. 62) as to bring up with Dorothea Ladislaw's relationship with Rosamond. The resulting confusion gives Dorothea
her memorable sleepless night and her morning view of figures
moving in the landscape, her view from home, which determines
her not to rest in mere observation and complaint: 'she felt the
largeness of the world and the manifold wakings of men to labour
and endurance. She was part of that involuntary, palpitating life'
(Ch. 80). It is neither a benevolent Romantic nature with beautiful
scenery nor a divinely created order that inspires Dorothea. It
is the varied human world we recognise today.[10] It is partly a
biological phenomenon to be studied and discussed, partly a social
construct to be investigated and improved, but it is not wholly
subject to rational control or intellectual measurement. There
are certainly *very* few literary works that do it more justice than
does *Middlemarch.* Dorothea responds to her experience of the
external world by acting positively where she can, in the sphere
of personal relations and local affairs where her social privilege
gives her influence and later, through marriage, on a wider stage.
But the ideal of consentaneity of development[11] between the inner
life of the individual and the external life of society, provincial and
national, can only be approached gingerly, with many setbacks and
unscheduled advances to be accepted.

7

George Eliot Criticism

The critics' response to George Eliot is usually regarded historically as a story of fall and rise. After adulation in her own day she was denigrated for half a century and then rehabilitated for good. Evidence can be adduced to support this view, but it has been done rather too selectively, I think. I am aware of an instability of critical opinion about her all the way along, of constant shifts of approval and disapproval, with both arising on varying grounds. Two factors have always weighed for and against her simultaneously; she is both a difficult writer and a woman writer. The sheer volume of comment which these issues have aroused inevitably involves controversy and disagreement.

That she was by no means universally admired in her own day has been amply demonstrated by David Carroll, who refers to the steep 'ups and downs' of her contemporary reputation.[1] Writing fiction from what was very much a minority point of view on religious, racial and philosophical issues, she could expect a variability of response, especially after she dropped the incognito. As a former reviews editor, she knew about the prejudices of literary critics and used G. H. Lewes as a filter to keep from her attention the more discouraging printed comments. Much Victorian opinion of her novels was handicapped by basic inhibitions: the dislike of the slight sexual audacity detectable near the end of *The Mill on the Floss*, for example, the feeling that stories written by a woman should display charm rather than intellect, the idea that a Midlander should stick to the landscapes and folk she knew, and the assumption that a morality not underpinned by religion must be gloomy. Considering the self-critical spirit in which she wrote her novels, George Eliot needed what support she could get. She complimented R. H. Hutton, for example, on his understanding of what she was expressing in her presentation of Bardo and Baldassare in *Romola*, namely that sense of the power of language which was felt so strongly at the Renaissance. It was rare for her to admit to an intention like that; she told Hutton tantalisingly, 'if I had been called upon to expound my own book, there are other things that I should want to say, or things that I should say somewhat otherwise'.[2] But she never did. Her aim was to influence opinion rather than to please it. She risked her reputation knowingly with elements like the Jewish nationalism in *Daniel Deronda*, as is clear from an entry in her journal dated 1 December 1876: 'I have been made aware of much repugnance or else indifference towards the Jewish part of *Deronda*, and of some hostile and some adverse reviewing. On the other hand . . . there are certain signs that I may have contributed my mite to a good result.'[3] The tone is not that of one who expects her work to become uncontroversial; for her the challenges were worth it.

The attacks on George Eliot's prestige which ensued for decades after her death alongside a steady output of appreciation are to be viewed, then, as a continuation of critical habits already established. George Saintsbury is an example of a critic of this period whose views on George Eliot retained a fairly consistent basis though the balance eventually tips in her disfavour. In 1876, while rejecting Deronda as an impossible prig and insisting that no perfect novel can ever be written 'in designed illustration of a theory' such as the superior claims of kinship and duty to those of love, Saintsbury found in the 'wonderful creations' of Gwendolen and Grandcourt evidence of 'a capacity of rendering minute effects of light and shade, attitudes, transient moods of mind, complex feelings and the like, which is simply unparalleled in any other prose writer',[4] views not so far away from those of Leavis seventy years later. In 1895, however, in the rashly entitled *Corrected Impressions*, Saintsbury refers to George Eliot's late novels as ungenial studies of immense effort which are 'on the whole dead'; *Daniel Deronda* is now 'a kind of nightmare, – a parochial and grotesque idea having thoroughly mastered the writer and only allowed her now and again to get free in the character of Grandcourt and (less often) in that of Gwendolen'. George Eliot, her scientific phraseology blamed on Lewes, is by then said to have passed out of 'contemporary critical appreciation'.[5] This was hardly the case; there had been studies by Matilda Blind (1883) and Oscar Browning (1890), and the substantial chapters or books on her by W. C. Brownell (1901), Leslie Stephen (1902) and others were still to come. Saintsbury in the 1890s was probably influenced by the aesthetic distaste for long novels as such and may have been disinclined to re-read them. G. S. Haight has pointed out that several slips or omissions suggest that George Moore, Oliver Elton and Arnold Bennett all wrote against George Eliot's work without being clear as to its exact contents.[6] The last named, believing absurdly that George Eliot never had 'a genuine natural appreciation of the value of words', wrote in 1896 that he had only 'dipped into *Adam Bede*' to have his impression that she would never be among the classical writers 'made a certainty'.[7] Dipping in or skimming seems also to lie behind the most notorious canard against George Eliot: W. E. Henley's contention that her men, with the exception of Lydgate, were all 'governesses in revolt' or 'heroes of the divided skirt' repeats a point made in 1881 by Leslie Stephen, but Henley tops it with an epigrammatic list of insults: '"the Death's-Head Style" of art', 'an Apotheosis of Pupil-Teachery', 'George Sand *plus* science and *minus* sex', 'Pallas with prejudices and a corset', 'the fruit of a caprice of Apollo for the Differential Calculus'.[8] Such jibes have enough puerile gusto to leave their object strengthened rather than weakened. Even Henley implies that there is a lot to learn from George Eliot.

The seriousness of George Eliot's appeal is the aspect emphasised by W. C. Brownell. Though he complains oddly that she has no style, a limited imagination and deficiencies in conveying sensuousness, he accepts that she has intellectual weight: 'no other novelist gives one such a poignant, sometimes such an insupportable, sense that life is immensely serious, and no other, in consequence, is surer of being read, and read indefinitely, by serious readers'.[9] That appeared in the first year of the twentieth century, and it was followed in 1902 by H. H. Bonnell's favourable analysis of her style, in which he not only approved her learned and scientific metaphors, but also found an inevitableness in her occasional obscurity. She is 'the reverse of a pedant', and yet you know she is not playing with you.[10]

Bonnell finds all sorts of linguistic fineness in George Eliot's prose. Leslie Stephen's work of the same date is more ambivalent though the fact that *George Eliot* was added to the English Men of Letters series, with Jane Austen the only other woman in a list of forty-nine, was itself a major tribute. Stephen's study is an expanded versions of his *Cornhill* obituary article of twenty-one years before. He again questions her touch in drawing male characters ('portraits drawn from the outside'), but praises the sympathetic quality of her irony, especially in the early works like *Adam Bede*, where it seemed to him to be more spontaneous and immediate than in the later ones. Stephen does, however, find George Eliot's 'reflective powers' and psychological insight 'fully ripened' in *Middlemarch*, yet that extraordinarily powerful novel leaves him with a 'rather painful impression' since the compromises made by its idealistic characters pass 'imperceptibly into surrender', giving 'a rather one-sided view of the world.'[11] Stephen consistently believed that George Eliot's speculative interest in philosophy distanced her from reality in her later novels.

A more subtly shifting view of George Eliot is provided by Henry James, who is, of course, in so far as he was her critic, a special case. As a novelist he consciously regarded himself as carrying on and modifying her work, especially in the *The Portrait of a Lady*, during the period of his composition of which she died. His early reviews of her works are less sympathetic than one might expect. In 1886 he found that *Felix Holt* illustrated 'her closely wedded talents and foibles. Her plots have always been artificial — clumsily artificial — the conduct of her story slow, and her style diffuse. Her conclusions have been signally weak'.[12] In 1873 *Middlemarch* was pronounced 'at once one of the strongest and one of the weakest of English novels.' James criticises it as merely a panoramic 'chain of episodes' rather than an organised whole with a 'definite subject', yet he insists on its importance as an imaginative form of 'History' which 'sets a limit, we think, to the development of the old-fashioned English novel'.[13] In his 1885 review of Cross's *Life* James aligned himself with Stephen and the other English critics who found George Eliot's intellectual knowledge or 'excess of reflection' a handicap to her spontaneous vitality; she puts herself at a disadvantage by regarding the novel as 'a moralised fable, the last word of a philosophy endeavouring to teach by example' rather than as 'primarily a picture of life, capable of deriving a high value from its form'. By form James means manipulation of narrative point of view, which he felt George Eliot subordinated to 'a certain greyness of tone . . . a kind of fragrance of moral elevation'.[14] But he stresses the extent to which she had helped on the cause of feminism by showing in the dedication of her life that there was nothing that was closed to women. When in 1908 he came to write his Prefaces to the New York edition of his novels, James focused more clearly on the significance of her heroines not only as precedents for his own, but in the development of literature itself.

James, in the preface to *The Portrait of a Lady*, quotes with approval George Eliot's defence of making intelligent young women
the centre of interest in fiction: 'In these frail [delicate] ves-
sels is borne onward through the ages the treasure of human
affection[s]', he slightly misquotes her conclusion to chapter 11
of *Daniel Deronda*, and mentions Hetty Sorrel, Maggie Tulliver,
Rosamond Vincy as well as Gwendolen Harleth, bracketing also
Shakespeare's Portia from *The Merchant of Venice*, all forerunners
of Isabel Archer. It was a 'deep difficulty' which George Eliot had
braved, but which Scott, Dickens and Stevenson failed to attempt.[15]
In the preface to *The Princess Casamassima* James broadens and
deepens his account of his indebtedness to his predecessor by
pointedly including her male characters in his list of those whose
treatment amounted to a psychological adventure, even if by mischance she occasionally left these figures too abstract 'by reason of
the quantity of soul employed'. He admits what he calls 'a weakness
of sympathy' with George Eliot's constant effort to show these
main characters' story (which constituted her subject-matter) 'as
determined by their feelings and the nature of their minds. Their
emotions, their stirred intelligence, their moral consciousness,
become thus, by sufficiently charmed perusal, our own very adventure.' James likens his own 'instinctive disposition' to place his
polished 'mirrors' like Mallet, Newman, Isabel, Densher, Strether,
Prince Amerigo and Maggie Verver, at the centre of his novels with
George Eliot's concentration of interest on Adam Bede, Maggie
Tulliver, Romola, Tito Melema, Felix Holt, Lydgate, Dorothea,
Gwendolen and Deronda.[16] This tribute is certainly substantial
and was, I think, influential, given James's eminence as a literary
arbitrator in the Edwardian period.

James followed up his comments in the Prefaces with several
further passages of praise of George Eliot in his autobiography,
recalling, for instance that *The Mill on the Floss* had seemed an
all-engulfing, 'incomparably privileged production' to the young
James and his contemporaries, and adding that its nobility was not
matched by that of any current (1914) production.[17] Finally in *The
Middle Years* (1917) James re-attested his commitment to George
Eliot, dismissing those critics who misdoubted her 'backing of rich
thought' or held that her philosophy, with its scientific vocabulary,
'thrust itself through to the confounding of the picture'. Henry
James concludes, 'I was to remain – I take pleasure in repeating –
even a very Derondist of Derondists, for my own wanton joy: which

amounts to saying that I found the figured, coloured tapestry *always* vivid enough to brave no matter what complication of the stitch.'[18] These extracts escape the usual collections of critical essays on George Eliot, but as far as her reputation went they undoubtedly kept it higher than convention would have it.

The crucial effect of her influence was on younger novelists; here there is plenty of evidence of enthusiasm and respect. Mrs Humphrey Ward, for example, refers in her autobiography to George Eliot as a great writer with a 'rich, absorbent mind' whose best work, like her talk, had a 'perfect ease and finish', with 'singularly complete and accomplished descriptions'.[19] In 1902 we find Conrad writing to his publisher about the design of his novels and linking George Eliot with Scott and Thackeray as novelists who developed their characters, commentary and situations slowly in the interest of honesty, truth and art: 'But these are great names.'[20] Edith Wharton not only wrote an appreciative essay on George Eliot in 1902, but when she was held up in writing *The Touchstone* regarded George Eliot's delays with *Middlemarch* as a comforting precedent.[21] Again the young D. H. Lawrence found Maggie Tulliver his favourite heroine, especially responding to the description of her arm, and when he came to plan *The White Peacock* in 1905 he told Jessie Chambers, 'The usual plan is to take two couples and develop their relationships . . . most of George Eliot's are on that plan'. Lawrence was conscious of George Eliot's originality as a psychological novelist: 'it was really George Eliot who started it all . . . and how wild they were with her for doing it. It was she who started putting all the action inside. Before, you know, with Fielding and the others, it had been outside.'[22] Lawrence regarded George Eliot as his first source. Another keen practitioner who knew where to look for examples was I. Compton-Burnett. On leaving college in 1900 she spent a gift of fifty pounds on complete sets of Jane Austen and George Eliot, who, with Thackeray and others, remained her 'staple favourites'; it is seldom, adds her biographer, that one major author submerged herself 'so completely in the personality of another as I. Compton-Burnett, at the start of her career, in George Eliot'. Compton-Burnett told an interviewer in 1962 that she had read a good deal of George Eliot about 1911. Resemblances in Compton-Burnett's early work are to *Middlemarch* and *Daniel Deronda* as well as to George Eliot's early novels.[23] Nor, of course, did Virginia Woolf – whose 1919 centenary essay is generally regarded as having rehabilitated the

later George Eliot, though really it was not isolated – acquaint
herself with her for the first time then. She wrote in 1906 about
her own experimental pieces of fiction to a friend who had already
given her a George Eliot book, 'perhaps I may get something better
as I grow older. George Eliot was near 40 I think, when she wrote
her first novel.'[24] Even the unkind Edmund Gosse seems to have
sensed in the centenary year that younger novelists might still tend
to go to school to George Eliot. Though Gosse could not find a word
to say in favour of *Daniel Deronda* and called *Middlemarch* 'a very
remarkable instance of elaborate mental resources misapplied,' still
he was unsure of his own impatience with George Eliot's 'strenuous
solemnity' and wondered if students yet unborn might not after all
'read her gladly.'[25] He was getting warm, you could say.

Virginia Woolf's celebrated essay takes up the case for George
Eliot's heroines where Henry James had left off, responding to
them not only for their inner development but also for their
struggle in a man's world to find a purpose for which to live,
in learning, in domestic life and in service to the community.
That this struggle ends in melancholy compromises is, according
to Virginia Woolf, a tribute to George Eliot's strong intelligence
and broad humour, since feminine consciousness had been dumb
for so long. Like James, Virginia Woolf stresses the invaluable
example of George Eliot's personal experience where she reached
out triumphantly for 'all that life could offer the free and inquiring
mind', but she takes the debate one step beyond James in relating
the life to the texts. For Virginia Woolf the real-life achievement
of the writer implicitly authenticates the mixed experience of her
characters, especially Dorothea Brooke's. It is Virginia Woolf's
grasp of the irony of this 'exacting and questioning and baffled
presence' in the fictional texts, even in the early novels, which
underlies her frequently quoted sentence, 'It is not that her power
diminishes, for, to our thinking, it is at its highest in the mature
Middlemarch, the magnificent book which with all its imperfections
is one of the few English novels written for grown-up people.'[26] The
comment, hardly judicious in respect of other writers, was probably
necessary in refuting a line of criticism associated with Leslie
Stephen, Virginia Woolf's father, that George Eliot's reflective
powers damaged her gift of charming spontaneity. For Virginia
Woolf, the obtrusive authorial commentary in George Eliot's novels
is not an *explanatory* presence; it is there precisely because it cannot
itself be explained by the experiences of the characters; that is its

point.

Views of George Eliot in the 1920s and 1930s were more conventional, on the whole, than Virginia Woolf's. There was a defence of her style in Oliver Elton's *Survey* of 1920, even of her confessional scenes.[27] In a period when debunking the Victorians was the fashion George Eliot tended to evoke little enthusiasm from those who valued experimental narrative techniques. There was, however, a by no means unfavourable assessment in Lord David Cecil's *Early Victorian Novelists* (1934). After some routine superior jokes about George Eliot's dowdy appearance and her books' solemn titles, which are compared with 'names in a graveyard', Cecil locates her as uneasily standing 'at the gateway between the old novel and the new'. She appears as forward-looking, in fact the first modern novelist; the first, that is, to construct novels around an idea. The idea is the moral code founded on Puritan theology with its supernatural sanction removed. Her intellectual acuteness over psychological essentials enabled her to penetrate to the mainspring of characters' actions. She is particularly good, according to Cecil, at tracing the changes in people and showing 'how temptation triumphs'. He agrees with Virginia Woolf that *Middlemarch* is George Eliot's masterpiece: it not only has 'the biggest subject of any English classical novel' but also reveals the cosmic process 'in a whole society' as Tolstoy does in *War and Peace*. Cecil considers her moral ethic limited, too drably pedagogic, failing to take account of life's chaos, 'its caprices, its passions, its mysticism', but she is still for him a great writer.[28]

F. R. Leavis's articles on George Eliot in 1945 and 1946 in *Scrutiny* were partly motivated by dissent from Cecil's suggestion that his enlightened contemporaries must forget their dislike of her Puritanism, her admiration of truthfulness, chastity, industry and self-restraint and her disapproval of loose living, recklessness, deceit and self-indulgence: 'I differ (apparently) from Lord David Cecil in sharing these beliefs, admirations and disapprovals . . . they seem to me favourable to the production of great literature.'[29] Leavis regards George Eliot as a peculiarly fortifying and wholesome author and recommends her as one of a group of writers whose work can be used to resist the debilitating influence of modern commercial and media culture. This 'great tradition' of English novelists includes Jane Austen, Henry James, Joseph Conrad and D. H. Lawrence. It has to be said that she might not have recognised herself in this company, since she never positively praised Jane Austen, as she did Fielding, Goethe, Scott and Mrs Gaskell. Nevertheless the ensuing controversy ensured George Eliot's position in the critical limelight. Leavis's main point is that George Eliot's intellectual interests go to strengthen and mature her work, not spoil its original charm. If her novels are partly spoiled it is by emotional self-indulgence, or day-dream self-idealisation. This discernment of psychological immaturity leads Leavis into finding Maggie Tulliver at one with the author in their lack of self knowledge; they also share the sense of Stephen Guest's 'irresistibleness'. Leavis seems determined to find no irony there. He can be very hard-hitting: 'Few will want to read *Romola* a second time.' But he praises the Transome sections of *Felix Holt* where George Eliot achieves 'dramatic constatation, poignant and utterly convincing',[30] asserting human dignity without moralising. The Casaubon, Lydgate and Bulstrode sections of *Middlemarch* are similarly approved, with skilfully chosen illustrations, but Dorothea and Ladislaw are regarded as re-runs of Maggie and Stephen, products of George Eliot's own 'soul-hunger'. On the Jewish part of *Daniel Deronda* Leavis writes with studied acerbity, likening the promotion of the higher life of Deronda's hereditary duty to 'the exalting effects of alcohol'. There is a sense in which the Puritan in George Eliot is not Puritan enough for Leavis; he finds the 'Shakespearean sprightliness of Hans Meyrick's letter' (*Daniel Deronda*, Ch. 52) to be 'utterly routing'. But the Gwendolen episodes show quickness, delicacy and precision; they have 'a complexity and completeness, the fulness of vision and response' that is too inclusive to be satiric; George Eliot renders the analysis 'with extraordinary vividness and economy, in the concrete.' So eloquent is Leavis's closing paean to George Eliot's achievement (her moral sensibility expresses itself 'with perfect sureness, in judgments that involve confident positive standards and yet affect us as simply the reports of luminous intelligence')[31] that criticism for a time seemed stunned.

Leavis's skill in highlighting powerful, detailed effects tended to make his notion of constatation, concreteness and completeness very persuasive as though the reader were coming across irrefutable facts practically demonstrated. Eventually critics questioned his negative judgments of George Eliot, finding more irony and variety of perspective in her 'soul-hungry' characters than he will allow. The positive, encouraging component in George Eliot's sympathy with energetic characters like Deronda also came to be appreciated more. Some of Leavis's points were too dependent on a simple biographical view and on too sharp a distinction between the writer's desires and the real world. More attention had to be paid to examining George Eliot's techniques.

Of the many New Critical studies which followed Leavis's the fullest is Barbara Hardy's *The Novels of George Eliot* (1959). Here the interest is in form, though not so much in plot structure or thematic contrasts as in 'the form of particularity,' which is explained in a later work as a complex and a mobile pattern with 'omissions made conspicuous' by 'suggestive reticence'.[32] Barbara Hardy's facility in exploring the minutiae of George Eliot's text is unrivalled. She analyses the use of coincidence as a formal device and of scene as image; she finds that images of water, animals, plants and objects, and literary allusions, are employed ironically or pathetically not only locally, but also more broadly, to express George Eliot's humanist views and personal experiences. The 'intense particularization for the moment' issues in 'dramatic display and professional description'; the novels show all human variables, successes as well as failures, 'the mixed cases, even the unacted possible lives that haunt all our commitments'.[33] The noting of these alternative lives for the characters in the 'Possibilities' section (Ch. 7) is Barbara Hardy's subtlest point. It was picked up by W. J. Harvey in his *Character and the Novel* (1965), where he argues that speculation that Lydgate could have turned into somebody rather like Farebrother is evidence of George Eliot's accurate imitation of the actual world of conditional freedom where people have unrealised potential.[34] Harvey's earlier *The Art of George Eliot* (1961) is largely a defence of George Eliot's use of the omniscient narrator against the detractions of Henry James's followers, who preferred the narrator to be close to one or more of the characters. Harvey approves George Eliot's 'steadiness of ironic contemplation' as well as her 'precise and varied use of narrative chronology', which contributes to the complexity of her 'control of historical perspective'.[35] It should be added, of course, that the George Eliot criticism of Barbara Hardy and W. J. Harvey is by no means wholly adulatory; in 1967 the former edited a collection of new essays on *Middlemarch* in one of which the latter compared contemporary (1960s) disappointment with George Eliot's limited ability to deal with sexual passion with Victorian reviewers' dissatisfaction with her moral bias in favour of a commonplace unworthy character like Ladislaw. Also Barbara Hardy admitted that, popular though its claim to be the greatest English novel was, *Middlemarch*

was still a work 'whose stature and status have had to stand up to a
fair amount of battering by controversy and attack'.[36]

The most influential of these attacks were beginning to come
from the Left. George Eliot's suspicion of full-scale social theory as
too abstract and reductive to provide a guide for action inevitably
was deplored by Marxists. At first they tended merely to disagree
with her on the level of political debate. For instance, in 1951
Arnold Kettle supposed that the 'total impact' of *Middlemarch*
was weakened by George Eliot's 'undialectical philosophy'; he
expressed some impatience that, since her view of society was
static and her outlook 'mechanistic and not revolutionary', no
one in the novel 'can fight Middlemarch or change it'.[37] In fact
her outlook was non-committal, not mechanistic, and she considered revolutionary fighting inadvisable and counter-productive.
Raymond Williams modifies the tone, but his political opposition is also very marked. Considering *Felix Holt* in 1958 as an
'industrial novel', Williams criticises the author for patience and
caution which are very easily converted into acquiescing in a vicious
society; it is obvious to him that George Eliot could not believe
that 'the common people were something other than a mob and
had instincts and habits something above drunkenness, gullibility
and ignorance'; hence her basic pattern was to dramatise 'the fear
of being involved in violence'.[38] Mob violence persists, however,
as a minority problem, and George Eliot's fear is defensible. In
the later *Country and the City* (1973) Williams is less interested
in George Eliot's putative class bias than in the form and tone
of her novels, which are said to reproduce in their disunity the
flawed social structures and disturbances of feeling in her subject
matter. For example, he finds a conflict between George Eliot's
placing value in the past 'as a general retrospective condition'
and placing value in the present only as 'the individual moral
action'. All that is left is 'a set of personal relationships' in a
history that has 'for all valuing purposes' ended.[39] Williams's distinction can hardly apply to Ladislaw; scepticism with regard to
a particular political programme may co-exist with activism and
commitment to reform. The search for contradiction is, however, developed and modified in Terry Eagleton's *Criticism and
Ideology* (1976), where George Eliot's forms are held to repress
and defuse the 'potentially tragic collision'[40] between corporate
and individualist ideologies, between regard for immutable social
laws and regard for romantic individuals' desire for self-fulfilment.

Eagleton's argument that George Eliot's 'naturalising, moralising and mystifying devices', are her way out of her failure to reconcile irreconcilable historical conflicts is based on the assumption that social formations are determined by the class war; 'turbulent issues are marginalised'. However varied in subtlety they may be, recent Marxist and Marxist-influenced New Historicist critiques forward a language of metaphoric bellicosity, coded as militancy, action, disturbance, struggle, collision, incompatibility, division, deformation, problem and so on, which deliberately excludes irenic notions like compromise, reconciliation and fairness and achieves little or no purchase on George Eliot's dense texts with their amused concern for existing and developing social forms. George Eliot presents the reader with characters living in what are immediate social structures, in what Burke calls the subdivision 'or little platoon we belong to in society',[41] the parish, the estate, the profession, the municipality, the market, and she respects the net of free choice, agreement seeking and mutual adjustments on which they rely in spite of the pressures which the individual experiences from prejudice, poverty, debt, vice and crime; she prefers these social forms to deceptive abstractions like collective correctness, political justice and socialist equality, let alone proletarian victory. Politically, George Eliot is no statist; she anticipates post-socialist ideas of a spontaneous order of tolerant conventions, a community formed by free association where people are entitled to their property and taxes are limited, ideas which Marxist critics show few or no signs of grasping.

Recent structuralist criticism has also engaged with George Eliot, partly because of her own curiosity as to the instability of meanings, signs and metaphors, but also because of her high reputation for psychological and sociological realism, a concept which has come under adverse, though also rather insecure, scrutiny. Structuralist belief in language as a self-enclosed system which does not transparently grant access to an external 'reality' so that languages and the various discourses which compose them may rather be said to speak us than we them, is highly controversial, but might be thought to have some affinity with the determinist ideas which interested George Eliot in her own time. The anti-scientific element in structuralism is alien to George Eliot, however; she accepted that language shifted with science, not that science shifted with language. For some structuralist critics George Eliot has therefore been a large target.

Did George Eliot claim to be a pure realist? Did she have a simple representationalist motive which can be easily deconstructed? In fact George Eliot was more influenced by Romantic critical theory of the reciprocal influence of subject and object on each other than by neo-classical mimesis. In her comparison of her approach in *Adam Bede* with that of the Dutch realist painters she noted that the effort 'to give a faithful account of men and things as they have mirrored themselves in my mind' is subject to qualification from the defects of the mirror; 'the outlines will sometimes be disturbed, the reflection faint or confused' (Ch. 17). George Eliot's aspiration to truthfulness is principally a rejection of one-dimensional idealised characters and exclusively high-life settings in favour of the ordinary and the in-between. Yet it *can* be construed as a privileging of the narrator's insight. So Colin MacCabe argues that George Eliot's narrator creates a metalanguage which 'refuses to acknowledge its own status as writing' and functions simply as a window on 'reality'. He notes her device of quoting her characters, not only in dialogue. In separating her narration from other types of speech and enclosing them in inverted commas, George Eliot creates 'a specific hierarchy of discourses' in which the reader is placed 'in a position of dominance with regard to the stories and characters'. This relationship between discourses is, according to MacCabe, the defining feature of the classic realist text. There are, however, within George Eliot's novels always 'images which counter the flat and universal showing forth of the real'.[42] MacCabe's point is weakened by his failure to consider the uncertainty factor introduced into narration by the use of *Erlebte Rede*, where words, phrases and syntax appropriate to the character are intermingled with words, phrases and syntax appropriate to the narrator, and not appropriate to the character, in an ambiguous way. A critique of MacCabe is to be found in David Lodge's *After Bahktin* (1990), in which George Eliot's deployment of this free, indirect style is held to complicate the relation between two types of narration: mimesis, confined here to meaning narrating by imitating another person's speech; and diegesis, narrating in one's own voice, *neither* of which is a metalanguage.[43] This debate is largely about the effect of George Eliot's novelistic technique.

A more fundamental defence of George Eliot's flexible intelligence as a novelist can be derived from the deconstructionist criticism of J. Hillis Miller, who points out that a novel like *Middlemarch* itself deconstructs naive notions about history, especially abstractions like unity, progress and causality:

> The concepts of origin, end, and continuity are replaced by the categories of repetition, of difference, of discontinuity, of openness, and of the free and contradictory struggle of individual human energies, each seen as a centre of interpretation, which means misinterpretation, of the whole.[44]

Seen in this way, George Eliot's characters' lives fit into no overall pattern (they have 'no unitary meaning'), though they have moral choice in a world of entanglements. The narrator too can be said to deconstruct the idea of omniscience, if only by acknowledging that metaphors cut across pretensions to total coherence or comprehensiveness of understanding. Miller's deconstructionism can be perceived as a modern, more negative version of George Eliot's own scepticism; it demonstrates how modern she was, if only through her intelligent modesty. Her interest in chance and unpredictability, as with Ladislaw, for instance, points forward to modern chaos theory. She was well aware of the random elements involved in both personal and historically important decisions. She illustrates concepts like moral inertia and short-term reversibility quite familiarly: the riot scene in *Felix Holt*, for example, has more to do with crisis management than class conflict. Recognition of George Eliot's acuteness on such matters reminds us how difficult it is to categorise her as merely a middle-class Victorian.

It also puts into perspective the impatience felt by some feminist critics who regard her as not having endorsed the campaign for women's rights with the unambiguous certitude which they feel it deserves. In 'Why Feminist Critics are angry with George Eliot' Zelda Austen wrote in 1975, 'The feminist critic calls for a literature that will show women active rather than docile, aggressive and ambitious rather than retiring and submissive.'[45] Anger was to George Eliot a very treacherous emotion, and she no doubt would have reasoned that her women-characters, particularly at the end of the stories, fail to transcend the conventions imposed upon them because it was so rare to do. She had done so herself, but it was a story, mainly, of intense study, which she did not want to make central to her fictions. Nevertheless there are questioning and challenging elements in her novels, especially in the humour, which make any idea of male superiority seem historically transient. Theoretical feminists are able to approve these thrusts and interpret George Eliot's explorations of women's psychological tensions as tending to subvert a patriarchal system and male-dominated language within which the writer still works. Other women critics have stressed George Eliot's close connections with the women's movement. Gillian Beer in her *George Eliot* (1986) concentrates on the women writers whom she read and brings out her sensitivity to women's needs, making the additional necessary point that her 'presence at the centre of literary culture in the past hundred years is of immense worth to other women'.[46] Her novels are, of course, of equal worth to men's, for whose problems they show a constructive concern – she seems to have regarded gender differences as complementary and believed that male and female roles could be adjusted gradually overall to the mutual benefit of both sexes. She was convinced that men would thus be the equal beneficiaries of female emancipation, as her own case indubitably proved, and as indeed was beginning then to be belatedly acknowledged.

Virtually unceasing as the discussion of her work has been since her own day, with no wildly inconstant proportion of unfavourable comment to favourable at any one time, and only very exceptional contestation of her prominence, it cannot be said that George Eliot has yet met her match in the critical world. In the early years dislike of her scientific knowledge weakened her critics. Since then there has been hostility to her authorial commentary, to her idealistic ardour, to her sexual decorum, to her political scepticism, to her suspicion of abstraction, and to her fair-mindedness with regard to men. On the other hand her immense assimilation of past culture, her combination of radicalism with conservatism, her recognition of the role of the market, her concern for national stability and international harmony and the sheer variety of her fictional scenes and situations continue to commend her to an enthusiastic readership. George Eliot is not self-evidently, however, a popular author. She appeals to the student in all of us. Intensely bookish herself, she elicits in the reader a sense of his or her contextual inadequacy. Her style, where it is not immediately lucid, requires the reader to remember previous learning or to catch up with background reading, even to the extent of learning new languages and investigating new disciplines. Her novels control, then, a kind of curriculum, resist cultural disposability and defy the death of literature by their own momentum. One captive audience they will surely always have: other writers. Philip Larkin, for example, wrote in 1949 that *his* ideal writer would be a 'mixture' of D. H. Lawrence, Thomas Hardy and George Eliot.[47] And so it goes on, with other peers. In a *Times* straw poll of authors published on 20 February 1992, among those chosen as essential books for to-day's educated reader, alongside Homer, Dante, Shakespeare, Milton, Jane Austen, Dickens and Tolstoy (seven, that is, of her predecessors and contemporaries) appeared George Eliot.[48]

Notes

1 George Eliot's Life

1. In G. S. Haight's *George Eliot; a Biography* (Oxford: Clarendon Press, 1968), p. 7, evidence for George Eliot's early devotion to Scott is found in the epigraph of Chapter 57 of *Middlemarch*: Scott was still 'living far away' while young Mary Anne Evans's reading of *Waverley* was interrupted. Scott's balanced and tolerant view of historical change was a permanent influence on George Eliot's thinking; see V. A. Dodd, *George Eliot: An Intellectual Life* (New York: St. Martin's Press, 1990), pp. 72–74.
2. Included in *Biography* as 'Edward Neville' in Appendix I, pp. 554–60.
3. *The George Eliot Letters*, ed. G. S. Haight (New Haven, Conn: Yale University Press), IX vols., vols. I–VII, 1954–1955, vols. VIII–XI, 1978; vol. I, p. 23. Letter of George Eliot to Maria Lewis, 16 March 1839.
4. *Letters*, vol. I, p. 206. Letter of Mrs C. Bray to Sara S. Hennell, 14 February 1846. See D. F. Strauss, *The Life of Jesus Critically Examined*, ed. P. C. Hodgson (London: SCM Press, 1972), pp. xlviii–xlix.
5. J. W. Cross, *George Eliot's Life as Related in her Letters and Journals* (Edinburgh and London: Blackwood, 1885), 3 vols; new edn (revised with additions and deletions), 1 vol., (1887), pp. 55–58.
6. I. Taylor, *George Eliot: Woman of Contradictions* (London: Weidenfeld and Nicolson, 1989), p. 60.
7. *Letters*, vol. I, p.284. Letters to Charles Bray, May 1849, and to Charles and Cara Bray, 30 May 1849.
8. *Ibid.*, vol. II, p. 49. Letter to John Chapman, 24–25 July 1852.
9. *Ibid.*, vol. VIII, p. 57. Letter to Herbert Spencer, 16 July 1852.
10. See R. F. Anderson, 'A note on George Eliot's "Escapade" to Germany with George Henry Lewes', *The George Eliot–George Henry Lewes Newsletter* (September 1991), nos. 18–19, pp. 66–69.
11. G. H. Lewes, *The Life and Works of Goethe* (London: D. Nutt, 1855), vol. II, p. 340 (Part VI, chapter vii).
12 *Biography*, pp. 160–61.
13. Information given to Edith Simcox by Cara Bray in June 1885; see *Biography*, p. 179.
14. 'The Natural History of German Life', *Westminster Review*, vol. LXVI, p. 55 (July 1856).
15. *Letters*, vol. II, p. 407. George Eliot's journal, 6 December 1857.

16. *Ibid.*, p. 277. Letter of G. H. Lewes to John Blackwood, 22 November 1856.

17. *Ibid*, p. 292. Letter of George Eliot to William Blackwood, 4 February 1857.

18. Information supplied to Ina Taylor by A. A. Phillips; see her *George Eliot*, pp. 158 and 240.

19. *Letters*, vol. II, p. 362. Letter of George Eliot to John Blackwood, 12 July 1857.

20. See W. Gareth Jones, 'George Eliot's *Adam Bede* and Tolstoy's Conception of *Anna Karenina*', *Modern Language Review*, vol. LX, pp. 473–81 (July 1966), p. 473. In 1898 in *What is Art?* Tolstoy placed *Adam Bede* alongside works by Dickens, Mrs H. B. Stowe and Dostoevsky as a modern example of religious art, an art which transmits positive love of God and neighbours and also transmits negative indignation and horror at the violation of love. See *Biography*, p. 279, n. 4, and *Critics on George Eliot*, ed. W. Baker (London: Allen and Unwin, 1973), p. 11.

21. *Letters*, vol. III, p. 98. Letter of S. S. Hennell to George Eliot, 26 June 1859.

22. See *Biography*, pp. 396–97.

23. *Letters*, vol. IV, p. 287. Letter of F. Harrison to George Eliot, 18 July 1866.

24. *Ibid.*, p. 300. Letter of George Eliot to F. Harrison, 15 August 1866.

25. *Ibid.*, p. 496. Letter of George Eliot to Mrs R. Congreve, 16 December 1868. W. M. Simon, however, believes that the Comtism of the poem, found in no more than a half-dozen brief passages, is overshadowed by its nationalism; see his *European Positivism in the Nineteenth Century* (Ithaca, NY: Cornell University Press, 1963), P. 210, n. 32. The suggestion that *Middlemarch* shows the influence of Harrison's Comtist plot-sketch is discussed by A. S. Byatt in her introduction to *George Eliot: Selected Essays, Poems and Other Writings* (Harmondsworth: Penguin, 1990), p. xxxii. The moral and artistic triumphs of *Middlemarch* are said to be 'ultimately more Feuerbachian than Comtean', however.

26. *Biography*, pp. 405–6.

27. *Henry James Letters* (ed. L. Edel), vol. I, 1843–1875 (London: Macmillan, 1974), pp. 116–17. Letter of Henry James to Henry James senior, 10 May 1869.

28. *Letters*, vol. V, p. 175. Letter of George Eliot to Alexander Main, 9 August 1871.

29. *Ibid.*, p. 278. Letter of G. H. Lewes, 19 June 1872.

30. *Ibid.*, p.352. Letter of G. H. Lewes to Mrs Anna Cross, 29 December 1872.

31. *Biography*, p. 502. G. S. Haight reports, however, from Lady Gray (Sophia Williams) the question in the mind of one young lady present at that party; why 'genius was so terribly homely'?

32. I. Taylor, *George Eliot*, p. 217.

33. *Letters*, vol. VII, p.212. Letter of George Eliot to J. W. Cross, 16 October 1879.

34. *Biography*, p. 544, n. 3. The authority is Lord Acton.
35. The very little may include work on an unwritten novel set in the Napoleonic wars, for which there are two notebooks extant, one at Princeton University Library, the other in the Hugh Walpole collection at the King's School, Canterbury. Four pages in George Eliot's hand from the latter were published with an introduction and annotations by William Baker as 'A new George Eliot manuscript' in *George Eliot: Centenary Essays and an Unpublished Fragment*, ed. A. Smith (London: Vision Press, 1980), pp. 9–20. A period of either 1877–1878 or 1879–1880 has been assigned to this fragment of a novel, which has a Midland sitting and details of two land-owning families by the name of Forrest and Pollexfen, allusions to the Isle of Man, Ireland and Nova Scotia, a reference to the telephone and a gentle nudge against fox-hunting; 'as many foxes were allowed to remain and enjoy their known pleasure in being hunted . . . handsomely provided with covers', p. 11.
36. J. W. Cross, *George Eliot's Life* (1885), vol. III, p. 439. See also *Letters*, vol. VII, p. 351. Letter of J. W. Cross to Elma Stuart, 23 December 1880.

2 Country Life: *Adam Bede*

1. *Letters*, vol. III, p. 176. Letter to Sara Hennell, 7 October 1859.
2. *Ibid.*, vol. II, p. 502. George Eliot's Journal, 30 November 1858.
3. *Ibid.*, vol. II, p. 387. Letter to John Blackwood, 17 October 1857.
4. J. W. Cross, *George Eliot's Life as Related in her Letters and Journals* (Edinburgh and London: Blackwood, 1885), vol. I, p. 5.
5. W. J. Harvey in *The Art of George Eliot* (London: Chatto and Windus, 1961), p. 77, regards Dinah as '*too* articulate' with her Methodist idiom; 'once she opens her mouth she fails'. But this criticism is based on too simple a realism, for her speech is not designed to succeed as such.
6. See S. Dentith, *George Eliot* (Brighton: Harvester, 1986), p. 20, on the 'Feuerbachian saints' in George Eliot's novels, who 'inspire to submission rather than revolt'.
7. J. Goode is particularly forceful on George Eliot's achievement in precisely 'delimiting Dinah's religious emotion in the superbly structured sermon'. He argues that there is 'no attempt to sentimentalize Methodism's ruthless exploitation of social injustice'. See his '*Adam Bede*', in *Critical Essays on George Eliot*, ed. B. Hardy (London: Routledge & Kegan Paul, 1970), pp. 38–39.
8. W. Myers, however, in *The Teaching of George Eliot* (Leicester: Leicester University Press, 1984), pp. 148–49, accepting Lacan's point that love of neighbour will be contaminated by narcissism and violence, suggests that in Dinah's intervention with Hetty in Ch. 15 of *Adam Bede* George Eliot 'maladroitly' illustrates the connection between the sympathetic and aggressive instincts.

9. Myers, *ibid.*, p. 138, goes too far in claiming that the climactic meeting of Adam and Dinah on the hill is emptied of erotic content. Given Victorian reticence on sex, George Eliot does well to have Adam 'with the fine instinct of a lover' first speak to Dinah while her head is turned away (Ch. 54).

10. G. Beer, in *George Eliot* (Brighton: Harvester, 1986), pp. 72–73, criticises the narrative of the Epilogue for feeding the fact that Dinah is now forbidden by the Methodist Church to preach 'too gratefully into the stabilising and making private' of the poised close. Noting that Dinah 'no longer travels', G. Beer sees her as finally 'contained within the family, back in the conventional ordering'. Nevertheless, the mention of *Arthur*'s conviction of Dinah's exceptionality, suggests that she is not to be excluded from a wider role.

11. *London Quarterly Review*, vol. XVI, p. 307 (July 1861); 'we are merely left to infer some excusing weakness in the fall'. See D. Carroll (ed.), *George Eliot: The Critical Heritage* (London: Routledge & Kegan Paul, 1971), p. 108.

12. *Letters*, vol. III, p. 115. Letter of 10 July 1859.

13. George Eliot's own considerable experience of butter-making led, as she believed, to one of her hands being specially large. G. S. Haight, *George Eliot: A Biography* (Oxford: Clarendon Press, 1969), p. 28.

14. George Eliot and G. H. Lewes practised birth-control themselves, or so G. S. Haight deduced in his *Biography*, p. 205. Haight had a description of a destroyed letter to go on.

15. E. D. Ermarth, in *George Eliot* (Boston, Mass.: Twayne, 1985), p. 75, finds Hetty's hardness 'not entirely surprising in a community based on hierarchical social bonds rather than a sense of common ground'.

16. U. C. Knoepflmacher, in *George Eliot's Early Novels* (Berkeley, Calif.: University of California Press, 1968), pp. 2–3, has *Adam Bede* 'located in the tranquil, mythical world of Hayslope' and finds Loamshire 'semi-mythical and self-contained', p. 163.

17. J. Goode, in '*Adam Bede*', *loc. cit.*, p. 22, points out that the early parts of *Adam Bede* 'show a persistent tendency to resolve the narrative into pictures. We begin with the static picture of the workshop, and when the men begin to talk it is as though a painting were to begin to move'.

18. Jane Welsh Carlyle shrewdly linked the novel's humanity with its interest in dogs; 'it is a beautiful most *human* Book! Every *Dog* in it, not to say every man and woman and child in it, is brought home to one's "business and bosom", an individual fellow-creature!' *Letters*, vol. III. p. 18. Letter of 20 February 1859.

19. S. Shuttleworth, in *George Eliot and Nineteenth-Century Science* (Cambridge: Cambridge University Press, 1984), p. 37, links Adam's love of mathematics with Herbert Spencer's view of society as the 'aggregate of component parts' (mathesis) and regards Adam's progress as sustaining 'the unchanging structure of Hayslope society', p. 36. She believes George Eliot uses an a-historic pastoral mode in *Adam Bede*, her classificatory or static theory of order excluding 'the dimension of change or progress', p. 28.

20. C. Palliser's essay, '*Adam Bede* and "The Story of the Past"', in *George Eliot: Centenary Essays and an Unpublished Fragment*, ed. A. Smith (London: Vision Press, 1980), is especially perceptive in tracing the way in which our 'initially satisfied' literary expectations of a rosy picture of Hayslope life are altered by the enlarged perspective, p. 59. Palliser considers that the balancing of advantages and disadvantages suggests both objectivity and ambivalence. He interestingly analyses the 'proleptic nostalgia' involved in the presentation of the characters' false hopes, pp. 62–63.

21. I. Gregor's point that Hayslope is a pastoral world of a different order from the world of moral enquiry into which Hetty has strayed is contradicted by many details in the novel. See I. Gregor and B. Nicholas, *The Moral and the Story* (London: Faber, 1962), p. 30; 'the gap between the world of description and the world of analysis is never bridged'. For a strong presentation of the case that 'George Eliot's comprehension of life cannot allow for the contingent, the incongruous, the unframed, the indefinitely questioned and receding aspects of experiences', see J. Bayley's 'The Pastoral of Intellect', in *Critical Essays on George Eliot*, ed. B. Hardy (London: Routledge & Kegan Paul, 1970), p. 201.

22. Compare S. Dentith, *op. cit.*, p. 49. 'Adam Bede signifies both a class of self-improving and self-confident artisans and the better and more progressive elements of humanity in general.' Dentith's subsequent hostile point that George Eliot obscures or hides the fact that 'class is a material distinction determining different positions and rewards in the labour process' seems to me to evade consideration of the subjectivity of 'class' as a concept and of the real fluidity and discontinuity of the barriers between 'classes', points which George Eliot herself did not evade.

23. A. Welsh, in *George Eliot and Blackmail* (Cambridge, Mass.: Harvard University Press, 1985), pp. 136–37, in suggesting that gossip and scandal indicate the cohesiveness and closeness of small communities like Hayslope, does not touch on the usefulness of outspokenness and free discussion there. It seems likely that George Stephenson the engineer served as 'a model for the temperament, intelligence, and affections of Adam Bede'; so suggests J. Wiesenfarth in his edition of *George Eliot: A Writer's Notebook 1854–1879 and Uncollected Writings* (Charlottesville, Va.: University of Virginia Press, 1981), p. xxi. See especially p. 20.

24. Contrast W. J. Harvey, *op. cit.*, p. 167, who remarks severely that Arthur's 'social view is not supported by any real sense of social responsibility. Instead we have a moral vacuum which is masked but not filled by a graceful observance of traditional forms and by lavish promises to the future.'

25. A. Welsh (*op. cit.*, pp. 122–23) points out that George Eliot was herself subject as an intellectual journalist and novelist to the forces of the market and publishing trade, a trader 'in the marketplace of ideas', and had once expressed relief that Dr Cumming's evangelical sermons had been fixed in 'black and white' too, where they were

open to Press criticism, expressed with 'thorough freedom'; 'Evangelical Teaching: Dr. Cumming', *Westminster Review*, vol. LXIV, p. 438 (October 1855).

26. W. J. Harvey's defence of George Eliot's use of the omniscient-author convention against the neo-Jamesians is still largely effective (see his *op. cit.*, pp. 64–89). A recent critic supports the defence, using more sophisticated vocabulary: G. Beer (*op. cit.*, pp. 28–29) notes that the 'observations within the writing are freed from circumscription, endowed with large as well as enigmatic meaning'; we are given intelligence 'through passionate inhabiting of diversity . . . by a method which challenges essentialism by *inclusion*.'

27. *The Times* review of *Adam Bede*, 12 April 1859, p. 5.

28. C. Palliser, *loc. cit.*, p. 76, stresses George Eliot's 'ironic alternation between reassuring and disconcerting the reader.'

3   A Story of Nature: *The Mill on the Floss*

1. *Letters*, vol. III, p. 133. Letter to John Blackwood, 17 August 1859.

2. The earliest reference to *The Mill on the Floss* comes in George Eliot's journal for 12 January 1859, when she 'looked in the annual register for cases of inundation', *Letters*, vol. III, p. 33.

3. G. H. Lewes reported that the novelist 'is getting her eyes redder and swollener every morning as she lives through her tragic story. But there is such a strain of poetry to relieve the tragedy that the more she cries, and the readers cry, the better say I', *Letters*, vol. III, p. 269. Lewes's letter to John Blackwood, 5 March 1860.

4. *Letters*, vol. III, p. 285. Letter to John Blackwood, 3 April 1860.

5. *Letters* vol. V, p. 52. Letter to Mrs Mark Pattison, 10 August 1869.

6. J. Fiske, *Life and Letters of Edward Livingston Youmans* (London: Chapman and Hall, 1894), p. 127.

7. U. C. Knoepflmacher, *op. cit.*, p. 192.

8. G. Beer, *op. cit.*, pp. 98–99, suggests that the drowning 'sloughs off compromise': Maggie's 'swollen trouble, the outrage' are 'naturalised as flood', her anger 'internalised' as self-doubt and inadequacy. The work is said to be 'combative towards its heroine'.

9. I. Adam, in 'The ambivalence of *The Mill on the Floss*', says that the Wordsworthian doctrine is put here to a 'painful test'; *George Eliot: A Centenary Tribute*, ed. G. S. Haight and R. T. Van Arsdel (London: Macmillan, 1982), p. 133. *cf.* 'Tintern Abbey', pp. 122–23.

10. Three times George Eliot regretted that she had permitted herself an 'epic breadth' in the early part of the story at the expense of a fuller development of the later part (see *Letters*, vol. III, pp. 317, 362 and 374. Letters to John Blackwood, 9 July 1860, on *Epische Breite*, and to F. D'Albert-Durade, 6 December 1860 and 29 January 1861, on 'epic tediousness' and 'love of the childhood scenes' which made her 'linger over them'). For arguments vindicating the novel's design, see my 'Education in *The Mill on the Floss*', *A Review of English*

Literature, vol. VII (July 1966), pp. 52–61, and R. T. Jones, *George Eliot* (Cambridge: Cambridge University Press, 1970), pp. 21–25.

11. *Letters,* vol. III, p. 374. Letter to F. D'Alberte-Durade, 29 January, 1861.

12. R. Ebbatson in *George Eliot: The Mill on the Floss* (Harmondsworth: Penguin, 1985), pp. 12–13, explains that 'warping' was a process undertaken in the Trent lowlands to produce rich agricultural soil; in refusing a contract Mr Tulliver showed himself opposed to the entrepreneurship values later to be endorsed by Tom in his dealings with Bob Jakin.

13. S. Dentith, *op. cit.,* p. 45, writes of Mrs Tulliver's and Aunt Pullet's sense of the sacred; 'Their level of religious culture is primitive – indeed it is strictly fetishistic in the Comtist sense'.

14. *The Times* review of *The Mill on the Floss,* 19 May 1860, p. 10. George Eliot was aghast at finding the Dodsons 'ticketed with such very ugly adjectives'; see *Letters,* vol. III, p.299. Letter to William Blackwood, 27 May 1860.

15. G. Beer, *op. cit.,* p. 93, says that *The Mill on the Floss* 'excels at taut humour which catches the sound of women gossiping, pinched into forms of their narrow society. The aunts with cheerful gloom give voice to the domestic powers and repression of St Oggs'.

16. R. Ebbatson, *op. cit.,* p. 41.

17. J. Bennett, *George Eliot* (Cambridge: Cambridge University Press, 1948), p. 128.

18. F. R. Leavis's hard-hitting argument that the flooded river is only 'the dreamed-of perfect accident that gives us the opportunity for the dreamed-of heroic act – the act that shall vindicate us against a harshly misjudging world, bring emotional fulfilment and (in others) changes of heart, and provide a gloriously tragic curtain' makes too much of supposed perfection and glory in an episode full of human error and imbalance. See *The Great Tradition* (London: Chatto and Windus, 1948), pp. 45–46.

19. The attempt by G. S. Haight in his appendix A to the Clarendon Edition of *The Mill on the Floss* (Oxford: Clarendon Press, 1980), p. 467, to prove that the catastrophe reveals George Eliot's 'ignorance of hydraulics' is highly dubious. Haight believed that the boat and the large objects were drifting 'in the same current' and could not have collided, but it is surely clear that in floods different currents can meet. The Ripple is said to be 'strangely altered', producing a current which Maggie 'passed', on her way to fetch Tom, so something similar *could* happen on the way back (VII, 5).

20. See Miriam H. Berlin, 'George Eliot and the Russians' in *George Eliot A Centenary Tribute,* eds, G. S. Haight and R. T. Van Arsdel (London: Macmillan, 1982), pp. 90–106, p. 103 and n. 25 The conversation, with Sophia Kovalevskaia, a mathematics professor, is reported as having taken place in 1880, two weeks before George Eliot's death, though it is not listed in George Eliot's diary.

21. Barbara Hardy, arguing that the flood answers Maggie's prayer, attacks the ending of *The Mill on the Floss* as unauthentic. The

ending contrasts, she suggests, with the novel's earlier point that
renunciation does not make you feel 'noble and striking and secure';
instead the novel 'ends with a combination of several strong fanta-
sies', including the fantasy of reconciliation. See her 'The Mill on
the Floss', in *Collected Essays on George Eliot*, ed. B. Hardy (London:
Routledge & Kegan Paul, 1970), p. 50. I question, however, if
most readers feel that Maggie's 'long deep sob of that mysterious
wondrous happiness that is one with pain' (VII,5) is conclusively
problem-solving and productive of a sense of security, especially in
view of the fatal decision to row straight to Lucy's house.

4 George Eliot's Shorter Fiction, including *Silas Marner*

1. *The Art of the Novel: Critical Prefaces by Henry James*, intro. R. P.
   Blackmur (New York: Scribners, 1934), p. 233. James states that,
   with the anecdote, his effort was to follow a 'little situation' from
   'its outer edge in, rather than from its centre outward'. See also
   pp. xxviii–xxix, 181 and 221.
2. *Letters*, vol. II, p. 407. George Eliot's Journal, 6 December 1857.
3. Of Trollope's series of Barchester novels, which present more consistent scenes of clerical life than do George Eliot's tales, only *The
   Warden* (1855) precedes *Scenes of Clerical Life*.
4. U. C. Knoepflmacher, in *George Eliot's Early Novels: The Limits of Realism*
   (Berkeley and Los Angeles, Calif.: University of California Press,
   1968), p. 56, argues that George Eliot idealises Milly Barton exces-
   sively as an 'angelic mate', dropping irony and indirection in favour
   of hortatory sentimentality. T. A. Noble, whom Knoepflmacher aims
   to refute, is surely nearer the mark in defending George Eliot's sure
   'sense of reality' in this tale's scenes of pathos (see his *George Eliot's
   Scenes of Clerical Life*, New Haven, Conn.: Yale University Press, 1965,
   pp. 113–15).
5. George Eliot, *Scenes of Clerical Life*, ed. T. A. Noble (Oxford: Clarendon
   Press, 1985), p. 9, n. 8.
6. Dianne F. Sadoff, *Monsters of Affection: Dickens, Eliot, and Brontë on
   Fatherhood* (Baltimore and London: Johns Hopkins University Press,
   1982), pp. 66–67. The daughter, encouraged by the dying mother
   to replace her, 'reaps the structural rewards of familial desire' as
   substitute wife and housekeeper. Hence George Eliot's first story
   'obscures its sexual meaning'. See also S. Marcus, 'Literature and
   Social Theory: Starting in with George Eliot', in *Representations:
   Essays on Literature and Society* (New York: Random House, 1975),
   pp. 183–213.
7. T. A. Noble's view (*op. cit.*, p. 134) that in this tale the 'foreign
   background seems thrown in simply for glamour and romance'
   excludes both the humour and the tension which George Eliot
   derives from the situation of the aristocratic English family's adoption
   of an alien child, a theme which still exercised her as late as *Daniel
   Deronda* (1876).

8. 'To a Mouse, On turning her up in her Nest, with the Plough, November, 1785', ll. 7–12.

> I'm truly sorry Man's dominion
> Has broken Nature's social union,
> An' justifies that ill opinion
>   Which makes thee startle,
> At me, thy poor, earth-born companion,
>   An' *fellow-mortal!*

   R. Burns, *Poems, Chiefly in the Scottish Dialect* (Kilmarnock: John Wilson, 1786), pp. 138–39.
9. George Eliot assured her publisher that everything in 'Janet's Repentance' was 'softened from the fact. . . . The real town was more vicious than my Milby; the real Dempster was far more disgusting than mine', *Letters*, vol. II, p. 347. Letter to John Blackwood, 11 June 1857.
10. The manuscript of 'Janet's Repentance' contains several cancelled and dropped passages, which coarsen the behaviour of the people of Milby in the 1820s and 1830s; e.g. 'Drunkenness was indulged in with great candour' (*ed. cit.*, p. 204). The mitigating effect of the alterations also serves to bring the present and the past closer together in the narrator's implied view.
11. G. H. Lewes (*Letters*, vol. II, p. 378. Lewes's letter to John Blackwood, 23 August 1857) accepted that the story of Tryan's past misdemeanour was a 'hacknied episode'; yet it does explain Tryan's ability to make what T. A. Noble calls the 'imaginative identification upon which the fullest sympathy depends' and thus to express 'the practical side of Christain ethics' (*op. cit.*, p. 90).
12. *Letters*, vol. III, p. 41. Letter to John Blackwood, 31 March 1859. K. M. Newton observes that recent George Eliot criticism regards 'The Lifted Veil' as 'an integral part of her *oeuvre* and not as a strange anomaly.' See his *George Eliot* (London: Longman, 1991), pp. 25 and 28, n. 40.
13. Henry James, review of 'George Eliot's Newly Published Tales', i.e. 'The Lifted Veil' and 'Brother Jacob', *The Nation, XXVI* (25 April 1878) p. 277, reprinted in A. Mordell (ed.), *Literary Reviews and Essays by Henry James* (New York: Grove Press, 1957), p. 291. James Diedrick discerns the influence of German novellas like Gottfried Keller's in the grotesque images and 'detached and harshly ironic style' of 'Brother Jacob', which in its turn anticipates the presentation of Gwendolen Harleths's 'grotesque alter-egos' in *Daniel Deronda*; see his 'George Eliot's Experiments in Fiction: "Brother Jacob" and the German *Novella*', *Studies in Short Fiction*, vol. XXII (Fall 1985), pp. 464 and 468.
14. *Letters*, vol. III, p. 371. Letter to J. Blackwood, 12 January 1861; the story came across other plans 'by a sudden inspiration'; it was finished in four months, *ibid.*, p. 387. Letter to John Blackwood, 11 March 1861. Several critics have commented on the economy of means in

the composition of *Silas Marner*. R. Speight, in *George Eliot* (London: Arthur Barker, 1954), p. 66, says, 'one feels that she has put into it exactly the right weight of writing', and L. Haddakin, in 'Silas Marner', in B. Hardy (ed.), *Critical Essays on George Eliot* (London: Routledge & Kegan Paul, 1970), p. 64, remarks, 'when you turn back to the book itself you are surprised by its brevity'.

15. John Blackwood , George Eliot's publisher, reported a conversation which he had had with her shortly after *Silas Marner* was published, in which she said that the work had sprung 'from her childish recollection of a man with a stoop and expression of face that led her to think that he was an alien from his fellows', *Letters*, vol. III, p. 427. John Blackwood's letter to Mrs John Blackwood, 15 June 1861.

16. Still the most severe analysis of George Eliot's underlying theme in *Silas Marner* is Richard Simpson's in 'George Eliot's Novels', *Home and Foreign Review*, III (October 1863), pp. 522–49. He argued that the tale contained an ironic apology for Providence in a 'specious defence of the truth' which was achieved by 'planting opinions' which George Eliot wished to eradicate. The irony consists in 'making Marner's conversion depend altogether on human sympathies and love, while he, simple fellow, fails to see the action of the general law of humanity, and attributes every thing to the "dealings" which regulate the accidents', p. 529. See D. Carroll (ed.), *George Eliot: The Critical Heritage* (London: Routledge & Kegan Paul, 1971), p. 229.

17. David Cecil, arguing that there is 'no inherent reason in the nature of things why a morally-feeble man should not beget twenty children', regards Godfrey Cass's discontent as 'a gratuitous piece of poetic justice imposed on him by the arbitrary will of his creator'. *Early Victorian Novelists: Essays in Revaluation* (London: Constable, 1934), p. 323.

18. Henry James, 'The Novels of George Eliot', *Atlantic Monthly*, vol. XVIII (October 1866), p. 482.

19. The suggestion of I. Taylor in her *George Eliot: Woman of Contradictions* (London: Weidenfeld and Nicolson, 1989), p. 175.

20. Q. D. Leavis in her wide-ranging introduction to the Penguin English Library edition of *Silas Marner* (Harmondsworth: Penguin, 1967) stresses George Eliot's 'complete emancipation from restrictive ideas of class' as well as her penetrating criticisms of its causes and manifestations. When the Casses retire helpless and humiliated in Ch. 19, Q. D. Leavis goes so far as to say 'we feel impelled to cheer', pp. 32–33. Sally Shuttleworth in 'Fairy Tale or Science? Physiological Psychology in *Silas Marner*', in *Languages of Nature: Critical Essays on Science and Literature*, ed. L. Jordanova (London: Free Assocation Books, 1986), pp. 250–88, argues that George Eliot is 'far from confirming organicist theories of social or economic development' in *Silas Marner*, 'yet requires an image of essential social order' to show Silas and Eppie as 'participants in an integrated community' at the close; hence it is a 'fundamentally divided' text, pp. 273 and 285.

21. L. C. Emery, in *George Eliot's Creative Conflict: The Other Side of Silence*
     (Berkeley and Los Angeles, Calif.: University of California Press,
     1976), p. 71; she finds in the ending evidence of a disguised Oedipal
     wish with Silas perhaps representing 'the return of the repressed',
     p. 77.

5 Europe and Beyond: *Romola, Daniel Deronda*

1. A. McCobb, *George Eliot's Knowledge of German Life and Letters* (Salzburg:
    University of Salzburg Press, 1982), Salzburg Studies in English
    Literature: Romantic Reassessment, 102, p. 76.
2. *Letters*, vol III, p. 300. Letter to William Blackwood, 27 May 1860.
3. The story of 'noble vengeance' or *edle Rache* which is the source
    of Baldassarre's relations to the adopted Tito was told to George
    Eliot in Berlin by General Pfuhl in 1855. In it the murderer says
    of the son, 'I wish to go to Hell, for *he* is there, and I want to
    follow out my revenge'. See *Biography*, p. 352, and *George Eliot: A
    Writer's Notebook 1854–1879 and Uncollected Writings*, ed. J. Wiesenfarth
    (Charlottesville, Va.: University of Virginia Press, 1981), p. 23.
4. *Letters*, vol. IV, p. 97. Letter to R. H. Hutton, 8 August 1863.
5. *Ibid.*, vol. IV, p. 104. Letter to S. S. Hennell, 23 August 1863.
6. D. Barrett, in *Vocation and Desire: George Eliot's Heroines* (London:
    Routledge & Kegan Paul, 1989), p. 83, notes George Eliot's concern
    in *Romola* with economic evolution as the base on which philosophical
    evolution takes place. F. Bonaparte, however, sees Bratti as 'another
    symptom of the moral disintegration of Florence', mentioning that
    he was based on an actual merchant who reputedly died in great
    prosperity; see her *The Triptych and the Cross: The Central Myths of
    George Eliot's Poetic Imagination* (Brighton: Harvester, 1979), p. 164.
7. F. D. Maurice, who praised George Eliot for her *Romola* (*Letters*,
    vol. IV, p. 59. Letter of G. H. Lewes to S. S. Hennell, 12 Sep-
    tember 1862), argued in his *Modern Philosophy* (London: Griffin,
    Bohn, 1862) that Savonarola's theocracy was a protest against civil
    and ecclesiastical tyranny; it undermined the foundation of Roman
    autocracy by the pronouncement that the Pope was 'infallible only
    as Pope', pp. 90–92. Maurice added significantly, 'A student who will
    give himself to the history of Florence, will not be able to dispense
    with the study of the history of England, of Germany, of Bohemia,
    but he will have a light which may reveal what was working secretly
    in all these countries', p. 94.
8. F. Bonaparte, however, argues that the philosophy of self-interest
    has brought both Tito *and* Florence 'to a state of moral anarchy',
    which 'reason is entirely powerless to overcome', though Romola
    makes a more promising effort through her discovery of the power
    of sympathy (*op. cit.*, pp. 138 and 241).
9. J. Bayley in 'The Pastoral of Intellect' (*Critical Essays on George Eliot*,
    ed. B. Hardy, London: Routledge & Kegan Paul, 1970, p. 207) sees

Tito as 'the accommodating man whose virtues depend on equiva-
lent accommodation in others'; he is thus destroyed by Romola's
'highmindedness and penetration (George Eliot's own qualities)'.

10. J. McMaster comments on this indirect account of Tito's and Romola's
love-making, rendered by their mingling hair, 'The imagery is perhaps a touch banal'; see her 'George Eliot's Language of the Sense',
in *George Eliot: A Centenary Tribute*, ed. G. S. Haight and R. T. Van
Arsdel (London: Macmillan, 1982), p. 23.

11. W. J. Harvey, in *The Art of George Eliot* (London: Chatto and Windus,
1961), pp. 182–83, argues tendentiously that Romola is a character
'inadequately placed in any real contact with the network of other
characters in the novel', She 'illuminates and realizes others without
being realized or illuminated herself'.

12. J. K. Gezari, in '*Romola* and the myth of Apocalypse', in *George Eliot:
Centenary Essays and an Unpublished Fragment*, ed. A. Smith (London:
Vision Press, 1980), pp. 79 and 91, comments that, though Dino's
vision of Romola's arid marriage does anticipate the frustration of
her moral yearnings which that will involve, its effect is spoiled by
intolerance. J. Gezari detects also in Romola's reservations about
Savonarola the influence of Feuerbach's view of faith as intolerant.
Compare L. Feuerbach, *The Essence of Christianity* (1841), tr. George
Eliot (1854), Harper Torchbook (New York: Harper, 1957), p. 255,
'faith is essentially a spirit of partisanship . . . it understands no neutrality; it is preoccupied only with itself. Faith is essentially intolerant,
essentially, because with faith is always associated the illusion that its
cause is the cause of God, its honour his honour . . . God himself is
interested: the interest of faith is the nearest interest of God'.

13. To argue, as G. Levine does in '*Romola* as Fable' (see *Critical Essays
on George Eliot*, ed. B. Hardy, 1970, p. 93), that Romola, in relation
to the political activities in Florence, is 'an utterly passive figure',
sustaining her purity 'by remaining in the world of romance', ignores
such episodes as her intervention on behalf of Savonarola's safety in
Ch. 47, which is perceived by Tito as an interference in 'political
affairs' (Ch. 48).

14. Palmerston's government had discussed plans for an autonomous
Jewish settlement in the Middle East. In 1865 the Palestine Explo-
ration Society was founded. In the *Jewish Chronicle* of January 1875
George Eliot noticed advertisements for plots of land for sale near
the agricultural school at Jaffa; see W. Baker, *George Eliot and
Judaism* (Salzburg: University of Salzburg, 1975), pp. 9 and 136–39.
The historical background to Deronda's plan is clear, but whether
George Eliot foresaw the international problems caused by Zionism
is disputed. J. Bennett's view that the 'claims of the Arabs in Palestine did not enter her head' (*George Eliot: Her Mind and her Art*,
Cambridge: Cambridge University Press, 1948), p. 186 is countered
by W. Allen's point that Deronda's reference to Arab nationalism
shows that George Eliot was 'certainly thinking' (*George Eliot*, London:
Weidenfeld and Nicolson, 1965, p. 166).

15. *Letters*, vol. VI, p. 301. Letter to H. B. Stowe, 29 October 1876.

16. J. Bennett, *op. cit.*, p. 185, is a representatively hostile critic of Mordecai. She says that the reader is left 'at worst, irritated by his prophetic posturing' and complains that 'he speaks in rhythms that no one hears, unless from a Nonconformist pulpit'.

17. Deronda certainly might have been made to be more explicit on this point, though an early detractor (A. V. Dicey), who found Deronda 'incurably weak', is surely hypercritical in commenting that when 'Deronda wanders off to the East we feel sure that he will travel about year after year doing deeds of kindness and cherishing noble aspirations, but further removed than even a passionate dreamer like Mordecai from working out any deliverance either for his people or for mankind'; unsigned review of *Daniel Deronda* in *Nation*, vol. XXIII,, pp. 245–46 (19 October 1876). See D. Carroll, *George Eliot: The Critical Heritage* (London: Routlege & Kegan Paul, 1971), p. 404. The association of Deronda with portraits by Titian, especially his 'Young Man with a Glove', is explored by H. Witemeyer in his *George Eliot and the Visual Arts* (New Haven, Conn.: Yale University Press, 1979), pp. 101–4.

18. G. Orwell, *Homage to Catalonia* (London: Secker and Warburg, 1938), p. 314. George Eliot and G. H. Lewes had visited Hampshire and Wiltshire for locations for the country scenes of *Daniel Deronda* in 1874. For four years they were searching for a country residence of their own, mainly in the Haslemere area of south-west Surrey, before settling on 'The Heights' at Witley, nearer Guildford, in 1876; there they had eight or nine acres of ground. See *Biography*, pp. 462, 474–75 and 499–500.

19. Cynthia Chase's argument that George Eliot overlooked the fact that Deronda would have known he was a Jew already since he would have been circumcised (see her 'The Decomposition of the Elephants: Double-Reading *Daniel Deronda*', *PMLA*, vol. XCIII, pp. 215–27, 1978) is countered by K. M. Newton in his *In Defence of Literary Interpretation* (London: Macmillan, 1986), pp. 197–211, who suggests that in the Victorian period Gentile male infants as well as Jewish ones were circumcised, so that Deronda would not have been sure. Both essays are reprinted in *George Eliot* (ed. K. M. Newton), Longman Critical Reader (London: Longman, 1991).

20. Several critics regard the English society potrayed in *Daniel Deronda* with a hostility which exceeds the narrator's. U. C. Knoepflmacher, for example, in *Religious Humanism and the Victorian Novel: George Eliot, Walter Pater, and Samuel Butler* (Princeton, N.J.: Princeton University Press, 1965), p. 129, calls the England of *Daniel Deronda* 'a nation which has become totally purposeless'. A. Mintz, in *George Eliot and the Novel of Vocation* (Cambridge, Mass.: Harvard University Press, 1978), p. 167, talks of the 'moral brutalization' of the English society of the novel; and S. Dentith, in *George Eliot* (Brighton: Harvester, 1986), p. 132, in connection with it refers to 'a world made sterile in part by male values of empire and competitiveness'.

21. S. Dentith challenges the view that the various political discourses in a novel like *Daniel Deronda* are necessarily 'sorted into a hierarchy by

the authoritative or "master" discourse'. Some examples which 'draw
on different ideological resources from the ostensible meanings of
the novel and thus work against those meanings, cannot easily be
integrated into a coherent, integrated or organic view of the novel',
op. cit., pp. 122–23. The reader of *Daniel Deronda* is, however, pressed
in the end to consider caution and moderation as valuable and
prioritised reactions to political problems such as those surrounding
land ownership.
22. W. Wordsworth, *The Prelude*, (1850), book I, l. 460.
23. See 'The Importance of Elsewhere' (1955), 'Here no elsewhere
underwrites my existence', in P. Larkin, *Collected Poems* (ed. A.
Thwaite, London: Marvell Press and Faber, 1988), p. 104.

6 Political Change and the Home View: *Felix Holt, Middlemarch*

1. *Biography*, pp. 381–82.
2. George Eliot may have been influenced by Dante's 'signs of
tenderness and compassion' for those who destroyed their own
lives, in Canto 13 of the *Inferno*, in her restrained account of Mrs
Transome's sufferings; see *George Eliot: A Writer's Notebook 1854–1879
and Uncollected Writings*, ed. J. Wiesenfarth (Charlottesville, Va.: University of Virginia Press, 1981), p. 43.
3. Florence Sandler in 'The Unity of Felix Holt', in *George Eliot: A
Centenary Tribute*, ed. G. S. Haight and R. T. van Arsdel (London:
Macmillan, 1982), pp. 137–52, gives a more positive version of Felix
Holt's refusal to jockey for power, reminding us that 'the meek may
inherit the earth', p. 146.
4. There is little in the novel to evoke the look of Middlemarch, its
buildings, streets, spaces, distances, much less than there was in
Romola, or to excite the visual imagination. The many illustrations
later used by publishers to evoke the appearance of Middlemarch,
including the hill-backed landscape chosen by the author herself for
the frontispiece of the 1874 edition, inevitably mislead. Middlemarch
is too fictionally intricate to be illustrated.
5. George Eliot wrote to John Morley, a supporter of Female Enfran-
chisement, assuring him that his attitude here was 'very nearly' hers.
She was against the view that Nature fixed women in their subservient
role; if women have 'the worse share in existence' biologically,
George Eliot contended, then 'in the moral evolution we have "an
art which does mend nature" – an art which "itself is nature"'. The
quotation from Shakespeare's *The Winter's Tale*, IV, iv, is used by
George Eliot to suggest that human intelligence applied morally to
social and political reform (e.g. votes for women) is itself natural.
See *Letters*, vol. VIII, p. 402. Letter to John Morley, 14 May 1867.
6. As D. A. Miller points out in his *Narrative and its Discontents: Problems
of Closure in the Traditional Novel* (Princeton N.J.: Princeton University
Press, 1981), 'The Bulstrodes' story is brought to term, but the term
seems only a permanent state of suspensiveness. The actual meaning

of their scene together remains in the air: blindness matching up with
concealment? or both transcending themselves?' See the excerpts
reprinted in *George Eliot*, ed. K. M. Newton (Longman: London,
1991), pp. 187–97, p. 193.

7. The many references to the turns of Rosamond's neck, which F.
R. Leavis believes 'the reader certainly catches himself, from time
to time, wanting to break' (*The Great Tradition*, London: Chatto
and Windus, 1948, p. 68), may owe something to the sensuous
and ominous passage on Gretchen's neck in Goethe's *Faust*, Part
1 (1808), Walpurgisnacht section;

> Welch eine Wonne! welch ein Leiden!
> Ich kann von diesem Blick nicht scheiden,
> Wie sonderbar muss diesen schönen Hals
> Ein einzig rotes Schmürchen schmücken,
> Nicht breiter als ein Messerrücken!

8. On Fred Vincy's relations with Farebrother, see my 'The Study of
Provincial Life in *Middlemarch*', in *English*, vol. XXVIII, pp. 219–47;
229–30 and p. 246, n. 15 (Autumn, 1979).

9. For a different view of Mr Brooke as possibly reflecting a too indul-
gent presentation of the gentry by the narrator, see K. McSweeney,
Middlemarch (London: Allen and Unwin, 1984), pp. 77–78. George
Eliot may have taken the name Brooke from the Parliamentarian
Lord Brooke who raised an anti-Royalist force in Coventry in July
1642 and won the first engagement of the English Civil War between
mobile forces at Southam on 23 August 1642 before his troops took
over the houses of their opponents in and around Coventry, the
Middlemarch of the novel. The Brooke ancestor, 'discernible as
a Puritan gentleman who served under Cromwell, but afterwards
conformed' (Ch. 1), is not the actual Brooke, who died at Lichfield
in 1643.

10. K. Chase, in *George Eliot: Middlemarch* (Cambridge: Cambridge University Press, 1991), p. 44, argues that the moral of *Middlemarch*'s
method is that 'art, like human community, should seem not a
unity that can reconcile life's multiplex variety, but should seek
instead a sympathy prepared to adjust to all the irregularities of
the human landscape'. We should, however, still remember that
some of the worst irregularities are not there. The home epic has
a certain in-built security.

11. In her anonymous review of W. H. von Riehl's *Naturgeshichte des Volks*
in the *Westminster Review*, vol. LXVI, pp. 51–79 (July 1856) George
Eliot had summarised Riehl's argument that parallel mutation is the
secret of successful social development: 'The external conditions
which society has inherited from the past are but the manifestation
of inherited internal conditions in the human beings who compose
it; the internal conditions and the external are related to each other
as the organism and its medium, and development can take place
only by the gradual consentaneous development of both', p. 69.

7 George Eliot Criticism

1. D. Carroll, *George Eliot: The Critical Heritage* (London: Routledge & Kegan Paul, 1971), p. 1.
2. *Letters*, vol. IV, 96. Letter of George Eliot to R. H. Hutton, 8 August 1863. See Carroll, pp. 198–207.
3. *Letters*, vol. VI, p. 314. George Eliot's Journal, 1 December 1876.
4. G. Saintsbury, review of *Daniel Deronda, Academy*, vol. X, pp.253–54 (9 September 1876).
5. G. Saintsbury, *Corrected Impressions: Essays on Victorian Writers* (London: Heinemann, 1895), p. 172.
6. G. S. Haight, *A Century of George Eliot Criticism* (London: Methuen, 1966), p. xiii; 'their knowledge of her novels grew dimmer with the years.'
7. A. Bennett, *Journals* (London: Cassell, 1932), pp. 5–6. Entry for 13 May 1896.
8. W. E. Henley, *Views and Reviews: Essays in Appreciation* (London: Nutt, 1890), pp. 130–32. Leslie Stephen in the unsigned obituary article in the *Cornhill*, vol. LXIII, pp. 152–68 (February 1881), commented that her 'men were often simply women in disguise', p. 160.
9. W. C. Brownell, *Victorian Prose Masters* (New York: Scribner, 1901), p. 145.
10. H. H. Bonnell, *Charlotte Brontë, George Eliot, Jane Austen: Studies in their Works* (London: Longman, 1902), p. 237.
11. L. Stephen, *George Eliot* (London: Macmillan, 1902), pp. 74 and 182–83.
12. Henry James, anonymous review of *Felix Holt, Nation*, vol. III, p. 127 (16 August 1866).
13. Henry James, anonymous review of *Middlemarch, Galaxy*, vol. XV, pp. 424–28 (March 1873).
14. Henry James, *Partial Portraits* (London: Macmillan, 1888), pp. 46, 50 and 61.
15. *The Art of the Novel: Critical Prefaces by Henry James*, intro. R. P. Blackmur (New York: Scribner, 1934), p. 49.
16. *Ibid.*, pp. 69–71.
17. Henry James, *Notes of a Son and Brother* (London: Macmillan, 1914), pp. 442–43.
18. Henry James, *The Middle Years* (London: Collins, 1917), p. 85. James is echoing here, I think, Matthew Arnold's final word on Wordsworth; 'I am a Wordsworthian myself . . . No Wordsworthian has a tenderer affection for this pure and sage master than I, or is less readily offended by his defects', Preface to Arnold's selection of *The Poems of Wordsworth*: (London: Macmillan, 1879). See *The Complete Prose Works of Matthew Arnold*, vol. IX, ed. R. H. Super, *English Literature and Irish Politics* (Ann Arbor, Mich.: University of Michigan Press, 1973), p. 55.
19. Mrs Humphrey Ward, *A Writer's Recollections* (London: Collins, 1918), pp. 108–9.
20. *The Collected Letters of Joseph Conrad* ed. F. R. Karl and L. Davies, vol. II,

1898–1902 (Cambridge: Cambridge University Press, 1986), p. 418. Letter of J. Conrad to William Blackwood, 31 May 1902.

21. R. W. B. Lewis, *Edith Wharton: A Biography* (London: Constable, 1975). *Middlemarch* 'was one of the two or three English novels Edith Wharton most respected.' Her review of Leslie Stephen's *George Eliot* in *Bookman* (15 May 1902) suggests that the later novels are used by George Eliot as unconscious vehicles of rehabilitation.

22. E. T. [Jessie Chambers], *D. H. Lawrence: A Personal Record* (London: Cape, 1935), pp. 97–98 and 103–5.

23. H. Spurling, *Ivy when Young: The Early Life of I. Compton-Burnett* (London: Gollancz, 1974), pp. 163–71.

24. *The Flight of the Mind: The Letters of Virginia Woolf*, vol. I, 1888–1912, ed. N. Nicholson (London: Chatto and Windus: 1975), p. 227. Letter of Virginia Woolf to Madge Vaughan, June 1906. In 1929 Virginia Woolf was again reading *Middlemarch*, 'with even greater pleasure than I remembered;' *A Reflection of the Other Person: The Letters of Virginia Woolf*, vol. IV, 1929–1931 (1978), p. 402.

25. E. Gosse, *Aspects and Impressions* (London: Cassell, 1922), pp.14–15.

26. Virginia Woolf's anonymous 'George Eliot', *The Times Literary Supplement*, vol. XVIII, pp. 657–58 (20 November 1919) was significantly expanded for inclusion in *The Common Reader* (London: Hogarth Press, 1925).

27. O. Elton, *A Survey of English Literature 1830–1880* (London: Arnold, 1920), vol. II, pp. 272–75.

28. D. Cecil, *Early Victorian Novelists: Essays in Revaluation* (London: Constable, 1934), pp. 283, 304, 310, 322 and 328.

29. F. R. Leavis, *The Great Tradition* (London: Chatto and Windus, 1948), p. 13.

30. *Ibid.*, pp. 42–44, 50 and 59.

31. *Ibid.*, pp. 84–85, 91, 99 and 123.

32. B. Hardy, *The Appropriate Form: An Essay on the Novel* (London: Athlone Press, 1964), pp. 3 and 130–31.

33. B. Hardy, *The Novels of George Eliot: A Study in Form* (London: Athlone Press, 1959), pp. 233, 235 and 237.

34. W. J. Harvey, *Character and the Novel* (London: Chatto and Windus, 1965), pp. 148–49.

35. W. J. Harvey, *The Art of George Eliot* (London: Chatto and Windus, 1961), pp. 88 and 114–15.

36. *Middlemarch: Critical Approaches to the Novel*, ed. B. Hardy (London: Athlone Press, 1967), pp. 3 and 141–42.

37. A. Kettle, *An Introduction to the English Novel*, vol. I, *To George Eliot* (London: Hutchinson, 1951), pp. 171, 174 and 177.

38. R. Williams, *Culture and Society, 1780–1950* (London: Chatto and Windus, 1958, repr. Harmondsworth: Penguin, 1961), pp. 115 and 119.

39. R. Williams, *The Country and the City* (London: Chatto and Windus, 1973), p. 180.

40. T. Eagleton, *Criticism and Ideology* (London: New Left Books, 1976), pp. 111–12 and 124–25.

41. E. Burke, *Reflections on the Revolution in France* (1790), ed. C. C. O'Brien (Harmondsworth: Penguin, 1968), p. 135.
42. C. MacCabe, *James Joyce and the Revolution of the Word* (London: Macmillan, 1978), pp. 15–21.
43. D. Lodge, *After Bakhtin* (London: Routledge & Kegan Paul, 1990), pp. 48–51.
44. J. Hillis Miller, 'Narrative and History', *English Literary History*, vol. XI, pp. 467–88 (Fall 1974).
45. Z. Austen, 'Why Feminist Critics are angry with George Eliot', *College English*, vol. XXXVII (1976), p. 551.
46. G. Beer, *George Eliot* (Brighton: Harvester Press, 1986), p. 1. Four searching and up-to-date surveys of George Eliot criticism, to each of which I am indebted, are Graham Handley, *State of the Art George Eliot* (Bristol: Bristol Press, 1990), J. Russell Perkin, *A Reception History of George Eliot's Fiction* (Ann Arbor, Mich.: UMI Research Press, 1990), K. M. Newton (ed.), *George Eliot* (London: Longman, 1991) and J. Peck (ed.), *New Casebooks: Middlemarch* (London: Macmillan, 1992).
47. See *Selected Letters of Philip Larkin 1940–1985* (ed. A. Thwaite, London: Faber, 1992), p. 156. Larkin's letter to J. B. Sutton, 30 October 1949.
48. *The Times*, 20 February 1992. Later authors were Proust and Rushdie.

Bibliography

GEORGE ELIOT'S PRINCIPAL WORKS

Fiction

Scenes of Clerical Life (1858). Periodical publication in *Blackwood's Magazine* (1857).
Adam Bede (1859).
'The Lifted Veil' (1859). Anonymous in *Blackwood's Magazine* (July).
The Mill on the Floss (1860).
Silas Marner (1861).
Romola (1863).
'Brother Jacob' (1864). In *Cornhill Magazine* (July).
Felix Holt (1866).
Middlemarch (1872). Instalments (1871–72).
Daniel Deronda (1876). Instalments (also 1876).

Other Works

The Life of Jesus Critically Examined, by D. F. Strauss. Translated from the fourth German edition (by Marian Evans, anonymously, 1846).
The Essence of Christianity, by L. Feuerbach. Translated from the second German edition by Marian Evans (1854).
The Spanish Gypsy: A Poem (1868).
The Legend of Jubal and Other Poems (1874).
Impressions of Theophrastus Such (1879).

Collections

Cabinet Edition of the Works of George Eliot, 19 vols. (Edinburgh and London: Blackwood, 1878). *Theophrastus Such* added in 1880 as the 20th volume.
Clarendon Edition of the Novels of George Eliot (Oxford: Clarendon Press, 1980, continuing). 6 volumes published, variously edited.
Essays of George Eliot, ed. T. Pinney (London: Routledge & Kegan Paul, 1963).
George Eliot: A Writer's Notebook 1854–79 and Uncollected Writings, ed. J. Wiesenfarth (Charlottesville, Va.: University of Virginia Press, 1981).

George Eliot: Selected Essays, Poems and Other Writings, ed. A. S. Byatt and N. Warren (Harmondsworth: Penguin, 1990).

CORRESPONDENCE AND BIOGRAPHY

Crompton, M., *George Eliot the Woman* (London: Cassell, 1960).

Cross, J. W., *George Eliot's Life as Related in her Letters and Journals* (Edinburgh and London: Blackwood, 1885), 3 vols; new edn (revised with additions and deletions), 1 vol. (1887).

Deakin M. H., *The Early Life of George Eliot* (Manchester: Manchester University Press, 1913).

——, *The George Eliot Letters*, ed. G. S. Haight (New Haven, Conn.: Yale University Press), 9 volumes, vols I–VII, 1954–1955, vols VIII–XI, 1978.

Haight, G. S., *George Eliot: A Biography* (Oxford: Clarendon Press, 1968).

Haight, G. S., *George Eliot and John Chapman* (New Haven, Conn.: Yale University Press, 1940).

Haldane, E. S., *George Eliot and her Times* (London: Hodder and Stoughton, 1927).

Hands, T., *A George Eliot Chronology* (London: Macmillan, 1989).

Hanson, L. and E., *Marian Evans and George Eliot* (London: Oxford University Press, 1952).

McSweeney, K., *George Eliot (Marian Evans): A Literary Life* (London: Macmillan, 1991).

Redinger, R. V., *George Eliot: The Emergent Self* (New York: Knopf, 1975).

Taylor, I., *George Eliot: Woman of Contradictions* (London: Weidenfeld and Nicolson, 1989).

Williams, B. C., *George Eliot: A Biography* (New York: Macmillan, 1936).

SELECTED CRITICISM

Adam, I., *George Eliot* (London: Routledge & Kegan Paul, 1969).

Adam, I. (ed.), *This Particular Web: Essays on Middlemarch* (Toronto and Buffalo: University of Toronto Press, 1975).

Allen, W., *George Eliot* (London: Weidenfeld and Nicolson, 1964).

Ashton, R., *George Eliot* (Oxford University Press, 1983).

Auster, H., *Local Habitations: Regionalism in the Early Novels of George Eliot* (Cambridge, Mass.: Harvard University Press, 1970).

Baker, W. (ed.)., *Critics on George Eliot* (London: Allen and Unwin, 1973).

Baker, W., *George Eliot and Judaism* (Salzburg: University of Salzburg, 1975).

Barrett, D., *Vocation and Desire: George Eliot's Heroines* (London: Routledge & Kegan Paul, 1989).

Beaty, J. *Middlemarch: From Notebook to Novel* (Urbana, Ill.: University of Illinois Press, 1960).

Beer, G., *Darwin's Plots* (London: Routledge & Kegan Paul, 1983).

Beer, G., *George Eliot* (Brighton: Harvester, 1986).

Bennett, J., *George Eliot: Her Mind and her Art* (Cambridge: Cambridge University Press, 1948).

Blind, M., *George Eliot* (London: Allen, 1883).

Bonaparte, F., *The Triptych and the Cross: The Central Myths of George Eliot's Poetic Imagination* (Brighton: Harvester, 1979).

Bonnell, H. H., *Charlotte Brontë, George Eliot and Jane Austen: Studies in their Works* (London: Longman, 1902).

Brady, K., *George Eliot* (London: Macmillan, 1992).

Brownell, W. C., *Victorian Prose Masters* (New York: Scribners, 1901).

Browning, O., *Life of George Eliot* (London: Walter Scott, 1890).

Bullett, G., *George Eliot: Her Life and Books* (London: Collins, 1947).

Carroll, D. (ed.), *George Eliot: The Critical Heritage* (London: Routledge & Kegan Paul, 1971).

Cecil, D., *Early Victorian Novelists: Essays in Revaluation* (London; Constable, 1934).

Chase, K., *George Eliot: Middlemarch* (Cambridge: Cambridge University Press, 1991).

Cockshut, A. O. J., *The Unbelievers: English Agnostic Thought 1840–1890* (London: Collins, 1964).

Cox, C. B., *The Free Spirit* (London: Oxford University Press, 1963).

Creeger, G. R. (ed.), *George Eliot: A Collection of Critical Essays* (Englewood Cliffs, N. J.: Prentice Hall, 1970).

Cunningham V., *Everywhere Spoken Against: Dissent in the Victorian Novel* (Oxford: Clarendon Press, 1975).

Daiches, D., *George Eliot: Middlemarch* (London: Arnold, 1963).

Dentith, S., *George Eliot* (Brighton: Harvester, 1986).

Dodd, V. A., *George Eliot: An Intellectual Life* (New York: St. Martin's Press, 1990).

Doyle, M. E., *The Sympathetic Response: George Eliot's Fictional Rhetoric* (East Brunswick, N.J.: Associated Universities Presses, 1981).

Eagleton, T., *Criticism and Ideology* (London: New Left Books, 1976).

Ebbatson, R., *George Eliot: The Mill on the Floss* (Harmondsworth: Penguin, 1985).

Elton, O., *A Survey of English Literature, 1830–1880*, 2 vols (London: Arnold, 1920).

Emery, L. C., *George Eliot's Creative Conflict: The Other Side of Silence* (Berkeley and Los Angeles, Calif.: University of California Press, 1976).

Ermarth, E. D., *George Eliot* (Boston, Mass.: Twayne, 1985).

Gilbert, S. M. and Gumar, S., *The Madwoman in the Attic* (New Haven, Conn.: Yale University Press, 1979).

Graver, S., *George Eliot and Community* (Berkeley, Calif.: University of California Press, 1984).

Gray, B. M., *George Eliot and Music* (London: Macmillan, 1989).

Haight, G. S. (ed.), *A Century of George Eliot Criticism* (New York: Houghton, Mifflin, 1965; London: Methuen, 1966).

Haight, G. S. and Van Arsdel, R. T. (eds), *George Eliot: A Centenary Tribute* (London: Macmillan, 1982).

Handley, G., *State of the Art George Eliot* (Bristol: Bristol Press, 1990).

Handley, G., *George Eliot's Midlands: Passion in Exile* (London: Allison and Busby, 1991).

Hardy, B., *The Appropriate Form* (London: Athlone Press, 1964).

Hardy, B. (ed.), *Middlemarch: Critical Approaches to the Novel* (London: Athlone Press, 1967).

Hardy, B., *Critical Essays on George Eliot* (London: Routledge & Kegan Paul, 1970).

Hardy, B., *Particularities: Readings in George Eliot* (London: Peter Owen, 1982).

Harvey, W. J., *The Art of George Eliot* (London: Chatto and Windus, 1961).

Harvey, W. J., *Character and the Novel* (London: Chatto and Windus, 1965).

Holmstrom, J. and Lerner, L. (eds), *George Eliot and her Readers* (London: Bodley Head, 1966).

Kettle, A., *An Introduction to the English Novel*, 2 vols (London: Hutchinson, 1951 and 1953).

James, H., *The Art of the Novel: Critical Prefaces*, with an intro. by R. P. Blackmur (New York: Scribners, 1934).

Jones, R. T., *George Eliot* (Cambridge: Cambridge University Press, 1970).

Knoepflmacher, U. C., *Religious Humanism and the Victorian Novel* (Princeton, N. J.: Princeton University Press, 1965).

Knoepflmacher, U. C., *George Eliot's Early Novels* (Berkeley and Los Angeles, Calif.: University of California Press, 1968).

Knoepflmacher, U. C., *Laughter and Despair: Readings in Ten Novels of the Victorian Era* (Berkeley and Los Angeles, Ca.: University of California Press, 1971).

Leavis, F. R., *The Great Tradition* (London: Chatto and Windus, 1948).

Leavis, F. R., *'Anna Karenina' and Other Essays* (London: Chatto and Windus, 1967).

Lodge, D., *After Bahktin: Essays on Fiction and Criticism* (London: Routledge & Kegan Paul, 1990).

MacCabe, C., *James Joyce and the Revolution of the Word* (London: Macmillan, 1979).

McCobb, A., *George Eliot's Knowledge of German Life and Letters* (Salzburg: University of Salzburg Press, 1982).

McSweeney, K., *Middlemarch* (London: Allen and Unwin, 1984).

Mintz, A., *George Eliot and the Novel of Vocation* (Cambridge, Mass.: University of Harvard Press, 1978).

Myers, W., *The Teaching of George Eliot* (Leicester: Leicester University Press, 1984).

Neale, C., *George Eliot: Middlemarch* (Harmondsworth: Penguin, 1989).

Newton, K. M., *George Eliot: Romantic Humanist* (London: Macmillan, 1981).

Newton, K. M. (ed.), *George Eliot* (London: Longman, 1991).

Noble, T. A., *George Eliot's Scenes of Clerical Life* (New Haven, Conn.: Yale University Press, 1965).

Paris, B. J., *Experiments in Life: George Eliot's Quest for Values* (Detroit, Mich.: Wayne State University Press, 1965).

Paxton, N., *George Eliot and Herbert Spencer* (Princeton, N. J.: Princeton University Press, 1991).

Pearce, T. S., *George Eliot* (London: Evans, 1973).

Peck, J. (ed.), *Middlemarch: George Eliot* (London: Macmillan, 1992).

Perkin, J. R., *A Reception-History of George Eliot's Fiction* (Ann Arbor, Mich: UMI Research Press, 1990).

Pinion, F. B., *A George Eliot Companion* (London: Macmillan, 1981).

Roberts, N., *George Eliot: Her Beliefs and her Art* (London: Elek, 1975).

Sandoff, D. F., *Monsters of Affection: Dickens, Eliot, and Brontë on Fatherhood* (Baltimore, Md.: Johns Hopkins University Press, 1982).

Saintsbury, G., *Corrected Impressions: Essays on Victorian Writers* (London: Heinemann, 1895).

Showalter, E., *A Literature of their Own: British Women Novelists from Brontë to Lessing* (Princeton, N.J: Princeton University Press, 1977).

Shuttleworth, S., *George Eliot and Nineteenth-Century Science* (Cambridge: Cambridge University Press, 1984).

Simon, W. M., *European Positivism in the Nineteenth Century* (Ithaca, N.Y.: Cornell University Press, 1963).

Smith, A. (ed.), *George Eliot: Centenary Essays and an Unpublished Fragment* (London: Vision Press, 1980).

Speaight, R., *George Eliot* (London: Barker, 1954).

Stephen, L., *George Eliot* (London: Macmillan, 1902).

Swinden, P. (ed.), *George Eliot: Middlemarch* (London: Macmillan, 1972).

Thale, J., *The Novels of George Eliot* (New York: Columbia University Press, 1959).

Uglow, J., *George Eliot* (London: Virago, 1987).

Viner, A. E. S., *George Eliot* (Edinburgh: Oliver and Boyd, 1971).

Welsh, A., *George Eliot and Blackmail* (Cambridge, Mass.: Harvard University Press, 1985).

Willey, B., *Nineteenth Century Studies* (London: Chatto and Windus, 1949).

Williams, R., *Culture and Society 1780–1950* (London: Chatto and Windus, 1958).

Williams, R., *The English Novel from Dickens to Lawrence* (London: Chatto and Windus, 1970).

Williams, R., *The Country and the City* (London: Chatto and Windus, 1973).

Witemeyer, H., *George Eliot and the Visual Arts* (New Haven, Conn.: Yale University Press, 1979).

Woolf, V., *The Common Reader*, 2 vols (London: Hogarth Press, 1925).

Wright, T. R., *Middlemarch* (London: Harvester-Wheatsheaf, 1991).

Index

Smith, A.   140, 142, 149
Smith, B.L.   5
Socialism   2, 4, 17, 35, 77, 98,
     108, 132–3
Society and social work   4, 20–1,
     30, 66, 70, 71, 75, 76, 84, 90,
     96–7, 106, 107, 117, 120, 121,
     132–3, 141, 142, 150, 152
Spain   12, 91, 120
  Spanish language   100
Speaight, R   147
Spencer, H.   5–6, 10, 12, 16, 44,
     138, 141
Spinoza, B. de   4, 7, 8
Spurling, H.   154
Sophocles   8
Stephen, L.   16, 123, 124–5, 128,
     153, 154
Stephenson, G.   142
Stevenson, R. L.   126
Stowe, Mrs H. B.   139, 149
Strauss, D. F.   3, 5, 138
Stuart, E.   14, 140
Super, R. H.   153
Sutton, J. B.   155
Switzerland   4, 11, 14

Taylor, I.   138, 139, 147
Tennyson, A.   8, 13, 15
Thackeray, W. M.   114, 127
Theatre and drama   5, 6, 7, 11,
     116, 130
Thoreau, H. D.   8
Thwaite, A.   151, 155
Times, The   9–10, 41, 50, 137,
     143, 144
Titian   150
Tolstoy, L.   10, 129, 137, 139
Tomlinson, E.   18
Trade and commerce   35, 43, 60–1,
     73, 77, 82–3, 84, 97, 102, 104,
     133, 136
Trade unions   103

Trollope, A.   11, 64, 145
Turgenev, I.   15
Turkey   91

United States of America   12,
     13, 91, 92
  American Civil War   96, 99
Utilitarianism   2, 23, 107

Van Arsdel, R. T.   143, 144,
     149, 151
Vaughan, M.   154
Violence   29, 55, 83, 102, 119, 132
Voce, M.   18

Wagner, R.   15
Walpole, H.   140
Ward, M. A. (Mrs Humphrey)   127,
     153
Warwickshire and the Midlands   1,
     4, 6, 10, 17, 19, 43, 63, 101, 105,
     122, 140, 144, 146, 151, 152
Watteau, A.   66
Welsh, A.   142–3
Wesley, J.   20
Westminster Review, The   5, 7, 8, 109,
     138, 152
Wharton, E.   127, 154
Whitman, W.   8
Wiesenfarth, J.   142, 148, 151
Wilberforce, W.   109
Williams, R.   132, 154
Williams, Sophia (Lady Grey)   139
Witemeyer, H.   150
Woolf, V.   127–8, 129, 154
Wordsworth, W.   23, 44–5, 68, 74,
     78, 88, 95, 100, 143, 151, 153
Work   6, 23, 46, 48, 77, 117,
     118, 121

Youmans, E. L.   143
Young, A.   38